DATE DUE

OCT 0 9 2013	

BRODART, CO.   Cat. No. 23-221-003

CAPTAINS
CONTENTIOUS

Studies in Maritime History
William N. Still, Jr., Series Editor

RECENT TITLES

Iron Afloat: The Story of the Confederate Armorclads
William N. Still, Jr.

To California by Sea: A Maritime History of the Gold Rush
James P. Delgado

Lifeline of the Confederacy: Blockade Running during the Civil War
Stephen R. Wise

The Lure of Neptune: German-Soviet Naval Collaboration and Ambitions
Tobias R. Philbin III

High Seas Confederate: The Life and Times of John Newland Maffitt
Royce Shingleton

The Defeat of the German U-Boats: The Battle of the Atlantic
David Syrett

John P. Holland, 1841–1914: Inventor of the Modern Submarine
Richard Knowles Morris

Cockburn and the British Navy in Transition:
Admiral Sir George Cockburn, 1772–1853
Roger Morriss

The Royal Navy in European Waters during the American Revolutionary War
David Syrett

Sir John Fisher's Naval Revolution
Nicholas A. Lambert

Forty-Niners 'round the Horn
Charles R. Schultz

The Abandoned Ocean
Andrew Gibson and Arthur Donovan

Northern Naval Superiority and the Economics of the American Civil War
David G. Surdam

Ironclads and Big Guns of the Confederacy:
The Journal and Letters of John M. Brooke
Edited by George M. Brooke, Jr.

High Seas and Yankee Gunboats:
A Blockade-Running Adventure from the Diary of James Dickson
Roger S. Durham

Dead Men Tell No Tales: The Lives and Legends of the Pirate Charles Gibbs
Joseph Gibbs

Playships of the World: The Naval Diaries of Admiral Dan Gallery, 1920–1924
Edited by Robert Shenk

Lewis Coolidge and the Voyage of the Amethyst, *1806–1811*
Evabeth Miller Kienast and John Phillip Felt

Captains Contentious: The Dysfunctional Sons of the Brine
Louis Arthur Norton

CAPTAINS CONTENTIOUS

The Dysfunctional Sons of the Brine

LOUIS ARTHUR NORTON

The University of South Carolina Press

© 2009 University of South Carolina

Published by the University of South Carolina Press
Columbia, South Carolina 29208

www.sc.edu/uscpress

Manufactured in the United States of America

18 17 16 15 14 13 12 11 10 09   10 9 8 7 6 5 4 3 2 1

Library of Congress Cataloging-in-Publication Data

Norton, Louis Arthur.
    Captains contentious : the dysfunctional sons of the brine / Louis Arthur
Norton.
        p. cm. — (Studies in maritime history)
    Includes bibliographical references and index.
    ISBN 978-1-57003-807-5 (cloth : alk. paper)
    1. United States. Continental Navy—Biography. 2. Ship captains—United
States—Biography. 3. United States—History—Revolution, 1775–1783—
Biography. 4. United States—History—Revolution, 1775–1783—Naval
operations. I. Title.
    E206.N676 2009
    973.3'5—dc22

                                                                    2008049201

This book was printed on Glatfelter Natures, a recycled paper with 30 percent
postconsumer waste content.

To my wife, Elinor Sue,
and to the future, our grandchildren: Sara Emily, Jacob James,
Samuel Matthew, and Caroline Elizabeth

Contents

List of Illustrations viii

Acknowledgments ix

Introduction 1

1   Maritime Naval Service during the Revolutionary War 7

2   The Continental Army Commodore: John Manley 29

3   The Army Privateer: Silas Talbot 46

4   The Naval Patrician: Dudley Saltonstall 64

5   The Lieutenant Commodore: Joshua Barney 87

6   Captain Paul: John Paul Jones 108

7   Issues of Leadership, Personality, and Psychology 133

Notes 147

Bibliography 161

Index 171

About the Author 187

Illustrations

Gun crew below decks 3

Two warships in naval combat 8

John Manley 30

Commodore Silas Talbot 47

Hull of the USS *Warren* 71

Map of Bagaduce on the Penobscot River, Maine, 1779 76

Joshua Barney 88

The *Hyder-Ally* and HMS *General Monk* 100

Bust of John Paul Jones 109

Bon Homme Richard and HMS *Serapis* 125

John Paul Jones 130

Below decks with crew's hammocks 137

Acknowledgments

I am grateful for the help and encouragement I have received from my wife, Elinor. Her patient reading of many drafts and her suggestions, support, and particularly her incredible good spirits kept me on track. I appreciate the mentoring of John Hattendorf and William Fowler, who aroused my interest in naval history. I also wish to thank James Bradford of Texas A&M University, who edited my previous biography of Joshua Barney. His patience and scholarly manner stimulated me to write another book based on officers of the Continental Navy; and his favorite, John Paul Jones, ended up playing a prominent role.

I am forever grateful to George and Libbie Merrow for allowing me to have free access to their treasure trove of primary source papers related to the Continental Navy. I also want to thank Kevin Haydon, Justine Ahlstrom, and Deirdre O'Regan, former editors and the current editor, respectively, of *Sea History*, who have used many of my manuscripts and reviews for the National Maritime Historical Society. Many of the books that they sent to me have provided inspiration for my current work. I am also indebted to members of the staff at Mystic Seaport Museum. I particularly wish to recognize Andrew German, William Cogar, and Paul O'Pecko, who have been helpful to me over my many years of association with this extraordinary facility.

I thank the eagle-eyed Robert Andrews Kingsbury and Tido Holtkamp for their constructive criticism and staunch support. I am indebted to Joan Durham and Roberta Buland for editing early drafts of this book and to the Merrows for generously allowing me access to their Dudley Saltonstall papers. I am particularly grateful to Alexander Moore and the fine people at the University of South Carolina Press for bringing this project to the public and to William Dudley and Michael Crawford of the Navy Historical Center in Washington, D.C., for their help in sorting out some historical details concerning the Continental Navy. I also thank the reference librarians at the Massachusetts Historical Society and the Connecticut State Library for their help in tracking down many obscure references. It has been a pleasure to work with so many generous, talented, and gracious people. Finally I am grateful for perhaps having a little genetic assistance from a family member—the late, noted maritime historian Arthur Jacob Marder.

Introduction

In the middle of the eighteenth century, Britain emerged as the most powerful nation in Europe and arguably in the world. Her North American colonies, a source of badly needed raw materials and trade, supported this effective hegemony. The abundant raw materials indigenous to America included the following: timber, especially a variety of oaks for vessel construction and tall, straight pines for masts; tobacco, an increasingly valuable commodity; hemp and similar fibers needed for rope making as well as pitch and tar (commonly called naval stores) from southern pines, used for wood and rope preservation; and fish, mainly dried salted cod, a source of inexpensive protein that fed some of the poor of Europe and especially the African slaves who toiled on West Indian and southern American colonial plantations.

This book is about a subset of naval officers who served in America's Continental Navy during the Revolutionary War and their acrimonious behavior toward one another, but it is more than that. It is a study of the expression and the occasional failure of leadership. In addition all naval officers are only as good as the men they command. Because of this, it is prudent to sketch a portrait of the American seamen available for this nascent navy at the time of the Revolutionary War, including their political aspirations or allegiances.

Seventeenth- and eighteenth-century transatlantic trade produced men of distinct character who would later become the backbone of the Continental Navy—for example, fishermen. Codfish was both plentiful and easily harvested off the New England coast, and the men who sailed these fishing vessels lived in communities near their boats. Because the crews were neighbors, the boats were run in a democratic fashion. Those who became fishing boat captains usually had little formal education but knew the waters to and from the fishing banks intimately. Other men elected to become "blue water sailors," men who chose to sail in merchant vessels on the oceans for extended periods of time. These skilled mariners, who often sailed with transient crews whose native languages were not English, were like interchangeable parts to be used to run complex and demanding vessels from all over the world. They manned the ships that transported goods among markets in Europe, Africa, the American colonies, or the Caribbean. Some of these "goods" were slaves; however, slave trading was an occupation in which few men lasted for more than a few years.

The merchant trade, regardless of the property transported, required sturdy ships, skilled shipwrights, knowledgeable shipmasters, and dependable crews. These men were recruited from ports of America's eastern seaboard, and some were relatively rootless seamen from abroad who signed on to any ship that needed them in any port of call. These merchantmen and fishermen made up the vast majority of the American maritime cadre, a source of recruitment for the Continental Navy at the start of the Revolutionary War.

When a man signed on as a crewman, his name, place of residence, and age were usually entered into the ship's log or roster/pay book. Ships' personnel logs from the era indicate that there were few American seamen beyond the age of thirty-five; this was likely because of either injuries or death working on an unkind sea.[1] Many men elected to go to sea because they were poor and in debt, and/or the sea offered an escape from mundane jobs ashore, demanding landlords, and family responsibilities. "[The merchant and fishing] fleet was manned by successive waves of adventure-seeking boys, officered by such of them as determined to make the sea their calling."[2] A young man who made an impression upon both his mates and his superiors had the opportunity to become an officer if he desired to stay at sea, but in this largely up-or-out environment there were few rewards for hardships endured. If found wanting, a seaman returned to labor ashore and was replaced by another in the almost endless stream of would-be adventurers. Those able forecastle crew members who persevered into middle age retired ashore, but often as "broken men."[3]

As colonial sea trade expanded, taxation of trade goods became a source of revenue used to support the colonies, the troops, and the navy that protected them. There were many layers of taxation that struck in waves and became burdens for the colonists; the most far-reaching for maritime trade were the complex Navigation Acts.[4] These acts required that nearly all manufactured goods and raw materials had to pass through British ports for duty collection before they could be marketed abroad. The acts also limited with whom the colonists could trade. Taxation became oppressive to those colonies actively engaged in foreign trade. Onerous British trade regulations and burdensome taxation caused an economic recession in North America and made it difficult for men to find employment related to commerce. Some British soldiers garrisoned in American ports supplemented their wages by taking work on wharves and rope walks, thus competing for scarce jobs ashore. Economic

Gun crew below decks. From Charles J. Peterson,
American Navy *(1858)*

strains in the colonies fueled displeasure with their brethren in Britain, while growing American patriotism made the idea of independence attractive to about a third of the colonial population.

In 1775 the Continental Congress decided that to fight for independence from Great Britain, Americans needed both a privateer fleet and a navy. The American men who made up the merchant fleet and New England's cod fishery became the backbone of the colonial fighting sailors.[5] Many were recent immigrants; few had naval experience, and those who had seen naval duty in their former nations' navies were mostly ordinary or able seamen.[6] Few were former naval officers in Britain or other countries, and most had little knowledge of naval strategy and tactics. These mariners were employed as the first American privateers who preyed upon British commerce in and around North America. Some of these men later volunteered as members of the Continental or states' navies.[7]

Since they were still British citizens, the threat of impressment of colonial sailors, laborers, tradesmen, and farmers into the British navy was constant. Many American men joined antiimpressment mob actions. Ironically, as the Revolution progressed, some Continental Navy commanders resorted to limited impressment of sailors.[8] During the war the Continental Navy lost major vessels to the British faster than new American warships could be built to go to sea. Yet, as it turned out, the Revolutionary War could not have been won without the support of the Continental Navy and especially the naval support of France.[9]

One might question why the Continental Congress opted to use scarce resources for a navy when the Continental Army would be doing most of the fighting and securing the land. An answer is evident in data gathered from the Napoleonic Wars; even though these took place some thirty years after the American Revolution, the theory of warfare was largely the same. The French army at Waterloo fielded 366 cannons that required about five thousand horses and nine thousand men for their deployment. This artillery train could move about twenty miles a day before resting the men and giving fodder to the animals. Nelson's Trafalgar fleet of twenty-seven warships carried 2,200 naval cannons that were sailed and manned by fourteen thousand men. These vessels, traveling day and night, could cover 100 or perhaps 180 miles per day. A bivouac area might require fifty hectares of land, while the main decks of Napoleon's fleet added up to about three hectares. Hence the Napoleonic navy could carry six times the number of guns as those of the army at more than five times the speed and for about 20 percent of the logistical cost. (The latter did not take into account that ships carried much larger guns with longer range and could store more shot and powder for battle.) Therefore warships were efficient and effective compact eighteenth-century military machines.[10]

Less has been written about the officers who served in the Continental Navy than about their Continental Army brethren, but it might be argued that Continental Navy officers lusted for honor and glory perhaps even more than their Continental Army counterparts did. These saltwater warriors displayed recklessness and sometimes self-destructiveness. This drive manifested itself as energy and zeal as well as devotion to duty and bravery. This leads to some important questions that will be explored in this book. Did the officers of the Continental Navy quarrel among themselves more than the officers of the British navy did? Who were these men who volunteered to serve as officers in this embryonic American navy, which seemed destined to be defeated? What made the enlisted men, sailors who served on board these armed sailing vessels during this time, different from their "ordinary seamen" brethren? How were the American officers and sailors different from their highly stratified and disciplined British naval officer adversaries? Because the American crews were largely volunteers from a society that was more democratic than any in Europe at the time, was the relationship of these officers with their crews different from that of the British?

There is a host of excellent secondary sources concerning the organizational and social history of the Royal Navy during this general period. Some of the best written, detailed, and accessible are Nichols A. M. Rodger's *The Wooden World* (1988) and *The Command of the Ocean* (2004), Brian Lavery's *Nelson's Navy* (1989),and for information on senior officers, most of whom began their careers during the Revolutionary War, Lee Bienkowski's *Admirals in the Age of Nelson* (2003).

Five biographical sketches of Continental Navy officers who had interactions with one another and were heroic at various times during the Revolutionary War can perhaps answer the questions regarding Continental Navy men. Although this concatenation is a limited sample of biographical data, it is evidence that the naval officers were a quarrelsome group—an unruly assemblage that was independent, aloof, and self-indulgent. The last chapter discusses some common leadership and personality traits that may account for the acrimonious actions of these men in the context of this time in American maritime history.

The aim in writing this book was to bring together sources, some of which are obscure, that would develop an insight into how the contentiousness might have occurred. The five Continental Navy officers whose overlapping biographies are sketched here could be considered representative models of the naval officers who served during the American Revolution. Of course, it is impossible to characterize the entire officer corps that served in the Continental Navy with such a small sample, but evidence indicates that it describes many. These five men were selected because they were contemporaries and essentially hailed from different colonies. They all joined the Revolutionary War at its start and, if only briefly during their naval services, displayed the broad pennant of commodore. Each of these officers had a contentious relationship with one or more of his peers. Except for John Paul Jones, they are not well known in naval history today.

Some previously published books have concerned themselves with the contentious behavior of some American naval captains. While they bear some literary similarities to *Captains Contentious,* the model used in this new book is different. For example, Leonard Guttridge and Jay Smith wrote *The Commodores* (1969), which has become a classic narrative about battles fought during the formative years of the United States Navy. In describing these battles, their book evolves into a collection of biographical sketches of naval officers, most of whom, in contrast to those in *Captains Contentious,* are well-known American naval commodores.[11] Although the authors of *The Commodores* skillfully depict accounts of naval battles, also revealed are the contentiousness, factionalism, distrust, and petty quarrels that developed among these officers in the new American navy. The authors offer many insights into the characters of these men by analyzing their responses and those of their colleagues to the combat events. In a more recent and elegantly written work, Ian Toll makes similar points in *Six Frigates* (2006).

Another well-written book that focuses on part of the maritime history of the Revolutionary War is Harold Larrabee's *Decision at the Chesapeake* (1964). The author uses the device of short biographical sketches in the first quarter of the book to help the reader understand how, by a series of odd events, the Battle of Yorktown was lost by the British. Larrabee presents a great deal of detail on how the acrimony among the leaders on both sides of the conflict contributed to the improbable outcome of this crucial battle. Unfortunately many of the quotes that appeared in his book were not attributed.

Captains Contentious uses the literary device of selected biographical sketches, but these focus on a small group of officers who served in the United States Navy's predecessor, the Continental Navy. The historical events surrounding the time of their service are only remotely comparable to those covered in Guttridge and Smith's *The Commodores*. This group of officers fought for an emerging republic with no national naval traditions except those borrowed from their enemy, the British. Another well-known naval history, William James Morgan's *Captains to the Northward* (1959), covers the same general period as that in *Captains Contentious* but is more focused on the Continental Navy captains from New England and is not generally concerned with the contentiousness of the officers. A more broadly encompassing narrative and highly readable book is William Fowler's *Rebels under Sail* (1976). In contrast to Fowler's book, *Captains Contentious* looks at actions and relationships among only five naval officers who joined the Revolutionary War from five different colonies.

This book recounts many of the important political and historical events that occurred during the time, while describing the interrelations between the captains. All of these men were at times ill-natured and occasionally narrowminded, yet prudent and cunning naval officers unrelenting in battle. These seemingly contradictory traits were the result of personality strengths, character flaws, and psychological drives. Charles Royster's *A Revolutionary People at War* (1979) gives analyses of strong and flawed character traits of the Continental Army commanders and their soldiers juxtaposed against the culture of the times. *Captains Contentious* concludes similarly, but with a more narrow focus on naval leadership. In preparation for writing *Captains Contentious*, the author has drawn on both primary and secondary sources for the narratives and the subsequent analyses.

Maritime Naval Service
during the Revolutionary War

His Britannic Majesty's ship *Serapis* was battering the hull and tearing the rigging of the smaller Continental Navy vessel *Bonhomme Richard* to pieces as the two ships fought on a moonlit sea. Bright flashes of light from exploding charges illuminated the billowing gun smoke. Two guns were still in service on the quarterdeck of John Paul Jones's *Richard,* and three or four 12-pounders were firing from the gun deck below. Combat might have been terminated if not for the courage of marines on the fighting platforms aloft, who fired their muskets down onto the vulnerable men on the deck of the *Serapis.*

After some delay, Continental Navy captain Pierre Landais set his ship, the *Alliance,* on a course to the windward of these warships locked in combat. Jones, his commodore, was in dire need of assistance. Once within range of the brawl between the British and American vessels, the *Alliance* opened indiscriminate fire that equally damaged both friend and foe. The *Alliance* moved to the starboard quarter of the *Richard* and, when almost abeam, discharged a broadside that killed or wounded many of Jones's men. A hail from a speaking trumpet and screams of sailors arose from the deck of the *Richard* to the captain of the *Alliance,* telling him that his gunners were firing on the wrong ship. Bright recognition signal lanterns had been hung aloft, and the black hull of the *Richard* sharply contrasted with the distinctive yellow hull of the *Serapis* in the beaming moonlight.

The *Alliance* hauled off for a time but still kept her station on the starboard side of the *Richard.* After a short interruption, the *Alliance* resumed the attack by crossing the bow of the *Richard* and the stern of the *Serapis* and firing grapeshot into both vessels. The *Richard* became so badly damaged that she began to leak and list, settling into the sea. Landais sailed the *Alliance* to leeward, stood off, and did nothing to help or hinder his commodore for the remainder of the conflict. John Paul Jones, surveying the carnage to his men and destruction of his vessel, now had to make the fateful

The Ranger and the Drake.

Two warships in naval combat. From Edgar Stanton Maclay,
History of the United States Navy from 1775 to 1898 *(1898)*

decision whether to strike his colors or fight on. He was infuriated that Landais, with whom he had had a professional disagreement, had not only declined to come to his aid but also appeared to hasten the fall of his American comrades by attacking the *Richard* rather than the *Serapis.*

Variations of this disturbing scene occasionally occurred during sea battles, particularly between Continental Navy ships. They were mostly due to misunderstood communications, signals not received or interpreted improperly, or confusion while sailing within the dense smoke from cannon broadsides. Unfortunately some were the result of frank animosities among allied naval captains and often affected military outcomes. It is impossible to objectively measure either the instances or the scale of this quarrelsome behavior among officers of all navies. Many were petulant and with fragile egos. Still, there is evidence that acrimony appeared more prevalent among naval officers in the Continental Navy than among their Royal Navy counterparts.

The American Continental Navy did not fare well against its British rivals during the Revolutionary War. The reasons were many. The Royal Navy was, at the time the most formidable maritime force on the seas. The British had recently triumphed against France during the Seven Years' War (1756–63). King George III had given his navy responsibility for the defense of the American colonies in major North American ports on the eastern seaboard from Halifax to the Caribbean. The Crown provided physical protection from foreign nations and pirates as well as supervising commerce. By commanding these eastern ports, the Royal Navy controlled the North American continental sea-lanes as well as the lucrative West Indian trade. The Admiralty was particularly interested in controlling American shipbuilding. The great North American forests contained large tracts of land with a variety of huge trees, vital and increasingly scarce raw building material, and naval stores for British shipwrights and riggers.

George Washington and the Continental Congress understood this. They authorized the formation of a small force of merchant vessels hastily converted to lightly armed warships with the mission of harassing the British as they approached the eastern ports. This nascent navy would require the strengthening of merchant ships and the acquisition of many cannons and small arms. Most important was the recruitment of brave men and particularly competent ship captains. Few of the first captains selected for the Continental Navy had naval experience, and some appeared to have been combative, vituperative, and manipulative malcontents.

The rhetorical question is, how were men chosen to ascend to the rank of commissioned naval officer? There were great differences in the selection processes for British and American ships' officers. British naval officers originated from restricted social strata. What is striking is that sons of nobles and persons of social rank such as clergymen, academicians, barristers, wealthy merchants, and particularly commissioned naval officers with political connections had an advantage at being selected as midshipmen. They also were more apt to have had a rudimentary education, particularly in mathematics, a skill vital for navigation.

The highest levels of British society had broad rules about what sons did with their lives. As William Shakespeare said, "Some are born great, some achieve greatness, and others have greatness thrust upon them" (*Twelfth Night*, 2.5). The first son generally inherited the family's estate and titles. The second son bought an army commission and served in a prestigious regiment. The third son often entered the navy, in which it was not necessary to purchase a commission and where prize money might make up for the lack of a substantial inheritance. Young men from the lower (working) classes or those who rose via the "hawse pipe" (enlisted men) were potentially skilled seamen, but they generally lacked the educational depth of their higher-born peers, especially in math and literacy. Some of these men from the lower strata of society went on to distinguished careers as naval officers, but relatively fewer advanced to senior officer rank.

The sons of the wealthiest American colonists may have been equally or better educated than their British counterparts, but they were commonly considered outsiders in the class-conscious British society. The North Americans rarely entered the ranks of midshipmen of the British navy unless they were Loyalists with strong political connections. Besides the social obstacles that were difficult to overcome, many in the upper classes suspected American maritime officers of harboring seditious political views. Ordinary British citizens considered Americans to be levelheaded Englishmen much like themselves. They had difficulty understanding why the colonists became impatient and did not choose a political rather than a military resolution to their grievances. Life on the whole in America was better than in England, certainly for the lower classes. Many Englishmen were envious of their relative freedom and wealth in terms of land. American colonial taxes were lower than taxes in England; there was far less aristocracy to contend with, and the plentiful land led to financial opportunity. The unruly Americans seemed like ingrates to the average Briton, and the Americans felt like exploited outsiders in His Majesty's expanding empire. Therefore, in the years prior to the Revolutionary War those few British naval officers who were natives of North America were mostly Tories from Canada and Nova Scotia, the latter a separate colony at the time.[1] These circumstances help to account for what appears to be the unique history of American naval officer personnel during the Revolutionary War.

Finding experienced and proficient officers was a difficult problem in the establishment of the Continental Navy. The officer pool for the Continental Navy came largely from merchant or fishing fleets and privateers. While some of these men had served in the British or other European navies and were familiar with naval tactics, none had served above the rank of midshipman or sailing master. Therefore naval command experience among American mariners was rare.

To join the rebellious Continental Navy against the well-led, well-trained, and well-equipped British navy appeared to be ill-advised; yet many Americans elected to serve as officers, and their reasons were diverse. All were eager, ambitious, and competitive. Most wished to prosper in this new, freer society. Had they spent their maritime careers as privateers—mercenary seaborne businessmen—they might have reaped greater monetary reward, but their motives appear to have been beyond mere self-interest. Material and social recompense cannot fully account for the motivation of the corps of Continental naval officers because of the self-sacrifice that many had to endure. Clearly most of these men risked their lives and fortunes for a cause in which they believed. A prime motive for the majority appeared to be a sense of patriotism and a strong identification with the revolutionary cause. Many of these men had developed strong anti-British sentiments based on personal instances of ill treatment at the hands of the British and their irritating high-seas arrogance.

In the eighteenth century, the standards for the attainment of personal success were found in the ill-defined and yet idealized terms "fame," "glory," and "honor." These somewhat ambiguous nouns did not connote celebrity or even moral courage, but they referred to one's reputation. These attributes were not the results of simple popularity (status devoid of achievement where one becomes famous largely for being well known) but the products of an illustrious eminence, a stature accrued from having led a consequential life. Service in the Continental Navy afforded the opportunity to pursue this noble military trinity: fame, glory, and honor. Yet the trinity resided on a narrow podium: a dais that few could share. These men fought for the same cause, but their disparate conduct, integrity, and character flaws affected their paths toward this elusive goal.

Naval service in America also afforded the chance to enhance one's social standing in a society that was in its formative stages. A selective aristocratic order had developed in colonial America as landholdings were amassed and wealth accrued. One time-honored way for an outsider to ascend the social ladder was to acquire the title navy captain.[2] In Britain many naval heroes became knights, and a few were granted the title of duke, baron, or earl. Although it seemed unlikely that similar titles would appear in the developing United States, a naval hero might receive a sizable land grant as well as a generous pension. Naval service also gave one the opportunity for financial reward through prize money from captured goods and vessels. Perhaps a few overconfident officers calculated the risk/reward ratio as being in their favor. In addition there were those who were simply driven by the challenges, the excitement of leading men in harm's way, and the opportunity to display manly qualities of leadership in the face of danger.

Most of the first American officers were appointed to positions of command because of personal, political, economic, or familial ties to the Continental Congress or the Marine Committee, the predecessor of the Department of the Navy. Nepotism was common in colonial societies. Because these were naval officers serving a rebellion, assurance of loyalty to the cause was extremely important. Congress did not want to lose a valuable ship, its arms, and men because of a captain's questionable loyalty. However, the usual route to command, including schooling as midshipmen and examinations for officer rank, establishment of leadership abilities, and reputation for seamanship, was not a primary factor in the selection process for American officers, as it was in many European nations. As a practical matter, there was insufficient time for what normally included years of apprenticeship. Also the Continental Navy was in competition for manpower with the Continental Army. During the recruitment of forces, the army actively enlisted fishermen and fishing boat captains as transporters of troops and armaments on the many waterways of the eastern seaboard.

Adding to the confusion, a political pecking order of influence surfaced among the colonies, creating discriminatory barriers for a man attempting to earn an officer's commission through the ranks. Strongly held opinions characterized the men of the New England colonies, and these men generally prevailed in maritime affairs. New England sea captains received most of the early command positions in the navy. For example the experienced John Paul Jones had difficulty achieving high rank in the command system because he was a Virginian, a southerner, a Scottish sojourner, and unfortunately a frequently vocal malcontent.

Many of the first officers appointed to command positions in the Continental Navy did not rise through the lower ranks as navy men. This may explain why their sense of compassion and understanding, a product of shared hardships under authority, was deficient or absent. Their method of dealing with their subordinates was by the power of rank rather than raison d'être. Parochial maritime custom also influenced attitude. Merchant sailors and fishermen were sources of experienced seamen, but these men were used to running their ships by way of a quasi-democratic system. Many lacked the rigid discipline needed for naval combat as they were "bloody-minded and objected to being bossed around."[3] Most believed in the two sentiments of the Declaration of Independence that "all men were created equal" and "governments [those in authority] derive their power from the consent of the governed," taking these sentiments literally.

Junior officers and crewmen often expected the captain to confer with them in a council of war concerning a mission. If the men thought the danger too great or the target not worthwhile, they wanted to influence a decision about whether or not to engage in an operation. This attitude could produce disciplinary problems among American crews, especially when a captain's judgment was questioned or an order contested. In contrast formal orders given by British naval officers were frequently followed by the phrase "if you please." This was a sign of courtesy that did not, in truth, ask permission.

During the American Revolution several options were available to the colonies for waging the war at sea. The first was the use of the Continental Navy and specially commissioned, relatively heavily armed naval vessels. The mission of the sailing navy was to destroy or disable enemy ships. Vessel capture was desirable and rewarding but less important than putting them out of action. Naval vessels readily confronted an undermatched enemy, but they would avoid placing themselves in harm's way if they were obviously overmatched. Being a navy sailor subjected men to strict and sometimes harsh discipline. Unquestioned obedience to naval hierarchy was expected. These men suffered from boredom, the result of long patrols. Nevertheless, because they represented the Continental government, they knew that they were obligated to fight honorably if challenged. The financial rewards afforded the naval crew for the collective dangers of capture, suffering wounds, and death were paltry. Each sailor received a small salary as well as a share of the money realized from prizes captured. Unfortunately the Continental scrip had little (or at best fluctuating) value, and a reading of the *Congressional Record* of the time indicates that ships' captains were constantly badgering Congress for payment of prize money due to them and their crews.

The second option provided "regional" naval protection. In July 1775 the Continental Congress gave each colony the authority to provide armed vessels to protect its harbors and navigation of its seacoasts at its own expense. In response, most colonial legislatures instituted independent navies largely manned by local residents and financed and controlled them through "state" Marine Committees. Although a few armed vessels were specially built for this purpose, most state navies comprised converted merchant ships. Their mission was to protect the shipping off or near their states' coasts. The individual state fleets varied in size and effectiveness from colony to colony. The colonies of New Jersey, Delaware, and the new republic of Vermont did not maintain formal navies, but the other colonies instituted individual and independent navies financed and controlled by state Marine Committees. State navies were successful in the recruitment of ships' officers and crews because most were residents of the states and had the distinction of being in a special naval service that protected their homes and the littoral waters of states.[4] Continental naval officers who could not find Continental Navy ships to command could temporarily serve in state navies, but they usually returned to duty when a federal vessel became available.

The third option, the most popular and profitable, was the quasi-naval enterprise of privateering. This was a government-sanctioned activity that was employed for many centuries and especially throughout the eighteenth century. Although not formally part of the Continental Navy, privateers joined some missions, such as the Penobscot Expedition (discussed in chapter 4). Their contributions in interdicting British shipping were of great consequence in the outcome of the Revolutionary War. Civilians were recruited to sail under privateers' letters of marque and reprisal issued by the governments of independent nations or states. Such letters were licenses to act as quasi-seagoing militiamen or a police force. On 27 July 1780, as the Revolutionary War progressed, all privateers were ordered to carry commissions from the secretary of Congress, making privateering an American-government-sponsored effort. A privateer captain was required to post a bond to the government (state or federal) issuing the license. The bond was the then-substantial sum of five thousand dollars for a vessel under one hundred tons or ten thousand dollars for heavier vessels. This did not seem to dissuade many, because 1,696 American vessels sailed under privateers' letters of marque during the Revolutionary War.[5] A mariner could make more money in a short period of time than during several years of peaceful employment. Thus, although the risks were great, the lure of the rewards outweighed the dangers for many.

In fact the bulk of the patriot maritime force of the Revolutionary period was composed of privateers, commerce raiders operating under letters-of-marque commissions from individual states. Most of the captains of the Continental Navy served as privateers at some point during their careers. Most of these privateers were inspired by motives of economic self-interest, with a modicum of patriotism added to the stew. Many thousands of men served on these private warships from 1775 to 1783, while far fewer served in the navy. Putting this fact into perspective, the Continental Congress could not afford to build and outfit many ships at the time. The important point is that in America, "the privateer system assumed approximately the shape of a marine militia or volunteer navy."[6]

American privateer vessels were not heavily armed but depended on surprise, speed, and cunning seamanship in order to capture vulnerable commerce. Once a vessel and its cargo were seized, a prize crew would make for a friendly American or foreign port. When the prize and its goods were sold, some of the crewmen who had taken the vessel to the port of sale were stranded. Thus, when another ship landed at this port, itinerant sailors signed on and thus began a career of wandering from one ship to another. The privateers were particularly successful at attacking British commerce near the Gulf of St. Lawrence and the West Indies. When emboldened they occasionally took ships off the English coast, fueling pernicious war-weariness among the population in England.

Privateer commissions recorded the shipowners' names, the ships' tonnage, their rigs, their armaments, and the numbers of men serving as crews.

Usually the captain and his lieutenant paid a fee for what could be a lucrative contract commission. When privateer vessels captured ships and their goods, the monetary gain for the owners, officers, and crews could be significant. The crews that signed to serve on board privateers understood the meaning of the saying "no prey–no pay"; but these men were often better fed and quartered than they had been onshore, and there was the financial incentive that came from the prizes taken by the ships.

A privateer captain had to be an excellent seaman and an enterprising, courageous, and quick-thinking leader, but not foolhardy. The key to success was often the intelligent application of measured aggressiveness to intimidate prey. Privateers avoided prolonged firefights, relying on the swiftness and maneuverability of their ships to outrun enemy guns.

A variation on privateering, non-letter-of-marque privateering, was a higher-risk option. This venture involved working outside the narrow edge of the law. Some European governments encouraged these noncommissioned privateers to prey upon enemy commerce and reap even greater rewards. The distinction between these non-letter-of-marque privateers and true pirates, men and some women who operated completely outside of the law and were given to plundering any quarry of any nation they could capture, was a fine line. However, privateers sailing under official letters of marque issued by a revolutionary colonial government had no standing in British courts. The king's magistrates did not recognize the legality of colonial governments issuing privateer commissions against the Crown. Therefore during the Revolutionary War the British merchantmen and Royal Navy officers generally considered American privateers as pirates.

Investing in a privateer vessel, or a fleet of privateers, could be a profitable but perilous business. Some well-known merchant families made their fortunes and reputations during the Revolutionary War from underwriting such speculations. Although there was money to be made, the significance to the American Revolution was that the privateer fleet had a detrimental impact on British commerce. Every vessel captured or sunk affected His Majesty's economy. Royal men-of-war had to be diverted from vital naval missions to escort merchant convoys. The British merchant fleet was under constant threat and could not guarantee delivery of goods. Insurance rates on vessels rose dramatically along with other costs of doing business. These expenses often changed the fortunes of marginally profitable merchant ventures from profit to loss.

Forty-seven vessels were commissioned as part of the Continental Navy during the Revolutionary War, but no more than thirty served at the same time. Altogether these vessels were armed with 1,242 cannons and swivel guns and captured 196 vessels valued at about six million Spanish dollars.[7] It should be noted that American privateers, who had far greater success, could carefully choose their battles when they perceived that they had a great advantage. By contrast the navy had what might be called a "professional obligation" to stand its oceanic ground when challenged and fight. Therefore, the Continental Navy became partially dependent on a quasi-militia of the sea—the large flotilla of profit-minded privateers—as their reserve.

To place their importance in an economic perspective, the Continental Congress recorded 1,491 privateer commissions during the duration of the Revolutionary War.[8] The men who obtained privateer commissions used 1,696 vessels during the war. These ships carried 19,745 guns and captured more than one thousand prizes valued in excess of eighteen million dollars.[9] According to Lloyd's of London, American privateers captured or destroyed an estimated 3,100 British vessels. Approximately 900 of these vessels were recaptured or returned after paying ransoms.[10] Using these data, the ratio of captured to commissioned vessels for the Continental Navy was approximately 4.2 to 1, while that of the privateer fleet was about 1.8 to 1. These facts reveal the military prowess of the Continental Navy; however, the navy was armed with about 26 guns per vessel and likely had heavier throw weight. By contrast the privateers had slightly fewer than 11 guns per vessel. The net loss of about 2,200 British merchant ships had a significant impact on insurance costs in Britain. Yet, although the costs were sorely felt, this disruption of British merchant commerce was not enough to decisively sway the outcome of the war.

On the other side of the ledger, British privateers and naval vessels combined to capture or destroy over one thousand American vessels and their crews to offset these losses.[11] Although the rebellious colonies had a smaller total number of ships and men at risk, interdiction by British privateers and warships had a greater impact on the American economy than did the American fleets on the economy of Great Britain.

Given the results of the Continental Navy during the Revolutionary War, was there anything extraordinary about the Americans who chose to serve as officers in the Continental Navy? One might assume that they represented a distinctive American spirit, a mindset of men caught up in a patriotic zeal of dedication to the War of Independence. This supposition also implies that at the dawn of the American Revolution the colonists had a national character. That generalization was too imprecise for a nation composed of immigrants from many countries, even though a majority at the time had British roots. Unfortunately with this meld came a few castoffs from their respective countries. Some of these were former European naval personnel who had immigrated to America in hopes of wangling commissions. Many of these men had competed against one another in "the old country," and they continued their feuds by being derogatory about each other's competence to command. The Continental Navy wardrooms could at times be characterized by hostility and rivalries. This acrimony clearly contributed to the genesis of contentiousness within the nascent navy in general.

What these men did share was a lack of commonality and a multiplicity of backgrounds that may have been unique to the American experience. Joseph Conrad wrote, "All ideals are built on the ground of solid achievement, which in a given profession creates in the course of time a certain tradition, or in other words a standard of conduct."[12] In the newly emerging nation of the United Colonies there were no American naval traditions or naval culture. John Adams had borrowed the British Admiralty Code as America's "standard of conduct" and applied it in almost its totality to the Continental Navy. Because the seniority system had to be created de novo in a crisis situation, the American rank scheme was controlled by local and federal politics. The Congress was justifiably reluctant to trust people whose backgrounds and allegiances were unknown. Nepotism was evident in the selection process, causing discord among many of the naval officers.

An example of nepotism was the selection of the captain whom the Continental Congress asked to be the first to lead the Continental Navy, Commodore Esek (or Ezek) Hopkins of Rhode Island. Like George Washington, Hopkins began his military career during the French and Indian War (1753–63), in this case as a successful English privateer captain. In 1764 he became a merchant ship captain for the Brown brothers of Providence, Rhode Island, commanding the eleven-ton brigantine *Sally* for a slaving venture to the Guinea coast of Africa. The vessel had a crew of eleven with a cargo of tobacco, highly prized Rhode Island rum, and some miscellaneous trading goods. The *Sally* also carried assorted small arms, thirteen cutlasses, plus forty shackles and an unknown number of long chains. The brigantine arrived on the coast of Guinea early in November, but the crew had difficulty in finding slaves offered by the local chieftains. By the time they had purchased enough slaves to make the venture profitable, they could not embark on their return voyage until the storm-ridden late December of 1765. Hopkins noted in his log that 109 of the original 167 individuals composing his slave cargo had perished during this harrowing Middle Passage. Of the 58 who survived, 24 were so ill that they brought a meager price on the Antigua slave market.

In 1768 Hopkins was elected second deputy to the Colonial Assembly of Rhode Island from North Providence. He returned to sea for a year, then was elected first deputy in 1771 for a term of three years. He served briefly as a brigadier general in the Rhode Island militia during October 1775 in defense of the island of Rhode Island. Hopkins's brother Stephen was a delegate to the Second Continental Congress and a member of the Naval Committee. On 6 November 1775 Stephen Hopkins wrote to his brother, "You will perceive by a letter from the [Marine] Committee dated yesterday, that they have pitched upon you to take the Command of a small Fleet."[13] Thus, through Stephen Hopkins's influence, Esek Hopkins resigned his army commission and was appointed commander in chief and commodore of a fledgling Continental Navy. Commodore Hopkins's history as a slave-ship master is evidence that political influence trumped what many considered immorality in the selection of the earliest officers of the Continental Navy. Then again slave trading was a legal and lucrative business in pre-Revolutionary days. This was particularly true in the colony of Rhode Island, arguably the center of the triangular trade: for example, rum shipped to Africa traded for slaves, slaves brought to North America in the Middle Passage for sale in the West Indies, and sugar bought for molasses made into New England rum for export.

The people one knew, the importance of one's family, and the colony or region where one lived or was born helped in obtaining a navy commission. The Marine Committee generally looked askance at officer candidates from less influential or less populous colonies. Disturbingly there is evidence of bias against recent émigrés, particularly those from economically poor or backward regions such as Ireland and Scotland. Perhaps this was an expression of social bigotry or possibly a question of a prospective officer's loyalty when in battle against Great Britain. The latter premise is unlikely since the Irish and Scots of the eighteenth century had little fondness for the English.

An atmosphere of prejudice was rampant at the onset of the Revolutionary War, perpetrated by the British Admiralty with their condescending attitude toward the Continental Navy. The rebels were denounced as cowardly rogues and villains who conducted war "like savages" and who were "the poorest mean-spirited scoundrels that ever surely pretended to the dignity of rebellion."[14] It is a common practice to vilify one's enemy in time of war, but the attitudes of the British seemed to transcend this customary exercise.

The highly structured tradition and culture of the Royal Navy sharply contrasted with the more ad hoc nature of its Continental Navy counterpart. This might lead one to believe that bickering among officers was an American affliction. British officers, in fact, were human and subject to the universal frailties of envy and occasional vindictiveness. Some complaints about or among British officers were very much in evidence. For example Admiral Cuthbert Collingwood, commander of the British fleet after Lord Nelson's death at Trafalgar, grousing about Captain Edward Rotheram, flag captain on the *Royal Sovereign,* wrote, "But such a captain, such a stick, I wonder very much how such people get forward. . . . Was he brought up in the Navy? For he has very much of the style of the Coal Trade about him, except that they are good seamen."[15] Rear Admiral Richard Lestock was described as "unconciliating in his manners, austere in command, restless when in a subordinate station, he had fewer friends than fell to the lot of most men, and that number . . . was gradually diminishing."[16] Admiral John Jervis, Earl of St. Vincent, spoke ill of the dead hero of Trafalgar some years after the event by saying, "Lord Nelson's sole merit was animal courage, his private character most disgraceful in every sense of the word."[17]

Even laypeople took the opportunity to castigate some high-profile naval officers. For example, a principled English lady lost patience with the renowned Admiral Richard "Black Dick" Howe, who took short cruises off Torbay interspersed with long anchorages in the port. Calling Howe the "Lord of Torbay," she said, "His lordship is not rapid, he moves like a king at chess at the end of the game, one square inch from Torbay, and the next back again."[18]

The most noteworthy clash of British commanders that occurred in America during the Revolutionary War, somewhat analogous to that of Dudley Saltonstall and Solomon Lovell (covered in chapter 4), was that between General Sir Henry Clinton and Admiral Marriot Arbuthnot.[19] Clinton was imaginative and aggressive, while Arbuthnot seemed predestined to procrastinate when faced with a decision. Midway in the war the two men were at loggerheads about co-coordinated military plans on land and naval support from the sea. At one point Clinton wrote to Lord George Germain (also known as Lord Sackville) that the admiral, "who from age, temper, and inconsistency of conduct is really so little to be depended on that, was I to continue to serve with him, I should constantly be under the most distressing apprehensions of the miscarriage of . . . enterprises we might engage in."[20] When the enigmatic Arbuthnot was reassigned, Clinton was very much relieved.

Admirals George Rodney and Samuel Hood produced a similar episode of clashes between temperamental social misfits. As one historian put it, Rodney had "an air of breeding, a fine distinction of manner, which his able subordinate [Hood] entirely lacked," thus leading to many clashes.[21] This was a case of Rodney's snobbishness expressed as an overbearing attitude when dealing with an inferior officer.

The illustrations above only scratch a deep surface, but squabbling and bickering among Royal Navy officers may have been less overt because British officers rose through the ranks from midshipman to post captain and beyond. One of the great communal centers and perhaps levelers in the British navy was the wardroom, a place in the afterpart of a vessel where the officers took their meals and socialized. This is where men from similar backgrounds and who largely had similar attitudes and concerns formed bonds and friendships that often lasted a lifetime. This small room was the place where the clan of the commissioned officer was founded, a place of civility and hospitality on board a crowded vessel, a compartment where career paths from midshipmen to junior and senior officers were charted. Still, because of human nature, it sometimes was the place where lasting enmities between officers were born. This wardroom culture was also found on board American Continental Navy vessels and functioned in a manner similar to that in the Royal Navy. However, because of the lack of an American naval tradition of rising through the pecking order of the ranks during the initial years of the Revolutionary War, its role was not as strong as with its British counterpart.

The British Admiralty had a naval officer procurement system that ostensibly provided for a steady supply of commissioned officers when needed. Unfortunately, as with many government operations, it malfunctioned, usually providing shortages during war and excesses during peace. First, the Admiralty tried to recruit a relatively fixed number of "volunteers," or what later were called midshipmen, per year so as to have trained junior officer replacements when needed. Second, they established a system of training these young officer candidates to assure their competence. Third, these new officers were assigned to posts to acquire experience so that they could be ready to assume a command position when needed. Fourth, they were given an opportunity for advancement, but nepotism and British class system gave certain junior officers advantages. Fifth, they entered a pyramid system of promotion; some would rise to the highest positions, while others would exit service in a reserve status. Last, for the officers and their dependents, there was a provision for retirement or pension as a result of sickness, wounds, or superannuation or not making the promotion list. This was deemed "service at half pay." This highly structured system was lacking for those who joined the Continental Navy.

British naval officers shared triumphs and hardships, creating a sense of camaraderie—a warrior brotherhood that, because of its lack of history, could not be duplicated in the nascent Continental Navy. Senior British captains would dine as a group at the admiral's mess, presenting their ideas for engaging an enemy in various circumstances. Their peers identified the best and brightest men and noted each other's strengths while perhaps avoiding their deficiencies, enabling them to work together as a team in battle. Because of these informal gatherings, signals between commanders and subordinates in battle took on subtle or deeper meanings; the inner thoughts of a well-known comrade were learned.[22] Naval officers who engaged in these discourses became "a Band of Brothers,"[23] developing bonds over years of shared service.

Education within the ranks of British naval officers was narrow, its greatest depth being in maritime professional knowledge and sea experience. Men who desired a sea officer's career usually went to sea when they were very young. "Of a sample of 100 officers who passed their lieutenant's examination in 1793 [a decade after the American conflict], at least thirty eight were not older than twelve when they first went to sea. Four were under eight years old, and the youngest was at least five."[24] If a young man aspired to commissioned naval service, it was wise to attend a special maritime school that gave basic instruction in mathematics and literacy (writing), and a few took foreign-language training, usually French. These were the academic tools needed for learning the advanced practical application of navigation and communicating with one's fellow officers and the occasional foreign or captured sailor.

A few men opted for admission to one of only forty places in the Royal Naval Academy at Portsmouth, established in 1737. Those who attended were mostly the sons of the elite. The cost was between seventy and eighty pounds sterling a year, a substantial sum in those days. The academy was poorly administered, and places in the classes were often left unfilled. Those line officers on shipboard valued sea experience over desk learning, so being an academy graduate in many cases was a disadvantage to promotion. Thus, during the eighteenth century the impact of the Royal Naval Academy for creating educated officers was trivial.

A young man accepted as a midshipman had to accumulate a minimum of six years of sea experience before he could sit for the lieutenant's examination. That meant that most were boys in their late teens to early twenties when they received their commissions. Less competent midshipmen stayed at this rank well into their thirties or forties. These officers were highly skilled as seamen, but the vast majority had little time for a formal education beyond what one might consider primary school. Their wide range in age, varied experiences in academic and maritime skills, together with an absence of an organized comprehensive midshipman curriculum made these officers a diverse lot. These factors also meant that when they became senior officers, "in the worst cases ignorant and monoglot admirals had to take on wide strategic and political responsibilities for which they were completely unqualified."[25] There were no admirals, ignorant or not, making policy decisions in America.

Buckling on an officer's sword and placing a cockade on one's hat did not automatically confer the social graces of a gentleman on a midshipman. Social polish was not easily acquired in the shipboard mess and blustering midshipman's berth. Manners and gentility were more likely the products of frequent social interactions with people of the upper classes. Thus social position played a prominent role in promotion to the highest ranks. In spite of this, "it was understood that sea officers had to demonstrate real professional competence and experience. . . . captains and admirals, whose professional credit was at stake . . . acted as a filter, receiving recommendations from political and personal connections, but adopt[ed] only those candidates whose abilities justified their endorsement and strengthened their authority."[26] Like their American counterparts, the British also appeared to have regional preferences in the selection of officer candidates. Over 70 percent of the officers who came from Britain hailed from southern England below the Humber and Mersey rivers, and most lived in the seaside shires as opposed to the inland counties.[27]

For advancement, having enlisted at the right time enhanced one's odds for promotion. The quickest rise from midshipman to lieutenant occurred in times of rapid mobilization. Conversely the least fortunate were those who enlisted just as a conflict was ending. They were at the bottom of an almost insurmountable seniority list when the promotion rate slowed to a near halt. Because most promotions occurred during wartime or in time of perceived threats, the Royal Navy seldom seemed to have the right number or desired mix of officers for any given length of time. Inactive officers received half-pay, and the necessity of earning a decent living rapidly reduced the ranks of midshipmen and lieutenants. Those officers who had seniority and were poised for promotion were required to wait through the long years of peace. Many became too old for further effective service and retired. Political patronage and social privilege were almost the only routes to promotion.[28] With the next need for navy mobilization, the numbers of qualified officers were insufficient again, and the vicious cycle repeated.

Since the American Revolutionary War was the first American naval war, this was not an issue in the Continental Navy. What became a problem was that American enlistments were often for specific durations; therefore, some essential crewmen and junior officers left service at inopportune times. An American naval officer who served in the Continental Navy could sign up for a state's navy, take temporary duty as a privateer, and then perhaps return to his previous rank in the Continental Navy. This recurring switching of military allegiances and roles rarely, if ever, occurred in the Royal Navy. In addition, there was a shortage of Continental Navy ships in service due to the time needed for building, conversion from other uses, or their repair from battle damage.

American naval captains had far less battle experience than their British counterparts; they were more diverse in their leadership skills, and most lacked formal education. In addition, some were army officers who were ordered to perform maritime missions. General Washington frequently used his troops as ships' crews on short inland missions in a quasi-naval capacity. If these men were later appointed as naval officers, the change of service was offensive to some who had served as "blue water" sailors. The unregimented nature of American captains made teamwork more of a goal than a reality. This was especially true in the relatively complex amphibious operations. In these instances troops had to be quartered, transported to a safe landing site, put ashore to accomplish a given mission, and supported by accurate fire from naval guns. Logistical requirements meant that food and ammunition had to be supplied by these vessels during battle, sophisticated military activities even by current standards. In summary, a multitude of well-honed leadership skills were vital attributes for the budding officer corps, skills to be developed from years of experience.

Contrasting naval tactics at sea may also account for some of the differences between American and British officers. Because King George had many vessels, the Royal Navy frequently employed large fleets in naval engagements for the numerical and firepower advantages. The potential downside of this strategy was that controlling many vessels in battle required both cooperation and coordination among the commanders. They had to maneuver and fight as a unit. The Continental Navy captains who had fewer ships with fewer cannons either fought one-on-one or as part of a small squadron of ships. Perhaps this reflected the American penchant for independence and was asserted in their preference for sea battle engagement.

The success of any navy depended on a crew of ordinary sailors who were called upon to perform dangerous tasks on the cruel sea. Life during the eighteenth century was difficult, but the man who went to sea had certain advantages: the assurance of decent food and grog, shelter and companionship, and rudimentary medical care. For a man with poor prospects and little education, the sea offered an escape. The routine of the vessel's rotational watch-keeping system varied his time on duty over a twenty-four-hour period, providing variety, stability, and most important, predictability. He also had the opportunity (though slim) for advancement, the possibility of the esteem of his fellows, and the chance for a share of prize money. The laborious way of life and shared hardship bound him to the exclusive society of his shipmates as well as loyalty to his ship and usually to its officers.

In the Royal Navy, little attention was paid to the career of the individual seaman. He was too often a mere entry on the muster books of his ship, a pawn in the grand maritime chess game of naval warfare. A seaman who volunteered for naval service would begin with the penning of his name in the pay book on board a commissioned man-of-war. In the case of a volunteer, it was possible to request to be assigned to a specific ship or captain, but this was not guaranteed. There was no provision for basic skills training or keeping men on shore bases. For those captured by press gangs or crimps, the formality of signing on as crewmen was essentially the same, but the ships they ended up on were usually vessels that had anchored in port and were in need of additional personnel. The merchant sailors were wise to quickly become patriotic and "volunteer." Doing so would likely assure better treatment than if they had resisted. If an inexperienced landsman fought against impressment and a press gang member was killed, he would be hunted down as a murderer.

An account of one of these expeditions from the log of the 36-gun *Flora* reads as follows: "I dropped [anchor] near the *Lord Harlow* Indiaman, which ship had acted in the most outrageous manner in [receiving] the boats from H.M. ships. . . . Afterwards veer[ing] alongside the Indiaman, when they received me armed, I told them the consequences of their resistance and to avoid the shedding of blood, I promised that if they would enter voluntarily, they would have liberty to do so; upon which they threw down their arms."[29]

Shipboard life for the novice sailor differed greatly from that of the landsman. In addition to being waterborne fortresses, wooden ships were vast storehouses of food and cordage that never seemed to lose their dampness. As a result they were floating breeding grounds for rats, lice, mites, and especially cockroaches. These despicable vermin were constantly in evidence, especially in the dimly lit areas below decks. Making matters worse, the gun decks also used for berthing and orlop decks harbored stale, fetid vapors that infiltrated the crew's living quarters in the ship's bowels. These damp, dirty, densely crowded spaces provided the center of a seaman's singular society, one of the male gender, ruled by an often brutal hierarchy. In this unpleasant social order, there were few options for mercy and even fewer for privacy. This was the pervasive microcosmic world within the bulwarks of the warship.

Theoretically all sailors were required to serve for a predetermined "enlistment" time, usually on a specific vessel, and were to be financially compensated when the cruise was over. In practice this rarely happened. Once at sea, a higher-ranking administrative commander could, as the need arose, trade recruited or impressed sailors from one ship to another. Because the British navy had worldwide commitments, a sailor might find himself far from home when his enlistment time was up. The faceless hierarchical body of the Admiralty bore no responsibility to the plight of an individual seaman. Its business was to provide vessels at specified locations for a certain span of time. At the local level it became the captain's responsibility to keep a sailor employed on his ship, trade him to another ship, or dismiss the seaman at a port of his choosing.

Because of being impressed against their will and the hardships of shipboard life, relatively few British seamen opted for long-term naval service. Sailors could rise through the ranks of landsman, ordinary seaman, and able seaman if they had ability and were fortunate enough to survive the rigors of an extended period of life on the gun deck. Cruelly, when a sailor was disabled, he could be dismissed or given humiliating duties when he was considered a liability in battle. A hand could descend in rank for many reasons, such as insubordination, insolence, drunkenness, or incompetence in performing his duty. The prospects for an enlisted seaman to rise above the lower decks to the ranks of a senior commissioned officer were slim; yet some men were successful and gained fame. James Cook was a sailor who became a renowned captain and explorer. From the century before, the highly regarded John Benbow rose all the way to admiral. Rear Admiral of the Blue Sir Samuel Hood was the son of a vicar and rose from able seaman to his lofty position. Still the most likely avenues of advancement in rank for the enlisted men were as warrant officer, sailing master, boatswain, master's mate, or gunner's mate.

In spite of the hardships, the British had a long tradition of naval service that seemed to transcend the shortcomings. Loyalty to king and country plus the perceived certitude that as sailors they were protecting their families and homes were strong motivational factors for those serving in the Royal Navy. These men had a sense of mission—the protection of the British Isles through the wooden walls of their ships, whose stout hearts were of British oak. Because of Britain's many years of naval conflicts, the crews were experienced in warfare and, regardless of rank, learned to obey the orders of their commanders without question (or suffered summary punishments) for the reward of victory and occasional glory.

Though they had an admirable heritage and were legendary for their intrepidity, most ordinary British seaman were from the lower rungs of British life. Undesirable aliens, rogues, vagrants, and a few criminals opted for naval service rather than time in prison. Admiral Edward Vernon is quoted as saying, "The men on whom depended the liberties of our country were the only people who had no liberty at all."[30] Impressed seamen frequently looked forward to poor or inadequate food, seasickness, corporal punishment, drowning, and wounding or death in battle, among other hardships. British sailors often complained of receiving meager quantity of rations and especially poor-quality rations. Pursers were known to misappropriate food by shortening the weight of the pound, keeping the overage for personal sale and profit. When a sailor was ailing from bad food, poor sanitation, or even wounds from battle, he could be docked pay because he could not work his watch. The only organized interruptions to the physical hardships and the monotonous routine were music and dance. "A casual visitor to a man of war, beholding the song, the dance, the reverie of the crew, might judge them happy. But I know that these things are often resorted to because they feel miserable, just to drive away dull care."[31]

British seamen performed their tasks out of fear of their officers but even more to gain or keep the respect of their fellow tars. They were often prevented from going ashore while on duty. When it was necessary to send a boat ashore, those who went had a sufficient number of officers on board to prevent the men from running. William Richardson, who had been impressed in the Royal Navy from a merchant vessel from 1790 to 1815, wrote, "I think it only fair and just, that when seamen are pressed, in coming home from a long voyage, they should be allowed a few weeks liberty on shore to spend their money among friends and relations; when that was gone, they would soon be tired of the shore, return contented to their ships, and by such means there would be half so much desertion."[32] Desertion was a major problem. Throughout 1775–80, at the time of the American Revolution, 176,145 men served in the Royal Navy; 1,243 were killed by enemy action, 18,543 died of disease or other causes (mostly accidents), and 42,069 deserted.[33]

By contrast, most American sailors were volunteers, and although impressment was not unknown, it was used far less than in Britain.[34] Seamen were recruited to sail on particular ships, usually based in ports that were close to their homes. For added inducement sailors could sign on for specific cruises. Like their British counterparts, the American sailors may have served longer than they had perhaps expected, being transferred from ship to ship or from captain to captain, but frequently this was by way of their own request. American sailors did not expect to make a career of naval service. Once independence was won, most thought that the navy would greatly downsize or even disband. Therefore, for most, naval service was looked at as interim duty for the patriotic cause and good preparation for a more lucrative career later in the merchant fleet. A record of desertion would likely be a blemish limiting opportunities or advancement.

Establishing a naval desertion rate among the Americans during the Revolutionary War is perhaps an impossible task. Some men had multiple enlistments, that is, they spent time in the Continental Navy and/or a state navy and occasionally served stints as privateers. The individual captains made log entries of the sailors who signed on board, but some volunteered for a limited enlistment period or a specific voyage. When a navy ship reached an overseas port, the crews were usually supplemented with foreign able seamen. Logs of all the captains were not necessarily made available to the Marine Committee of the Continental Congress. Thus there is a paucity of complete or dependable surviving records. An approximation could be calculated for those few major vessels for which muster rolls exist for an extended period, but extrapolating from this small data sample a general rate of desertion on every ship over the entire war would be erroneous.[35] Desertions varied depending on the period of the war and the operational history of each ship. Even so, one might reasonably assume that the desertion rate among sailors in the Continental Navy was proportionally less than that in the Royal Navy.

As the Revolutionary War progressed and the first flush of patriotism faded, many sailors became weary of the constant danger, strict naval discipline, and relatively paltry prize money—a fraction of that offered to privateers. It became increasingly burdensome for naval officers to recruit and control their crews. In addition some vain but qualified sea captains refused to accept commissions because of their place on the seniority lists. Their pride made it difficult, if not impossible, for them to subordinate themselves to more senior officers whom they did not respect. Since leadership and acquiescence is based on mutual respect, this produced calumny and venomous innuendos among some officers as well as members of the Marine Committee. After the war, some naval officers left America for service abroad and the opportunity for higher rank and greater prestige. Other, less fortunate Continental Navy officers were court-martialed for dereliction of duty, formally reprimanded for poor judgment, or lost their commands for a variety of other reasons. Some were well known, such as Esek Hopkins and Abraham Whipple; others, such as Nicholas Broughton, William Coit, Pierre Landais, Hector McNeill, and James Nicholson, were not as well celebrated.

Biographical sketches of five important naval figures are evidence of these disputations and the attendant character flaws. The Continental Congress recognized all of them for their service during the Revolutionary War. Each spent time as a privateer but readily served in his nation's navy with distinction. During this time they also found themselves mired in controversy and professional jealousies. John Paul Jones of Virginia emerged as a renowned hero, but John Manley of Massachusetts, Dudley Saltonstall of Connecticut, Silas Talbot of Rhode Island, and Joshua Barney of Maryland have largely been forgotten.

These men from different colonies had widely dissimilar backgrounds. Manley, a sometime fisherman and merchantman, probably deserted from the

British navy. Talbot was from a large New England Puritan family. Barney, the son of an upper-middle-class farmer, was from the then sparsely settled colony of Maryland. Jones, a Scottish immigrant with a checkered past, had a great deal of command experience in the British merchant fleet. Ironically the most patrician of the group, Saltonstall, became a fallen hero and perhaps a scapegoat for the shortcomings among army and navy officers as well as privateers. Manley and Saltonstall were among the earliest to be named captains in the Continental Navy. The other three ascended the ladder of rank after extraordinary service. The colorful Barney was the last man to be promoted to captain during the Revolutionary War. Jones, the most vexatious of the maritime quintet, had dealings with Manley, Saltonstall, and Barney, and he probably met Talbot in New London, Connecticut, when he returned from the Nassau Expedition raid. Talbot was the classic Revolutionary War hybrid, an army officer and a naval commander.

Each man found himself tossed about in the wakes of the others' naval careers. They possessed character flaws that now and again created enmity toward their peers. Remarkably all found themselves challenged by at least one potentially baneful adversary: Manley and Hector McNeill; Talbot and Barney and Thomas Truxtun; Saltonstall and Generals Peleg Wadsworth and Solomon Lovell; Barney and James Nicholson; Jones and Pierre Landais. Their stories are fascinating and their foibles all too human. The leadership abilities and deficiencies of this small sample is an insufficient model for all of the Continental Navy officers, but their actions give historians reasons to ponder the leadership skill set among the officer company.

The Continental Army Commodore

John Manley

John Manley may have been a deserter from the Royal Navy, but he became the second American Revolutionary War officer to be appointed by George Washington with the title of commodore.[1] The forty-three-year-old unassuming fisherman from Marblehead, Massachusetts, was somewhat of an enigma because he wrote little and was evidently relatively inarticulate. Manley actually held the rank of captain in the Continental Army, his bastion the bulwark of an armed fishing schooner. He commanded a ship in Washington's schooner fleet that harassed British shipping near New England. The Marbleheader captured the valuable British vessels, and his extraordinary record of successes helped convince General Washington of the value of forming a Continental Navy. Manley became the second captain in seniority in the Continental Navy and repeatedly distinguished himself in combat. In his final naval engagement he and his marines captured the last valuable British vessel of the Revolutionary War, the *Baille*. Although largely forgotten in the annals of American maritime history, John Manley set a lofty standard for initiative and bravery for the United States navy even by today's standards. However, his heroism did not prevent Manley from having his share of contentious encounters with his peers.

The powerful British navy controlled the Atlantic Ocean, the lifeline to and from the American colonies in the eighteenth century. Challenging the Royal Navy's might with relatively untrained leaders commanding seamen in small, lightly armed vessels seemed to be folly. Yet a strategic gamble and the emergence of a few unlikely maritime leaders gave shape to America's initial navy.

For over a century the British kings administered trade and navigation laws in order to develop a subservient colonial empire. However, oppressive policies of taxation and exploitation in the interest of English political factions shattered the allegiance of many colonists. The degree of damage differed in various sections of the country, depending on the way specific revenue acts

John Manley. Woodblock print.
Photograph courtesy of Peabody Essex Museum

were applied. Those colonies that suffered the largest prohibitions of free trade, the heaviest taxation, the most excessive fees, and seizure of property became the centers of the revolutionary movement.

The Acts of Trade and Navigation and the Stamp Act of the 1760s were particular irritants to the heavily trade-dependent Massachusetts colonists. Parliament passed laws known by the colonists as the Repressive or Intolerable Acts of 1774, which effectively shut down the port of Boston, giving rise to the Boston Tea Party. In March 1775 the New England Restraining Act, known locally as the "Fisheries Bill," was passed by Parliament. It became law on 20 July 1775, prohibiting fishing on the Grand Banks south of Newfoundland. This act economically fettered New England fishermen and produced a ripple effect, damaging the commerce of the coastal towns on Massachusetts Bay's shores. In addition, fishermen who were experienced sailors were extremely vulnerable for impressment into the British navy. Therefore these New England mariners were ripe for rebellion.

The repression of political liberty and economic freedom set the stage for insurrection, and on 15 June 1775 the Continental Congress of the United Colonies of America established the Continental Army and appointed George Washington as commander. Congress did not provide for a naval force; it was believed that to challenge the British navy, as Samuel Chase of Maryland said, "was the maddest idea in the world."[2] Indeed, the military strategic planners in London initially reasoned that the independence movement would collapse if they could cut off trade in American population centers, all of which were at or near seaports at the time. The British thought that if they could seal the ports and support the Crown's colonial governors, the rebellion could be quelled by naval control of North America—particularly since the insurgents essentially lacked a naval force of their own.

What they failed to take into account was that John Montagu, Lord Sandwich, had exaggerated both the readiness and seaworthiness of the British naval fleet and the competency of the navy's captains, many of whom had gained appointments because they were Whigs. Added to this was the vastness of the North American coastline that the thinly stretched Royal Navy was supposed to protect. There were significant distances between some of the major seaports; between them were many small harbors and estuaries that could shelter a harassing fleet of rebel vessels, and communication between ships of the line was relatively primitive.

In spite of the difficulties, the Admiralty was well aware of the Crown's advantages. Prior to 1775 the shipwrights of the United Colonies could not build warships under the eyes of the king's troops. Turning existing ships into men-of-war was problematic because the British forbade the colonists from casting cannons and even large anchors. In addition, smaller arms and munitions were in short supply, and merchant ships and fishing boats were no match for frigates or ships of the line. In spite of these tribulations, on 18 July 1775 the Continental Congress requested "that each colony, at its own expense, make such provision by armed vessels or otherwise . . . for the protection of their harbours and navigation on their sea coasts, against all unlawful invasions, attacks and predations, from cutters and ships of war."[3]

General Washington took command of the Massachusetts garrison on 3 July 1775, just prior to the declaration suggesting the formation of individual colonial (state) navies. The garrison's fortifications stretched from Roxbury on the southeast to Winter Hill and Prospect Hill on the northwest and looked down on Boston harbor. A dark forest of spars and masts of British warships and merchantmen populated the harbor. Near the harbor's piers stood warehouses; shipyards; chandleries; distilleries; a hodgepodge of pitched roofs, chimneys, and sporadic church steeples; and a few wooden stages for salting and drying fish. The British, under the command of Vice Admiral Thomas Graves, commanded Boston harbor and its waterways, while General Washington and his Continental Army controlled the land approaches to the city.

Washington's army service was limited to the French and Indian War. He knew little about naval affairs but reasoned that by harassing the sea-lanes (British supply lines), the Americans might slow their timely delivery of goods, and perhaps his troops might also gain some precious war materiel in the bargain. Colonel John Glover of the Continental Army was ordered to recruit fishermen from the ports north of Boston into his Massachusetts Continental Army regiment. These mariner-soldiers would be used to man converted, lightly armed fishing schooners. Their mission was to "Cruize against such Vessels as may be found on the High Seas or elsewhere bound inwards or outwards to or from Boston."[4] That meant that they were to interdict relatively nonthreatening armed British vessels as they beat southward down the Gulf of Maine from England and Halifax, as well as those running northward from the West Indies to Boston.

The colonists knew that privateering for a rebel cause was a dangerous pursuit. Raiding merchant ships or naval vessels of a sovereign nation without a recognized independent state's letter of marque was considered an act of piracy by most nations. Massachusetts boldly wrote legislation to legalize privateering on 1 November 1775, and the Continental Congress followed on 25 November. These governments were not internationally recognized sovereign states.[5] The captains and crews of these vessels were therefore placed in great jeopardy when performing their missions, including execution if they were caught.

On 24 August 1775, a little more than two months before Massachusetts passed privateering legislation, the Beverly schooner *Hannah*, under Captain Nicholas Broughton, a native of Marblehead, became the first to sail on behalf of the commander of American forces for the defense of the United Colonies. Regrettably Broughton (perhaps a prototype of other captains to follow) was irascible and independent. He showed little regard for orders from Washington's command and had little success in capturing prizes of value. To make matters worse, he grounded the *Hannah* on a muddy shoal outside Beverly harbor, damaging the ship and compromising Washington's ability to use the vessel as a privateer.

On 2 September, Colonel Glover leased the fishing schooners *Speedwell* and *Eliz* from their Marblehead owners, converted them to armed schooners, and then renamed them respectively *Hancock* and *Franklin*. In spite of his poor beginning, Broughton was appointed commander of the larger *Hancock*, while another Marbleheader, John Selman, was assigned to the *Franklin* to work in concert with Broughton. Both men successfully took small prizes, vessels, and cargoes of little strategic use. Small or not, their capture affected local commerce and insurance rates. Political controversy among prominent Massachusetts merchants ensued. Some merchants needed the ship's cargo delivered to stay in business; others were part owners of the ships, and their investments were in jeopardy. The disruption of Boston-bound commerce mostly managed to polarize the Boston populace.

The limited use of privateers was not working out as Washington had envisioned; the scheme apparently needed more time, more ships, and perhaps better captains. To answer this need, Washington ordered another pair of vessels made ready for combat against the British. They were the sixty-four-ton schooner *Warren,* owned by John Trisden of Marblehead, captained by Winborn Adams of Durham, New Hampshire, and crewed by New Hampshire men; and the seventy-four-ton schooner *Lee,* belonging to Thomas Stevens and commanded by John Manley, both of Marblehead. These two ship commanders were commissioned as Continental Army captains, a lesser pay grade rank, but assigned to sea duty as ships' officers.

The unrefined and sometimes gruff Manley sailed the *Lee* under the "Liberty Tree Flag," a white banner with a pine tree painted in the middle and emblazoned with the words "An Appeal to Heaven." His first act was to sail out of Beverly on 28 October 1775 in order to train his crew in naval defense, combat, and gunnery. Once his men were prepared for battle to his satisfaction, Manley sailed the *Lee* southward to Plymouth on 1 November to hunt for British ships based on the Massachusetts South Shore. Fierce gales kept him in port until 5 November. Shortly after putting to sea on 6 November, Manley's crew saw the lumber sloop *Ranger* with Captain William McGlathry in command. Manley approached the *Ranger* and discovered that a British boarding party from the frigate *Cerberus* had taken the lumber sloop as a prize, its cargo needed for the approaching winter. He threatened to fire on the sloop, but McGlathry surrendered before a shot was fired. Once on board, Manley ordered the American prisoners to be set free and sent the vessel to Marblehead as his first prize.

On 8 November, while cruising off Great Misery Island, he observed a schooner near the entrance to Beverly harbor and gave chase. As it neared the rocky shore, a boat loaded with armed local fishermen rowed out to intercept the schooner. The *Lee* came alongside the schooner just as the fishermen clambered on board the now-identified *Two Sisters* with Robert Robbins as master. The ship was bound for Boston from Ireland with foodstuffs and royal correspondence including the "Proclamation for Suppressing the Rebellion and Sedition" from King George III, which Manley knew would interest General

Washington. The colonists could use the food stores on board since it was past harvest time and winter was approaching. *Two Sisters* became the second prize of the *Lee* and also sailed to Marblehead for safekeeping. On 27 November, Manley spotted the eighty-ton merchant sloop *Polly*, with Samuel Smith as master, and seized the vessel laden with fresh produce and Spanish silver dollars. (An important point for the reader is that the *Lee*'s mission was to seize merchant vessels. Since ships' armaments varied greatly, only their tonnages are mentioned when known.)

The next day, near Boston, Manley encountered another ship, the 250-ton brig *Nancy*. Attacking a brig with a schooner one-third its size and with only four small cannons appeared to be bad judgment since the larger vessel usually carried more cannons and used heavier shot. Still, not all merchant vessels were well armed, and if they were, having guns did not mean that the crews were proficient in gunnery. Now good fortune smiled on Manley. Gales that had buffeted the New England coast in early November had damaged the *Nancy*. Robert Hunter, master of the *Nancy*, assumed that the *Lee* was a pilot schooner ready to take his partly disabled vessel into Boston. He sent up a signal flag asking a pilot to board. Manley saw his opportunity. He decided to send a longboat with armed crewmen to greet the captain cheerfully, and he then took possession of the vessel without a fight. This *ruse de guerre* became a common ploy for Manley and one imitated by other schooner captains.

The manifest disclosed that the *Nancy* was a windfall because she carried approximately two thousand muskets, thirty tons of musket shot, plus thirty thousand round shots, one hundred thousand flints, eleven mortar beds, and a huge cast brass mortar that weighed ten thousand pounds.[6] The seizure of the *Nancy* was the first major capture of military stores and munitions of the Revolutionary War. This confiscation vindicated Washington's vision of a paranaval fleet. It also brought Captain John Manley to the attention of General Washington and his military staff.

This loss, a blow to British pride, was elegized in Great Britain in the following poem:

> Retarded by a tedious long delay,
> The livestock perished on the blust'ring sea,
> And transport ships became provincial prey.
> Laden with apparatus for the train,
> Thrice strove the *Nancy* Boston's port to gain;
> Oft as she came, the wind unfriendly grew,
> (A rough opposing storm against her blew:)
> The *Cerberus* for her protection sail'd;

But in th' attempt the royal frigate fail'd;
In darkness wrapp'd but tempest rudely tost,
They parted, and the precious prize was lost;
This through the royal army spread damp;
And fill'd with pleasure the provincial camp.[7]

American colonies had at last found what appeared to be a competent naval captain. John Manley's early life is somewhat puzzling. He was born on 18 August 1732 in the village of St. Marychurch, Devonshire, England, a hamlet on the outskirts of Torquay not far from Torbay. Like many of the young men of the region, he went to sea.[8] The boy crossed the Atlantic, first landing in Boston on some unrecorded date but settling in colonial Marblehead, Massachusetts. It appears likely that he deserted a Royal Navy ship in Boston. At that time there was a Royal Navy officer called John Manley. This makes the reputed naval desertion story confusing. The well-born British navy's Manley rose from midshipman to fourth lieutenant on the Royal Navy ship *Dublin* in 1770 during the British mobilization over the eighteenth-century Falkland Islands crisis. Manley ascended to the rank of post captain in October 1782 just as the American Revolution ended, and he died at the rank of vice admiral.

Evidence that the John Manley from Marblehead served in the British navy appears in a defamatory comment by John Paul Jones: "[Manley] had lately the Honor, of being a Stick officer Vulgarly Called Boatswain's Mate in an English Man of War and was duely Qualified for that heigh Station, as Fame Says true as appears by his not Deigning to Read English."[9] Jones's cruel denigration of Manley's intellect and education was apparently written to negatively contrast him with Manley's chief rival, Hector McNeill, a colleague and close friend of Jones.

The alleged desertion from His Majesty's navy may account for Manley's dropping of his family name shortly after arriving in America. Manley went by the name of John Russell until 1775. On 27 September 1764 Russell was married to Martha Hickman of Marblehead. She bore him two sons and three daughters, all baptized under the surname of Russell. About the time that the fisherman and sometime merchantman Russell volunteered to serve General Washington as an army schooner captain, he had reverted to the name Manley, and he continued to use it for the rest of his life. The reason for either switch is not known.

Manley was a native of South Devon, England, a place where men were commonly perceived as taciturn and independent of thought. Indeed Manley was a quiet man, rarely speaking except under the trying circumstances of combat. This is reflected in his writing as well. Relatively few of his letters or documents survive, but those few samples are well written and to the point, lacking the flowery language frequently seen among the educated people of the late eighteenth century.[10] This calls Jones's disparagement of Manley's intellectual abilities into question.

Manley appeared to enjoy the hunt—the maritime chase—and probably also enjoyed the monetary rewards from his captured prizes. He seemed oblivious to the attendant dangers. Patrolling near the northern entrance to Boston harbor on 1 December 1775, a lookout on the *Lee,* a small schooner, spotted a large vessel lumbering toward port. It was the three-hundred-ton *Concord,* which had been at sea for about eleven weeks. Its captain, James Lowrie, had experienced a difficult transatlantic crossing. When he saw an approaching schooner, he, like the master of the *Nancy,* thought that it was a pilot schooner to guide him to his destination. When the *Lee*'s longboat came alongside, Manley's marines quickly mounted the gunwales and took possession of the only lightly armed *Concord.*

The vessel carried clothing and coal needed by the British garrisoned in Boston, but the manifest of the ship indicated that a Boston merchant had contracted it.[11] Technically this made its apprehension exempt from capture under Washington's rules for commandeering vessels. However, among the ship's documents was correspondence condemning the rebel cause and a note saying that the vessel would later be used in the king's service. Manley believed that these letters would be of interest to Washington's headquarters and decided that this was a legitimate reason to ignore the "rules of engagement" and take the prize to Marblehead. This correspondence had a far-reaching effect. Congress proclaimed that "all transport vessels having on board any troops, arms, ammunition, clothing, provisions, or military or naval stores of what kind soever . . . and all vessels employed in carrying provisions or other necessaries to the British Army . . . shall be liable to seizure, and, with their cargoes, shall be confiscated."[12] Thus the letters that Manley seized on the *Concord* ultimately led to the Continental Navy's recodification of official policy for taking British vessels.

On 9 December, Manley was back on patrol awaiting tempting prey on their way to Boston harbor. About five leagues (fifteen miles) out to sea he encountered the 400-ton *Jenny,* with Robert Foster as master. This vessel was even bigger than the *Concord* and was more heavily armed. Manley once again posed as a friendly pilot schooner captain, and his men took the *Jenny* without a significant fight.[13] While the Americans were inspecting the cargo of the vanquished *Jenny,* the 140-ton brig *Little Hannah,* with Robert Masters as captain, came into sight. The brig had sailed from sunny Antigua and, because of the wintry conditions of the North Atlantic, wanted to make harbor as quickly as possible. Although the *Little Hannah* was also armed, Masters assumed that the small schooner *Lee* was not a threat but was a pilot for the *Jenny*. Answering the signal for pilot assistance, Manley sent his marines in response and subsequently had two impressive prizes for little effort. There were no American casualties. Sailing orders were given, and the flotilla of three ships sailed to snowbound Beverly.

The *Jenny*'s cargo contained foodstuffs, including live hogs, and coal intended for the British garrison in Boston. The *Little Hannah* carried mostly alcoholic beverages, including rum and other spirits. In addition the vessel had bags of cocoa and tropical delicacies such as oranges, lemons, sugar, sweetmeats, and ginger—all of which would have been welcomed, as the winter solstice and Christmas were only weeks away. This loss would have a negative effect on British morale.

On 18 December, Manley encountered the sixty-ton sloop *Betsey,* which was seized after a short fight. The vessel was laden with more foodstuffs from Virginia royal governor Lord Dunmore and bound for the British garrison in Boston. More important were the five passengers on board and papers that they carried. One was Moses Kirkland, a wealthy Tory, who carried personal and confidential letters to General William Howe, the British army commander in Boston. From the first of November to the close of 1775 Manley had taken seventeen vessels, and he was by far the most productive captain of Washington's schooner fleet operating off the coast of Massachusetts. Because of Manley's fame many Massachusetts residents contended for the honor of claiming their town as his place of birth.[14]

Manley displayed natural leadership ability by taking care that his men received proper clothing and remuneration for their efforts. He also had a mysterious sixth sense or perhaps good luck in finding valuable prizes. More important, up until this time he had managed to capture his opponents with little bloodshed on either side. This celebrity apparently made him an American privateer role model. Lieutenant Colonel Stephen Moylan, muster master for Washington's army, when recruiting other skippers for privateer service, said, "Captain Manley's good fortune seems to Stick to him. He has taken three valuable prizes . . . this shews of what vast advantage to the Cause, these Vessels would be, if the Commanders were all as attentive to duty and interest [in capturing prizes] as Manley is. . . . Manley is truly our hero of the sea."[15]

Manley became the gallant subject of the following tavern song popularly used to recruit men as privateers in defiance of the British North American squadron:

Then Rouse up, all our Heroes, give MANLY [sic] now a cheer,
Here's Health to hardy Sons of Mars who go in Privateers . . .
They talk of Sixty Ships, Lads, to scourge our free-born Land,
If they send out Six Hundred we'll bravely them withstand . . .
Then rouse up all my Hearties. Give Sailor Lads a Cheer,
Brave MANLY . . . and [all] those Tars who go in Privateers.[16]

Because of Manley's leadership and performance, Washington named him as commodore of the schooner fleet on 20 January 1776, a sign to other maritime captains that the general was willing to reward accomplishment.[17] Although an army officer, John Manley was formally given this title and the privilege of flying the equivalent of the commodore's broad pennant at sea.[18] In actuality the title meant only that Manley had overall command of a group of vessels, usually on a specific mission. However, once a captain was given this designation, he was usually called commodore for the remainder of his maritime life.

Although Manley had significant achievements, he, like many accomplished men, also had many critics and a few enemies. Envy and plots of recrimination occasioned his rise to fame, particularly in a Continental Navy that had yet to form traditions. Of particular note was the spiteful Hector McNeill, just junior to him on the naval officer seniority list of the Continental Congress. McNeill said that Manley was "totally unequal to the Command with which he has been intrusted, he being Ignorant, Obstinate, Overbearing and Tyranical beyound discription, a man under whose command none can live with pleasure."[19] This Scottish immigrant sea captain publicly questioned Manley's competence both in speech and in writing to leaders in Congress and fellow naval officers, comments that appear to be invidious. Equally condescending and resolute was McNeill's fellow expatriate Scot John Paul Jones, who wrote, "There is a Fellow who calls himself a Commodore and who keeps us at an Awful distance by Wearing [Flying] an English Broad Pendant. . . . To be very serious, that such Despicable Characters should Obtain Commissions as Commanders in a Navy is truly Astonishing and [might] Pass for Romance with me unless I had been convinced by my Senses of the Sad Reality. . . . I need not therefore name this great Man this Commodore! Tho' I will if call'd upon and in the meantime I aver that he is Altogether Unfit to Command a frigate of thirty two Guns."[20]

Some British naval officers also made dispiriting comments about Manley, whom they considered an uncivilized pirate. Such epithets as "a thief like ugly dog" and "a man of savage courage, and a brutish ferocity of manners" were applied to him.[21] Probably the reason for the comments was that Manley was usually a reserved man, but in battle he became frenzied, running behind his men in a waistcoat and rolled up shirtsleeves and with an upraised cutlass, swearing to cut down the first who attempted to desert his post. This was not the way a proper and refined British officer of breeding conducted himself.

Broughton was discredited in the autumn of 1775, and Manley took command of the schooner *Hancock,* now armed with six 4-pounders and ten swivels. His small force of four schooners went on its patrol of the waters around Massachusetts Bay and captured seven vessels, Manley taking two of them by himself. The most difficult assault occurred when the British brig *Hope* chased the *Hancock.* The formidable *Hope* delivered hundreds of shots to the more lightly armed *Hancock.* During the melee Manley was sick in his cabin, and as he lay in his bunk, a ball crashed into the nearby bulwark, missing him by inches. Overmatched, the *Hancock* was forced to seek cover in the shallows, but in doing so she ran aground off Cohasset. Within forty-eight hours Manley recovered from his illness, floated the *Hancock* off the sandbar, and continued his quest for vulnerable strays on their way to Boston.

After that encounter the commodore decided that his seventy-two-ton ship was too small for its task and noted that the morale of his men had declined because remuneration for the captured prize vessels was slow in coming. The commodore petitioned General Washington for a better vessel and a more sympathetic ear for payment to his men, but Washington had moved his headquarters from Cambridge to New York and was not as focused as he had been on his Massachusetts schooner fleet. In time Manley prevailed. On 28 January 1776 Washington wrote to Manley, "You shall have Command of a Stronger vessel of War, but as it will take up Some time before Such a one Can be fitted out, my desire is, that you Continue in the Hancock, until the end [of the] Cruize. . . . [Upon your return] we will Confer Together in the subject of the other ship."[22] Out of frustration and hubris, and indifferent to his nation's need, Manley sent a letter resigning his army commission in early April 1776.

On 11 December 1775 the Continental Naval Committee had recommended that thirteen ships, some of thirty-two, twenty-eight, or twenty-four guns, should compose the fledgling navy and that they should be made ready to sail over the course of 1776. The mails were slow, and Manley's letter of resignation to Washington had not been received. Also Manley was commissioned for service in the army, and the formation of a navy was still a new congressional venture. Meeting in Philadelphia, the Continental Congress appointed Manley as captain in the Continental Navy on 17 April 1776. This placated the headstrong man from Marblehead, and he accepted the more prestigious new commission. His assignment was to supervise and outfit one of two frigates to be constructed in Newburyport, Massachusetts, at the mouth of the Merrimac River, a port protected by treacherous shifting sandbars.[23] Manley's powerful new frigate would have the same name as his second schooner command, the *Hancock*.

It was difficult to build stout armed vessels based on ways designed to construct lesser ships. Obtaining cannons, powder, and particularly crewmen for the navy was a daunting challenge. Privateer captains could deal in cash and thus more easily obtain munitions; profitable privateering was far more attractive to young seamen. In addition, Congress was, as usual, slow in appropriating funds for building and arming its frigates. Still, Manley was determined and prevailed, but these events kept him largely ashore until November 1776. While shore-bound, Manley was assigned to head a committee whose task was to design the first standardized uniform for American naval officers. This was also the first evidence that he had interactions with Dudley Saltonstall and John Paul Jones—the subjects of later chapters.[24]

There was continued disappointment that the new frigates were not being built or fitted with armaments so that they could put to sea. Reverend Samuel Cooper wrote in Boston on 24 March 1777, "It is astonishing to many that after so long a Time for Preparation, not a single Frigate this way has yet been made ready to put to Sea, while the British Frigates and Cruizers are distressing us everywhere, cutting off our most necessary Supplies. This has occasioned no small Clamor & uneasiness here. . . . There is Blame somewhere. I know not whether there be any Person or Persons here fully authorized to conduct and rectify these matters. I hope however they will soon be ready for sailing."[25] This attitude probably expressed Manley's frustration.

Once the *Hancock* was nearly built, the Marine Committee had difficulty locating cannons to arm the vessel. The temporary solution was to borrow weapons from vessels that were under repair. This led to the second Manley and Saltonstall relationship, although an indirect one. On 15 January 1777 Barnabas Deane, brother of Silas Deane, wrote to John Hancock from Wethersfield, Connecticut: "Capt. Manley Call'd on me with a letter from Govr. Trumbull . . . And Agreeable to his Advice I have Supply'd Capt. Manly [*sic*] with the Trumbulls Cannon which I hope will be Agreeable to the Honble Congress."[26] Therefore, the cannons were removed from the frigate *Trumbull*, being constructed in Connecticut under the command of Captain Dudley Saltonstall. This was a practical way out because the *Trumbull*, when armed, drew too much water to negotiate the Saybrook sandbars at the mouth of the Connecticut River. Therefore, Manley completed the fitting out of the new *Hancock* with "rented" guns.

During this time Manley continued to conduct himself as a senior Continental naval officer. On 29 April he sent a courteous note to Captain John Paul Jones requesting his presence at a court-martial on board the *Hancock,* in order to try a master's mate from the *Alfred* who was accused of striking Elisha Hinman, the ship's master, and using abusive language in conjunction with the assault. There is no documentation that Jones appeared to testify about the fate of the master's mate.

Over the months of preparation before Manley had orders to put to sea, McNeill, the new master of the frigate *Boston,* started to display more overt animosity toward Manley. This presented potential difficulties because they were assigned to patrol the North Atlantic together, and Manley, being senior in rank, was placed in command. McNeill showed his clear disdain for Manley in a 21 May 1777 entry in his personal journal: "Emplo'd my self and my clerke in Transcribeing Signals for the better Management of our Little fleet, as I had undertaken this at Capt. Manleys request I hope'd some satisfaction in Seeing for order reigne amoung us, but never was any use further Made of them."[27] After a near collision between the *Boston* and the *Hancock* toward the end of June 1777, McNeill composed a dispatch to Manley that spoke "my mind freely on his misconduct which nettle'd the Commodore Verey much."[28]

McNeill, increasingly concerned about Manley's signals, criticized his superior in a note to Captain Thomas Thompson of the *Raleigh,* complaining that he could never get any proper signals from Manley.[29] McNeill wrote that "never did a Pilotfish follow a Sharke, or a Jackall follow a lion, with more Assiduity and compliance then I follow'd him at Sea for Six or Seven weeks (chiefly in bad weather Latitudes), and that without my regular System of Signals, or instructions for my direction during which time he led me into several Scrapes by his misconduct, and at last left me to shift for myself."[30]

Manley curtly replied, "By your letter you tax me & my officers for not showing proper Signals Past Night but I was upon Deck & made the Exat [*sic*] Signals You gave me. . . . I am much surprised that you did not observe the Signals."[31] Manley ended his note with an expression of sympathy and humor, something lacking in any statement by McNeill: "I am sorry you met with that Accident in going aboard [the *Hancock*] hope your Leg is better . . . [I am suffering from a similar lameness that has me] laying upon my beem ends & what is worse than that I can not drink neither, Punch Wine nor Grog—Yrs John Manley."[32]

McNeill's response was another diatribe. It was becoming increasingly clear that Manley was losing patience with his comrade-in-arms. Although their relationship was mostly counterproductive and increasingly baneful, it was hoped that Manley's 32-gun *Hancock* and McNeill's 30-gun frigate *Boston* would be able to work better as a team. On their first mission the *Hancock* engaged and apprehended the small collier sloop *Britannia*. Shortly thereafter the *Hancock* challenged the British 28-gun *Fox*, commanded by Captain Patrick Fotheringham. Both vessels were badly mauled and fought to a draw. The *Boston* joined the fight belatedly, and the *Fox*, now outgunned, struck her colors. Manley admonished McNeill for his lack of support, but the British frigate became a prize, and that was the point of their mission. After hasty repairs to the *Hancock* and the *Fox*, Manley's command continued on North Atlantic patrol.

On 7 July 1777 the American frigates encountered three British vessels just south of Falmouth, Nova Scotia: the 32-gun *Flora*, commanded by Captain John Brisbane; the 10-gun brig *Victor*, with Lieutenant Michael Hydman in command; and the 44-gun *Rainbow*, under the well-known and formidable Sir George Collier. The *Flora* quickly attacked the *Fox*, then the vanguard of the American vessels. In time the recently repaired prize *Fox* struck her colors, once again resuming her former status as a king's vessel. The *Hancock* and the *Boston* cooperated for the moment and sailed to engage the *Rainbow*. Both American frigates discharged broadsides as they closed within a few hundred yards of the British man-of-war. Manley suddenly realized that this vessel was a double-decked warship with superior firepower to his *Hancock*. He continued to pursue his foe because it appeared that the battle would have been two against one. In an uncooperative maneuver, however, McNeill turned the *Boston* northward in an attempt to escape, presuming that the Americans were outmatched; Manley was left to fight alone.

Collier, on the other hand, quickly identified the *Hancock* and her captain as a man wanted by the Admiralty. The *Hancock* was swift and trim, but after suffering damage in the engagement with the *Fox*, Manley could not outrun the *Rainbow*. Soon the *Flora* and the *Fox* sailed to join the *Rainbow* in the anticipated fight. The 10-gun *Victor* was much slower than the other vessels and stayed in reserve in the distance. After exchanging heavy round shot and grapeshot off and on for what must have seemed like an interminable thirty-six hours, Manley decided to save his outgunned men by surrendering to Collier on 8 July 1777. When the Marbleheader presented his sword to the victorious Collier, the British captain noted that the rim of Manley's hat had been shot away. "You have had a narrow escape," said Collier. "I wish to God it had been my head," was Manley's reply.[33] Rather than damn McNeill for nearly costing him his life, Manley held the demeanor of an intrepid warrior, although his capture must have been deeply humiliating.

Meanwhile, instead of coming to Manley's aid, McNeill had sailed the *Boston* up the Sheepscot River in Maine to safe anchorage near Wiscasset.

When he was later questioned about his actions, McNeill haughtily claimed that Manley had signaled the *Boston* to take care of itself once the cannon fire started.

Manley, now a captive, suffered debasing imprisonment on a hulk in New York harbor, but he was eventually repatriated for a British naval prisoner. He returned to Boston on 21 April 1778 to face a court-martial for the loss of the valuable *Hancock*. The court-martial was presided over by Captain Dudley Saltonstall—another encounter between the two captains. At about the same time McNeill faced a court-martial on charges of dereliction of duty because he had not come to Manley's aid in the heat of battle. Manley presented credible evidence that he had fought valiantly and was overwhelmed by a superior force. The court found that he was guilty of some critical errors in ship handling during the battle, but certainly the captain did not surrender without a fight. The verdict in part said, "The Court are . . . of the Opinion that Manley did all in his power to save the *Hancock* and that he did not . . . discover any want of Courage but on the Contrary great Zeal for the good of the Service he was engaged in. . . . The Court therefore Acquit him of every part of the Charge and beg leave to recommend him to Congress as a Spirited and brave Officer."[34] McNeill, for his part, was found guilty of perfidy and summarily dismissed from the navy; his allegiance to command authority had been reproved. Thus Manley's most petulant and undependable colleague was no longer a direct threat.

By now the Continental Navy had lost several ships to the British and therefore had far more officers than vessels in which they could serve. As a productive and experienced captain, Manley was given temporary command of the 20-gun, Boston-based privateer *Cumberland*. This assignment was short-lived because the *Cumberland* was captured by the British brig *Pomona* within days of leaving port. Subsequently Manley suffered a harsh imprisonment in Barbados, although before long he managed to bribe a jailer and led a daring escape. When the band of escapees seized a British tender, Manley sailed the small vessel all the way to Boston, landing in April 1779.

By June, Manley assumed command of the 18-gun privateer *Jason*, which reportedly had good sailing qualities. In fact, the *Jason* outran two British warships, but in doing so found itself in a terrible squall. The vessel lost a mast, and a man was drowned while clinging to the wrecked rigging in the storm. The superstitious crew concluded that Manley was "a Jonah"—a marked, unlucky man—and some mutinied. Displaying leadership and courage, Manley challenged the mutineers and convinced the men that if they restored the damaged *Jason*, he would sail for home without bringing charges of mutiny. The repairs were made, and shortly thereafter the *Jason* encountered two

British privateers, the 18-gun *Hazard* and the 18-gun *Adventurer*. A frantic gun battle followed in which the British suffered thirty killed or wounded while only three Americans were wounded on board the *Jason*. In the face of such carnage the British struck their colors, and with the valuable prizes in tow, the crew lost interest in mutiny and willingly followed Manley.

On 30 September 1781 Manley had just secured another prize brig when misfortune revisited. The fast and nimble 28-gun warship *Surprise,* under Captain Robert Linzee, attacked the *Jason* off St. John's, Newfoundland. A roaring broadside-to-broadside battle ensued, taking fifteen British sailors' lives and wounding thirty. The men of the *Jason* fared better, suffering five dead and twelve wounded. The lethal gunnery of the *Surprise* toppled parts of the American vessel's rigging, affecting the *Jason*'s maneuverability and also making it impossible for Manley's men to work the gun deck. The *Jason* capitulated. Manley was a prisoner once again and was sent to be incarcerated at England's dreaded Old Mill Prison at Plymouth. While in custody Manley challenged fellow captain Daniel Brown to a duel, but the combat was refused.[35] In time Manley was exchanged for a British naval officer and returned to Boston in April 1782.

In September the Continental Navy, finding a last billet for Manley, assigned him to command the 550-ton, 32-gun frigate *Hague* (the former *Deane,* originally named for Captain Dudley Saltonstall's father-in-law). That autumn the potent *Hague* sailed for the West Indies, where Manley once again harassed British warships and shipping. He returned to Boston in May 1783. Independence had been won. By coincidence, having taken the *Nancy,* the first valuable prize of the Revolutionary War, Manley and the Continental marines had the distinction of serving on the last Continental Navy ship to capture a valuable vessel, the 340-ton *Baille,* in January 1783.

Once the terms of peace were announced, the *Hague* was ordered to return to Hancock's Wharf in Boston. In an unexpected turn of events, once Manley stepped ashore he was arrested by order of Robert Morris to answer to charges brought against him by one of the *Baille*'s officers. Manley apparently was never tried on these charges. There is no record of what it was all about, but it was a strange conclusion to his gallant naval career.[36]

After the War of Independence, Manley lived quietly in Boston until his death on 12 February 1793. His civilian activities faded into history, except for several petitions he presented to Congress. They gave him a half-pay pension of thirty dollars a month for his service and wounds suffered in battle.

James Warren wrote to Sam Adams, a year after the naval fiasco involving McNeill, that Manley was "a Blunt, Honest, and I believe Brave Officer. He was

first in the service, and merited much by his Conduct . . . he is extremely popular with Officers, and Seamen, and can Man a Ship with distinction. . . .
I would much rather trust him [with a naval command] even [though there
may be] another I could name, whose pretenses too . . . are more confident."[37] With those words Warren may have expressed how the self-confident
Commodore Manley would have wished to be remembered—as a brave, honest, trustworthy man who served his country with distinction. Manley had his
detractors among the officer corps of the Continental Navy. He was vociferously impatient with the Continental Congress, a trait he shared with many of
his peers.

The sentiment of the people of Massachusetts toward John Manley is
found in the following eulogy/poem composed at his death:

> What time the clarion's tone with echoing sound,
> Roll'd o'er the valley, shook the lofty mound,
> And summon'd to the crims'ning fields of strife,
> Columbian heroes prodigal of life—
> Then Manley rose, intrepid, dauntless, brave,
> He dar'd that power, whose naval thunders hurl'd
> From pole to pole, had aw'd the trembling word,
> And rul'd with force the foaming wave.
> The boreal blast, old ocean's angriest form,
> When work'd to madness by the wintry storm,
> Damp prison-ship, nor dungeon's dear abode,
> Apall'd his mind.—Firm steadfast, unsubdu'd,
> Mid adverse, variant scenes, tempestuous, rude,
> Where wild waves rag'd, and winds embattled blow'd,
> One course he shap'd: And leaves behind a wake,
> Where fame's keen searching eye, beholds no break.[38]

Manley had outbursts of ire and indignation at times, but he clearly left behind a substantial wake of admiration by his contemporaries.

The Army Privateer

Silas Talbot

The American Revolutionary War produced many men who were engaging figures. One of the most remarkable was Silas Talbot, a Continental Army officer, state naval officer, privateer, slaver, Continental Navy captain, United States Navy captain, and at the end of his career the second captain to command the frigate *Constitution*. Talbot's multifaceted career—including his exploits and changing fortunes during the Revolutionary War and the birth of the American political system—reflect the intrepidity of many of the first naval officers. These qualities also vividly portray why personalities often clashed.

During the time of the Revolution, waging war in the American colonies presented special military tactical problems. Population centers were concentrated at seaports or on navigable rivers. Sea-lanes, estuaries, bays, and river channels were highways for transport, particularly of heavy materials. On land, troops and supplies moved on sparse roads that were rutted in mud and roughened from log and stone paving. Overland travel brought the perils of broken axles, overturned carts, frayed hitches, and limited loads as well as the need for watering, feeding, and changing horses or oxen. Therefore the Continental Congress decided to acquire a flotilla of smaller ships such as brigs, cutters, schooners, galleys, lugsails, and barges to guard America's harbors and protect the free flow of commerce. Merchant sailors, fishermen, and men from other walks of life with maritime skills—all seamen with an intimate knowledge of local waters—manned these vessels. The role of these rebel warriors was to fight on land and sea, as hybrid infantrymen, artillery gunners, coastguardsmen, and marines. Of course the Royal Navy, stationed off America's shores and anchored in many of its major harbors, was engaged in similar duties, but for the benefit of King George III and Great Britain.

In 1751 Silas Talbot, the ninth of fourteen children, was born in Dighton, Bristol County, a part of the Massachusetts Bay Colony near the Rhode Island colonial border.[1] His parents taught their children self-reliance and

*Commodore Silas Talbot
wearing his Society of
the Cincinnati insignia.
Portrait by Ralph Earl.
© Mystic Seaport
Collection, Mystic,
Connecticut, #66–3–11*

independence; these attributes were tested when Talbot lost his last surviving biological parent at the age of twelve. In order to satisfy his youthful curiosity and love of adventure, Talbot became a sailor on a merchant vessel that traded goods among the villages on Narragansett Bay, then out into Long Island Sound, and eventually with the southern colonies. He was extremely intelligent, teaching himself reading and the skills of the mariner's trade. In 1772 Talbot married Anna Richmond, the daughter of a prominent Providence merchant.

Talbot developed a reputation as a bold and clever businessman who indulged in mercantile speculations. Once he raced other ships in Narragansett Bay to intercept a vessel loaded with southern lumber. Quickly hailing and boarding the vessel, he bought the cargo from the captain before it landed. Talbot turned this trading scheme into a large profit because of his knowledge of the rising price and increased demand for lumber in the local market. As the Americans grew discontented with King George, Talbot achieved enviable prosperity and much domestic happiness through the socially secure Anna Richmond and her numerous Providence connections.

In spite of his many-faceted personal success, the embers of patriotism smoldered in young Talbot, and he volunteered for the Rhode Island militia in anticipation of the war. After the battles at Lexington and Concord, Talbot was granted a commission as captain in one of the three Rhode Island Continental Army regiments. His first military assignment was to help Washington's troops in their siege of Boston. General Washington, however, learned of Talbot's maritime skills and reassigned him to help move two hundred volunteers from the port of New London to Providence, reorganize them, and sail these troops to fortifications at Brooklyn Heights and Paulus Hook, New York. By coincidence, Talbot was at the small coastal town of New London, Connecticut, when Continental Navy commodore Esek Hopkins's Nassau Expedition landed after the first successful Continental Navy raid of the Revolution. Dudley Saltonstall, John Paul Jones, and Joshua Barney, all participants in the expedition, were also there. Although it is not documented, it is likely that the four of them met there during this hectic time.

In the buildup for the battle of New York, the boredom of military encampment overtook Talbot and many of his comrades. In the latter part of the hot July 1776 on Brooklyn Heights overlooking the East River, Talbot got into a dispute with a Lieutenant Dunworth.[2] The young lieutenant became incensed by some trivial insult and, out of his eighteenth-century sense of honor, challenged Talbot to a duel. Rhode Island's General Nathanael Greene was informed of the impending clash and sought General Washington's advice about how to handle the matter. As the two distinguished American military leaders discussed the matter, tempers cooled and the duel challenge was withdrawn. Talbot now had a history of escaping a duel.

Meanwhile a formidable British fleet carrying the army of General William Howe arrived off Staten Island and sailed up the Hudson River to blockade the waterway and New York harbor. An indecisive standoff followed for a time. In an attempt to disrupt the British naval lines at anchor, Captain Talbot took command of a turpentine-impregnated fireship filled with combustibles and black powder, which was anchored fifteen miles up the Hudson from Fort Washington near Peekskill.[3] At about two o'clock on a cool September morning in 1776 he and his crew weighed anchor and slowly drifted downriver with the retreating tide. Talbot steered directly for the 64-gun ship *Asia* and grappled her. The British warship fired on her American foe at close range. The cannon barrage ignited the fireship, and the *Asia* found herself in the clutches of a floating incendiary bomb.

Captain Talbot lingered on the flaming deck to make certain that the fire-ship was securely fastened to the British vessel. If the warship went up in flames, it would be a warning torch to the British fleet now in control of the Hudson River. As the last to escape to join his waiting comrades, he was badly burned from head to foot and temporarily blinded by the intense flames and acrid smoke. His men rescued their officer and found shelter for him on the New Jersey shore. By chance and good fortune, General Henry Knox and his competent surgeon, Dr. William Eustis, were in this encampment. They arranged for Talbot's treatment and safe evacuation to Hackensack.

Talbot's mission, however, was only a partial success. The *Asia* was only badly damaged by its encounter with the fireship, and the British naval commander Vice Admiral Richard Howe noted their ships' vulnerability. Perhaps losing confidence, he ordered the fleet to move to a more defensible point south of Fort Washington. Talbot was cited by Congress for his gallant attempt to destroy the vessel. Given a vote of thanks for his maritime action, he was promoted to the rank of major in the Continental Army.[4] Talbot sent a petition to the Continental Congress for "the Value of my cloathing burnt and as charged is as near the Sum of thirteen pounds sixteen shillings as I am able to judge."[5] Recompense for the unanticipated expenses of combat was not unusual during the early stages of the American Revolution.

Upon his recovery from his burns, Talbot joined the garrison holding Fort Mifflin, at Mud Island on the Delaware River. The British had captured Philadelphia and now held the mouth of the strategically vital Delaware Bay. Needing to complete their link between Philadelphia and the bay, the British started a bombardment of the American defenses south of Philadelphia on the Delaware River on 2 October 1777. Most of the vessels of the Continental Navy fleet were assigned to protect the Delaware River channel leading to Philadelphia. Onshore Continental Army units prepared for battle, reinforcing their main defensive bases at Fort Mifflin, located at the mouth of the Schuyl-kill River below Philadelphia, and Fort Mercer, at Red Bank on the New Jersey shore of the river. The artillery batteries were erected with difficulty because of the marshy ground near the river. Transporting heavy cannons through swamps consumed a great deal of crucial time before they could be placed for maximum effect.

Meanwhile the British seized nearby Province Island and erected fortifications there. The Americans set up chevaux-de-frise as defenses; these were heavy timber poles set into the riverbed with sharp iron spikes set in their tops to impale unwary approaching vessels or force them to narrow points of vulnerability in the river. At that point the guns of the two forts located below the bend of the Delaware southwest of Philadelphia, the American galleys serving as floating gun batteries, and Continental Navy ships could engage and, it was hoped, destroy the vulnerable British vessels.

On 22 October the defenders of Fort Mercer repulsed a fierce assault from a mercenary Hessian unit of the British army. The battle was now in the hands of the American floating batteries and remnants of the Continental Navy to form a last-ditch attempt to keep the waterway from being seized by the British. Effective American cannon fire held British naval forces on the Delaware River below Philadelphia for forty days. The combined American forces bombarded the 64-gun *Augusta*. In an attempt to elude the rebel harassing fire, the *Augusta* ran aground, caught fire, and exploded. In spite of this significant loss, the persistent British military power, specifically their cannon fire, took a heavy toll on the American vessels and Fort Mifflin. The Continental Navy vessel *Andrea Doria* helped to defend the fort from only a few hundred yards out in the river. The ship's first lieutenant was Joshua Barney, a young naval lieutenant with whom Talbot would later clash.

By 15 November the British were prepared to strike Fort Mifflin. The *Vigilant* and an old hulk, both mounted with heavy cannons, passed between Hog and Province islands and the Pennsylvania bank to a position opposite the weakest part of the fort. The *Isis, Roebuck, Somerset,* and several small frigates sailed up the main channel of the Delaware River, to a line of chevaux-de-frise, and heaved to just offshore of these defense works.

Fewer than three hundred soldiers manned Fort Mifflin, but they valiantly fought against both the British fleet and the army that opposed them. The Americans answered British bombardment of Fort Mifflin with the fort's artillery, by the galleys that served as floating batteries on the river and defensive batteries based along the New Jersey riverbank. As the day progressed, the fort was largely demolished and many of the guns dismounted from their caissons or trucks. Talbot's artillery unit stationed in the Fort Mifflin bastion fought bravely, but the contest became futile. The British sent a floating artillery battery with two 32-pounders to within five hundred yards of Fort Mifflin to finish the siege by firing directly into the fort. Holding on to this garrison became no longer tenable, and Fort Mifflin was abandoned during the night, its residents ordered to evacuate to the safety of Red Bank.

During a lull in the onslaught, Talbot was found lying in the wreckage with a wrist shattered from a musket ball and a wounded hip.[6] He was totally disabled and was evacuated by boat to Red Bank and then on to a field hospital at Princeton for treatment. Later General Washington personally commended Talbot for his bravery, granting him a leave to Providence to recover from the trauma.

Meanwhile, because of the overwhelming British force, the inevitable conclusion played itself out. Two days later Fort Mercer at Red Bank was also evacuated. The American vessels in the river were now left unprotected. On 20 November 1777 an order was issued for the evacuation or burning of all ships of the Continental Navy and their supporting vessels. Some retreated upstream, keeping close to the Jersey shore and passing the newly erected British batteries at Philadelphia during the night to escape. The rest, almost the entire Continental Navy fleet, was set ablaze and abandoned, making the vessels relatively useless to the British.

Talbot's recuperation and return to the colony of Rhode Island did not place him far from action. The British captured the Narragansett Bay island known as Rhode Island in December 1777, enabling them to control the strategically important towns of Providence and Newport. The French commodore Comte d'Estaing, brought a French fleet and troops into Narragansett Bay in late July 1778. General John Sullivan, American commander of the Rhode Island forces, planned a coordinated attack on Newport with the French in order to recapture this vital port. Sullivan ordered Talbot to assemble eighty-six flat-bottom boats on Rhode Island's eastern shore. The simple vessels were built at the prodigious rate of about sixteen per day and were caulked by candlelight at night under the cover of marsh weeds and shore shrubs. When completed, each boat in the flotilla was loaded with up to one hundred men to cross over to the northern end of the island.

After assembling the boats, ferrying the troops, and supervising the landing, Major Talbot was assigned to lead a light infantry unit. Riding ahead of the troops to reconnoiter a British garrison, Talbot noticed three British soldiers rummaging in a garden. Astride his horse the major leaped over the garden wall, surprised the men, and ordered them not to move or call out. The soldiers mistook Talbot for a British officer, apologized for leaving their post, and offered to share with the officer on horseback what they had foraged. Instead Talbot identified himself, took the soldiers prisoner without firing a shot, and marched them back to American lines.

A British fleet was now being assembled and made ready for action in Narragansett Bay. Seeing the growing British armada, the French stopped landing troops and left to engage the enemy fleet off Point Judith. With little warning a fierce summer storm interrupted the fight, scattered both fleets, and left the isolated American troops on Rhode Island without support from the sea. The British defenders regrouped. The assault led by General Sullivan was outnumbered and outgunned. The American plan was doomed to failure.

On 29 August 1778 Talbot was ordered to help cover the tactical withdrawal of the invading American forces at Butts Hill, called the Battle of

Rhode Island. This engagement is historically significant because for the first time a battalion of freed African slaves fought as a unit for the Continental Army. They performed with distinction. Again Congress cited Talbot for his prompt provision of troop transport, his brave actions as part of the light infantry corps, and for providing a safe and orderly retreat from the island.

Still in control, the British continued to use their stronghold at Newport to command much of eastern Narragansett Bay. The most effective British naval defense was a stout two-hundred-ton galley called the *Pigot,* stationed at the mouth of the Sakonnet River, the gateway to many Rhode Island eastern shore communities.[7] The galley had a crew of forty-five, and girded with heavy antiboarding nets, the vessel was a formidable floating battery.

Although it is unlikely that Talbot ever met Captain John Manley, their paths tangentially crossed with the arming of the *Pigot.* When French ships bombarded Newport on 25 July, the British frigate *Flora,* which had aided in Manley's 1778 capture, was heaved down onto the beach so that its keel and bottom could be cleaned of barnacles and sea grass.[8] As a result of the French cannon bombardment onshore, the helpless *Flora* was heavily damaged and declared unserviceable. The recently built British galley *Pigot* was armed with twelve 8-pounders salvaged from the now-useless *Flora.* Therefore the guns that had helped to capture John Manley would now be used to face Silas Talbot.

Talbot was ordered by his Continental Army commander to refit the sloop *Hawke,* arm the vessel with two 3-pounders, and break the blockade. The *Hawke* was to be used as a floating platform to storm the *Pigot* with a boarding party of sixty men. Since the Continentals were obviously outgunned, military success required stealth and surprise. On 25 October 1778, staying close to shore so as not to present a telltale silhouette, Talbot maneuvered silently with the outgoing tide. Talbot planned to ram and grapple the *Pigot* with a kedge anchor tied to the end of the jibboom. When the *Hawke* encountered the *Pigot,* the kedge anchor tore a wide hole through the formidable netting that formed a secondary bulwark on the galley. Talbot led his raiding party and successfully breached these nets without a cannon being fired on either side.

Talbot and his crew captured the *Pigot* without loss of life on either side, bringing Talbot another letter of commendation from the Continental Congress: "[Talbot] showed great bravery, actually fighting alone on the deck, in his shirt, when every man of his crew had run below . . . . for his conduct and gallantry [he] was promoted to be a Lieutenant-Colonel. The following year [Talbot] was transferred to the navy, Congress passing an especial resolution to that effect, with directions to the Marine Committee to give him a ship on the first occasion. It does not appear that . . . the committee, at that period of the war, [had a Continental Navy vessel available for] Captain Talbot."[9] The British, however, had another view. The official Admiralty report of the embarrassing incident referred to Talbot as the great archrebel.

It is unusual to laud a failed military plan, but the next episode illustrates the creativity and cunning of Talbot.[10] In the late fall of 1778 the British had stationed the 50-gun warship *Renown* off Rhode Island to blockade the sea approach to Newport. Talbot had learned that morale on the vessel was low and that the officers onboard were not particularly vigilant, especially at night. He commandeered an old, four-hundred-ton, nondescript merchant vessel; moved it south of Providence into Narragansett Bay; and had a stage constructed on its upper deck. This gave the vessel the appearance of a common cattle carrier from a distance. Talbot calculated that the new staging made his vessel about seven feet higher than the upper tier of guns on the *Renown*. This added height would facilitate boarding if he could maneuver the lumbering merchant ship close to his unsuspecting prey. After boarding, his men would have command of the upper deck of the British warship and would be above the cannon fire of the enemy.

In preparation for the assault, his men placed on the newly built staging a large number of earthenware pots, each filled with three pounds of dry gunpowder and three charged hand grenades. The pots were then securely sealed with wax on dried sheepskins, with the wool inside for protection. A fuse, known as a slow match, was wound around each jar, leaving about a foot of slack to serve as handles. The men practiced throwing the pots filled with sand on deck and found that they could consistently hit a target about forty feet away. In combat the slow match would be lit, and when the pots fell and shattered on the deck, the gunpowder would spill and the small grenades scatter. The powder would explode and set off the grenades. The shrapnel imbedded in these bursting grenades should wound many of the men on deck. The assault plan called for one hundred men to cast two pots each into the *Renown* when they were within the forty-foot range. Musket fire and feral shouts would follow as they dropped into what should have been a terrible scene of enemy destruction. In addition Talbot planned to coordinate his attack from the sea by landing a four-hundred-man infantry assault on the nearby shore to distract British sailors and their garrisoned artillery support.

This was a clever and ambitious plan, but on the night that Talbot's men started on their mission, the weather turned bitterly cold. Ice formed on the deck and rigging, and they could not discharge the landing party. The river was frozen solid by morning, trapping both the converted merchantman and the crew of *Renown* within sight of one another. Talbot's imaginative and daring initiative was thwarted, and the *Renown* was now guarded against an attack. When the ice melted some weeks later, both ships were able to escape capture.

By this time Silas Talbot, a seaman in his youth and a soldier in manhood, had performed his army service as commander of a fireship, as a troop trans-porter, and as a boarding party leader. He was the prototypical hybrid mariner-soldier. His next military assignment, dated 14 April 1779, was as the commander of the sloop *Argo* and marked the beginning of a remarkable career as an American privateer.[11] The *Argo*, a small vessel armed with twelve guns of undocumented size, had a crew of sixty. The privateer vessel pos-sessed excellent sailing qualities and could easily outrun most of the small coasters in and around Narragansett Bay.

Under Talbot's aggressive seamanship the *Argo* successfully hunted prey. He applied for the cannon bounty (a financial bonus for the capture of scarce artillery pieces) on the following seven captured ships that were taken during the summer of 1779: the sloop *Lively,* the ship *Dragon,* the brig *Hannah,* the brig *King George,* the cutter *Dublin,* the galley *Pigot* (the prize from the sloop *Hawk*), and the unarmed merchant ship *Betsy.* The taking of the *King George* was of particular note because the brig's commander, Tory Rhode Islander Stanton Hazard, had plundered many Narragansett and Long Island Sound vil-lages. After Talbot boarded and took the privateer vessel, the imprisonment of Hazard in New London brought delight to the coastal people. However, the cost of these swashbuckling escapades was heavy; he sustained more multiple wounds from the taking of the *Dragon* and the *Hannah* on the same day and was awarded a three-hundred-dollar pension, an unusually large reward from Congress for a privateer. His record during this time was remarkable; he took eleven prizes and about three hundred prisoners.

Talbot thought that, because of his success at sea, he deserved a captain's commission and the command of a more formidable vessel than the little *Argo.* He petitioned the Continental Congress for this Continental Navy rank by way of his Rhode Island congressman Henry Marchand. In what appears as the first evidence of Talbot's petulance, he threatened to leave the Continental service if his request was not granted. Marchand challenged Talbot by saying that the colonel had won many honors and received rapid promotion. Accusing Talbot of being ungrateful, Marchand argued before members of the Marine Commit-tee that they could not create men and build ships for those "who hang on us for Command who are already in our Pay & who for want of Ships are eating the Bread of Idleness much against Their own as our Inclinations."[12]

On 17 September 1779 Henry Laurens successfully made the case before the Continental Congress that the talents of this seagoing soldier might, in fact, be better used in the Continental Navy. Lieutenant Colonel Silas Talbot was then promoted to captain in the Continental Navy; his army pay ceased, and he was assigned to command a man-of-war when one became available. The intentions of the Congress were admirable, but the body lacked the means to deliver on the promise. For compensation Talbot was given command of the 19-gun Rhode Island state naval ship the *General Washington* to continue in the cause of the Revolution. He captured one prize with the new vessel and then took a second prize, which was later recaptured by the British.

Unfortunately his luck took a bad turn when he found himself in the midst of a fleet of British men-of-war under the command of Admiral Marriott Arbuthnot. The *General Washington* ran before a gale but was ultimately captured in October 1780 by the warship *Culloden*. (The *General Washington* would later be recaptured by the Americans and go on to fame under Captain Joshua Barney.) This surrender led to Talbot's confinement on the infamous *Jersey*, a former 64-gun ship of the line now classified as a "prison hulk" and anchored in Wallabout Bay off Brooklyn, where he and others received ill treatment. In late 1780 he was transported to England. Henry Tuckerman, in his 1850 biography of Silas Talbot, gives the following stunning account of the voyage:

> In the midst of a hail storm [the prisoners] were marched . . . to the water's edge and put on board the *Yarmouth*. Not withstanding the extreme severity of the weather, they huddled together on the poop-deck, without the slightest refreshment until night; then they were driven into the hold, already nearly filled with casks of provisions, upon which loose planks were laid, the intervening space not allowing an upright posture. No light or air entered but what found their way through a scuttle only large enough to admit one prisoner at a time. Obliged to sit, kneel or crawl in this dismal abode, and deprived of the adequate means of respiration, they soon renewed the worst experience of the prison ship. Before morning there rose among them a desperate cry for water: a bottle was lowered, and such was the fierce struggle that ensued among the bewildered wretches, that scarcely one moistened his lips; and this miserable scene was again and again enacted. The air, at length, became so vitiated that a contagious fever broke out among the prisoners, and soon communicated to the sailors. Fear gained for the victims what pity had failed to yield. They were drawn up into squads, and placed in hammocks swung over the hog pens. By this process, continued through a winter voyage of seven weeks, these unfortunate men were alternately exposed to a putrid and suffocating heat and intense cold. . . . their appearance was frightful.[13]

When a prisoner died on board the *Yarmouth,* the others often concealed this fact from their jailers as long as possible so that the dead man's food allotment would continue and could be shared among the survivors. A total of eleven men perished, lying in their own filth during that voyage, and even the most weather-toughened seamen suffered from severe illnesses and delirium.

Upon reaching Plymouth, fifty-three days after leaving New York, the hatches of the *Yarmouth* were unlocked, but none of the poor wretches could climb out on his own. Most had to be hoisted by sling, and when dropped on the deck, few could stand unaided. Some fell helplessly into a limp heap. Bright sunlight, unseen for many weeks, blinded and tortured eyes that had long been confined in the darkness of the hold. Blinking, men shielded their faces with their hands or lowered their heads when the sun appeared from behind a cloud. Men stood in twos and threes to support each other. Those who were able to walk staggered across the deck, stumbling on painful, swollen feet and wobbly legs. Bearded, disheveled, unkempt, and soiled, they were unrecognizable as once proud and competent American seamen. Dazed, many seemed to have lost either the desire or the power to speak. The sight of the prisoners' matted hair and beards, yellow and red runny sores, and their odor surely must have caused shame among the civilized officers and crew of the *Yarmouth.*

The prisoners were moved to a nearby prison hulk that, although hardly commodious, was far less crowded. There they began to recover from the poor treatment. After a brief time they were transported ashore in small boats under heavy guard, probably more to hide them from the people of Plymouth than to guard them from an escape attempt. Once assembled in a courtroom for trial, they were placed before a quasi-civil/military tribunal and questioned about the "allegiance they owned to His Most gracious Majesty" and their "revolt." All were convicted of treason against the Crown for being "found in arms and Rebellion on the High Seas in various ships commissioned by the North American Congress."[14] They were sentenced to the desolate double-walled internment camp Old Mill Prison, on a peninsula, the former site of a windmill that projected into the sound off Plymouth. There they joined more than two hundred Americans in British custody, among whom were Continental Navy lieutenant Joshua Barney and Captain John Manley.

While incarcerated at the Plymouth prison for several months, Talbot made several futile attempts to escape. In October 1781 he won release in an exchange for a British officer at Cherbourg arranged through the patriots John Jay and Benjamin Franklin. In France, Talbot boarded a Nantucket whaling brig to return home.[15] Fifteen days outward-bound, misfortune returned. The British privateer *Jupiter* captured the whaler, but its British captain showed compassion for the long-suffering former prisoner and transferred him to a ship bound for New York City, which was still under Crown control. Talbot escaped once again, this time through Long Island, across the sound to Connecticut, and ultimately back to Providence. When he arrived home in late fall, he learned that his wife, Anna, had died of an illness in the spring of 1781.[16]

During Talbot's incarceration the Continental Congress passed a law designed to decrease the roles of officers and save scarce financial resources. Many idle officers were granted full pay, and according to the legislation in place, those officers who remained on the rolls through the end of the war were entitled to half-pay for life. The solution was insensitive and perhaps had unintended consequences. As of 1 January 1782 all officers who were not on active duty during the war were considered retired, and their pay ended as of the date of their inactive status.

By chance Talbot never received the documents appointing him as a naval officer. Therefore, since he resigned his army commission in September 1779, Talbot was not entitled to receive compensation from either the army or the navy for his last eighteen months of service. Because he was not assigned to a billet this soon after his imprisonment, he was without an income and suddenly was retired from military service. Much of the discussion about recompense had occurred while he was incarcerated, and he had no say in the matter. Talbot was furious. The next years found him at odds over his pay and allowances with the Congress. Like many of his fellow navy captains, he argued vociferously with the Marine Committee and Congress over his compensation. In the interim Talbot had received the promised title of naval captain, but he was not to receive captain's pay because there was no naval ship available for him to command. Captain Talbot was officially listed as a privateer commander without a ship but was required to produce his own remuneration through bounties—certainly an impossible task without a vessel. On 22 October 1783 Congress relented. Under the signature of Connecticut's Oliver Ellsworth, an adjustment and settlement were authorized so that Talbot could at least receive back pay at his old army rank for his time spent in the service of the Revolution.

Now that peace had arrived, during the next decade Talbot ventured into commerce and shipping as a civilian. In addition he became involved in landownership and development in Kentucky. Land on the Kentucky frontier was given to Revolutionary War veterans as the nation expanded westward. He returned east to become a resident of New York, where his son-in-law, George Metcalf, the husband of Talbot's illegitimate daughter, persuaded him to run for public office. Talbot was elected to the New York Assembly in 1792. When the term was over in 1793, he successfully won a seat in the federal House of

Representatives. According to Metcalf, liquor and other refreshments were provided, as well as free transportation to help assure the outcome of the election.[17] This electioneering stratagem became a widespread custom and continued into the early part of the twentieth century.

The British maritime policy after the Revolutionary War was that a person born under a British flag was forever considered British. Because the Royal Navy needed manpower, the British frequently boarded American vessels and impressed many sailors, accusing them of being expatriates or deserters, whichever met their "legal" needs. Because the congressman was a navy veteran, President Washington asked Talbot to intervene on behalf of daunted American sailors, but to no avail.

As a defensive and protective measure Congress reluctantly authorized the building of six naval frigates. They were to challenge the British or any other maritime nation with similar ideas. On 5 June 1794 Congressman Talbot was offered the position of third in seniority on the list of six original United States Navy captains. Until then Talbot was apparently relatively unnoticed within naval circles. This seniority ranking led to an acrimonious dispute, an altercation that led Captain Joshua Barney to decline his commission. Harsh words were spoken and written between the two men who had been former fellow prisoners at Old Mill Prison in Plymouth, England. Barney considered Talbot unfit to be his senior in the new branch of the service.

Talbot, however, coveted the rank and naval life that it afforded. He relinquished his congressional seat in 1795 and returned to New York as the captain assigned to superintend the construction of the frigate *President*. With the signing of the 1795 Treaty of Algiers, Congress ordered construction stopped on the ships that had not been completed and launched. Only the *United States,* the *Constellation,* and the *Constitution* had been commissioned. When the building of the *President* was suspended, Talbot was again without an assignment and pay. His bad fortune continued until President John Adams reinstated his commission for war service at the outbreak of the undeclared war with France in 1798. This led to another rank and seniority dispute, this time with Talbot as the plaintiff. Although his original commission was dated 1794, Talbot was deactivated when work was stopped on the *President,* while some more junior officers had continuous service, allowing them to move up on the seniority list. Because of this, Captain Thomas Truxtun, Talbot's junior during the Revolutionary War, was next in line for an appointment to command a frigate.

Truxtun had developed a reputation for being a tyrant at sea, probably more euphemism than fact. He could be harsh, a response to his arrogance and fastidiousness. He had the reputation for running a disciplined ship and was intolerant of disorderliness in any context. Punishment for infractions was swift, yet he disdained the use of the lash, substituting humiliation or deprivation in its stead. This practice evidently extended to his family as well. Truxtun disinherited one son and disowned another for not living up to his standards. Ironically he suffered from excessive self-importance, a result of the public adulation that he received from his victory as commander of the *Constellation* over the frigate *Insurgente* during America's Quasi-War with France.

Talbot and Truxtun now heatedly contested their placements on the seniority list. When the seniority dispute arose, Truxtun told President John Adams that he would not be subordinate in seniority to Talbot, a man whom he considered a landlubber who was changed by fiat into a sea captain. This was a manifestation of Truxtun's cockiness and ambition, but the charge against Talbot echoed that of Talbot's against Joshua Barney, also a member of the exclusive list of first captains of the new United States Navy. Meanwhile, Adams argued that Talbot's suspension of pay while the construction of his ship was on hold should "no more deprive him of seniority 'than shaking off the apples is cutting down the tree.'"[18] Adams, in what appeared to be an instance of regional nepotism, openly favored his fellow New Englander Talbot over the upstart Truxtun from New Jersey. He furnished Secretary of the Navy Benjamin Stoddert with a detailed account of Talbot's service to his country on land and especially at sea.

In an attempt at reaching a solution, Stoddert decided that Talbot would command the pride of the new fleet, the frigate *Constitution,* but that his seniority would remain below that of Truxtun. Now it became Talbot's turn to refuse the commission. Out of pride he refused to be subordinate to Truxtun. The relationship of these two naval heroes degenerated into a juvenile game of "if I can't be the team captain, then I refuse to play!" Stoddert diplomatically courted Talbot by saying that his services were greatly valued and that the seniority decision was an "accident and not designed on the part of Government [to make] Captain Truxtun your senior officer."[19] Nevertheless, Talbot objected, and Stoddert promised the Rhode Islander that "Truxtun will not be sent on any service to meet with you."[20] Therefore, if the two would never cross each other's path, seniority was essentially a moot point.

President Adams again intervened, writing that "in point of merit & services, there is not an officer in our navy who can bear any comparison to Talbot."[21] Talbot essentially regained his place of seniority in the chain of command, but in truth the naval hierarchy made a finesse by seeing that seniority would not become an issue between the two dissident captains. Talbot's reward was the command of the frigate *Constitution,* replacing Captain Samuel Nicholson, the vessel's first captain. Stoddert later noted to a fellow cabinet member that "this avarice of rank in the infancy of our service is the Devil."[22] Actually the "avarice of rank" appears to have been a naval officer birth defect, one that first appeared during the Revolutionary War.

The forty-eight-year-old Talbot, described by a senior marine as "a man grown gray in the service, who bears the scars he received in defense of his country,"[23] assumed command of the two-year-old *Constitution* at Boston on 5 June 1799. He supervised its caulking, refitting, and minor repairs. On 4 July 1799 Talbot sailed her into Boston harbor, where he ordered her cannons to fire a salute, one for each state in the union at the time, in honor of the nation's birthday.[24]

In spite of Talbot's important position in command of a premier frigate in the navy, he was still upset at being junior to Truxtun. Again he threatened to resign his commission. On 8 July 1799 John Adams wrote, "If you would accept the commission, altered so as to leave the question [of seniority] unde-cided, to be determined hereafter by a council of officers, this shall be done. Assurances have been given you, as I understand, by Mr. Stoddert, that you should not be ordered to serve with Truxtun, without absolute necessity. These assurances I am willing to confirm."[25] Talbot replied on 9 July: "notwithstand-ing I have command of so fine a ship as the *Constitution,* I will freely relin-quish my present station, and retire to private life. If there is a desire . . . to place captain Truxtun over me, I shall be silent on the occasion; but, at the same time I cannot sacrifice the little reputation I have . . . as an officer, by accepting a commission that would inevitably compel me to yield that grade or rank, which no officer can do, and preserve his honor in or out of service. I am free to grant that Captain Truxtun has much merit . . . [but] I have done some things that were, perhaps, thought at the time equally clever . . . and I should glory in the comparison."[26]

Ultimately Talbot made the decision to retain his command, but the depth of his indignation and dislike of Truxtun was apparent. As promised, the two men never served in the same theater of operations at the same time. There is irony in Talbot's stormy attitude toward his place on the seniority list. Joshua Barney had made quite a commotion when the original list was announced in 1796 by refusing a captain's commission in the United States Navy because he would be junior to Talbot, yet Talbot was equally sensitive to his place in the naval chain of command scheme.[27]

Truxtun once again showed his troublesome temperament during the Bar-bary War of 1801. When offered command of the American Mediterranean squadron that was to attack the corsairs, the captain refused the appointment because of a political policy dispute with Navy Secretary Robert Smith. In an attempt at appeasing Truxtun, Smith offered him command of the 36-gun frigate *Chesapeake*. At first he accepted; however, his personal shoal of pride interfered once again. Truxtun demanded that he be made flag captain or commodore of the Mediterranean squadron, and Smith consented. This briefly placated the hypersensitive captain. Shortly thereafter, in another clash with the secretary over policy differences, Truxtun angrily left his flagship. This act of hubris reflected his occasionally disputatious character, not unlike that of many of his peers.

Talbot's first overseas assignment was to take the *Constitution,* with a crew of four hundred officers and men, on a South American cruise along the Antilles to French Guinea. On 15 October 1799 he was stationed off Santo Domingo to patrol and oversee American commerce in the West Indies from Cayenne to Guadeloupe. At Cape François he became Commodore Talbot, the title of the senior captain of a naval squadron, and proudly flew the broad commodore pennant from the mainmast of his flagship the *Constitution*. This made him responsible for about thirty vessels of various descriptions, which he organized into convoys under flag protection.

Although many considered the *Constitution* a handsome vessel, British naval captains ridiculed the flagship, feeling that its sailing qualities were inferior to those of similar British vessels. While cruising in the West Indies, the *Constitution* met the British frigate *Santa Margaretta*. Her captain, an old acquaintance of Talbot, was invited to inspect the *Constitution*. The Royal Navy captain politely expressed admiration for the way the American frigate was constructed, but he wagered a cask of madeira against its value in cash that the *Santa Margaretta* could beat the American frigate on the wind. The good-natured challenge was accepted. A race was sailed some weeks later from sunup to sunset, with the capable First Lieutenant Isaac Hull of Connecticut serving as the *Constitution*'s sailing master and tactician. Long after the incident James Fenimore Cooper wrote, "the manner in which the Constitution [beat] her competition out of the wind was not the least striking feature of this trial, and it must in great degree be ascribed to Hull, whose dexterity in handling a craft under her canvas was remarkable. . . . he was perhaps one of the most skilful seamen of his time."[28] Thus, with the sweat from her crew and some clever maneuvering, the *Constitution* won the race, the cask of wine, and the respect of a periodic adversary. The victory also helped establish Hull's reputation as a seaman.

In early 1800 Secretary Stoddert gave Talbot some discretionary liberty in employing his command so that he might take advantage of any opportune use of his fleet for the protection of American commerce. Talbot was to follow his own judgment for the defense of trade and the capture of enemy vessels in the Caribbean region. In the precedent set by the British, naval presence and strength sometimes projected boldness of foreign policy. Talbot occasionally stretched the unwritten law to display America's naval skill and power. His years of experience as a privateer enabled him to capture a sizable number of prizes at sea in a remarkably short time. These included the ship *Amelia,* the schooner *Swift,* and, with his schooner-rigged tender *Amphitheatre,* the schooner *Esther,* the brig *Nymph,* and the sloop *Sally.* He also aided the frigate *Boston* in her capture of the ship *Two Angels.*

The most daring and ultimately distressing exploit of the *Constitution* under Talbot's command was the taking of the sloop *Sandwich,* which sailed as a privateer under a French letter of marque. The *Sandwich* was fast and able and armed with four 6-pounders and two 9-pounders. The vessel lay at anchor in the harbor of the neutral Spanish colony of Porto Plata under the protection of the town's fort shore battery.[29] Lieutenant Isaac Hull was ordered to place a detachment of ninety sailors and marines on the sloop *Sally,* which had recently been captured. The *Sally* had left port only days before and was expected to return. Talbot and Hull did not think that her capture had been reported. The lieutenant quietly sailed the *Sally* into the harbor with a small crew on deck and the remainder of his men in the hold out of sight. When the sloop came alongside the *Sandwich,* Hull and his men boarded and took her without the loss of a man killed or wounded. A small band of marines, with water up to their necks, waded ashore, breached the walls of the fort, spiked their cannons, and detained its commanding officer. Thus, on 11 May 1800, they were able to seize the *Sandwich* intact and unmolested.

The well planned and executed naval maneuver was, unfortunately, illegal. It occurred in a neutral Spanish port against a ship of a nation with whom America was officially at war. The orders of Captain Talbot may have justified the action in his mind, but the *Sandwich* had to be returned. The local merchants were impressed by Talbot's "dignified conduct, while on station, . . . with a high idea of American character . . . and produced an attachment to the Government of the United States."[30] Stoddert praised Talbot for his meritorious service in protecting American commerce, laying the foundation for permanent trade with the Dominican Republic, and causing the American character to be respected. Stoddert went on to cite Talbot for "the spirit which dictated & the gallantry which achieved an enterprise which reflects honor on the American Navy."[31]

In March 1801 a treaty ending the Quasi-War with France was signed. With peace at hand, the navy suffered another cutback, forcing the decommissioning and a two-year retirement (also known as being "placed in ordinary") of the *Constitution* at the Boston navy yard. Captain Talbot resigned from the navy and managed to have one last dispute. A provision of the Peace Establishment Act, which had recently been enacted by Congress, stated that an officer dismissed from service was entitled to four months separation pay. Since Talbot resigned voluntarily, he had forfeited this recompense. This resembled the shabby treatment that had occurred when he left the Continental Army and Navy. Once again Talbot felt that the government had betrayed him after his military service.

Talbot lost his second wife in1803 and shortly thereafter married a divorcee, Eliza Pintard of New York. This marriage proved to be miserable for the aging captain. Talbot died in 1813 in New York City at the age of sixty-two and rests in the graveyard at Trinity Church at the head of Wall Street. His body carried the scars of thirteen wounds, marks of severe burns from the *Asia* incident, and the remains of five musket ball fragments. Although he largely disappeared from the pages of American history, Talbot was among the founders of the United States Navy and a highly respected Rhode Island patriot. Certainly he was a man of courage, cunning, ingenuity, and patriotism; yet, like many of his compatriots, his vanity occasionally conflicted with his valor.

The eighteenth-century poem "Captain Silas Talbot" celebrates his legend:

> Talk about your clipper ships, clipper ships, clipper ships,
> Talk about your barquentines, with all their spars so fancy;
> I'll just take a sloop-o'-war, with Talbot, with Talbot (Si Talbot),
> An' whip 'em all into 'er chip, and just so suit my fancy.
>
> So heave away for Talbot, for Talbot, for Talbot,
> So heave away for Talbot, an let th' Capting [sic] steer;
> For he's the boy to smack them. To crack them, to whack them,
> For he's the boy to ship with, if you want to privateer."
>   (From "Ballads of Rhode Island," 1782)[32]

Talbot was an unusual Continental military officer. He was a true hybrid: a man who served as a soldier for much of the Revolutionary War but who was largely utilized as a skilled mariner. The Rhode Islander earned his commission as a Continental Navy captain and, like many of his peers, his self-esteem and temper hampered his effectiveness as a leader at times. Talbot's valiant exploits were admirable, but they were diminished by his occasional flashes of egotism.

The Naval Patrician

Dudley Saltonstall

Dudley Saltonstall was unique among the original captains of the Continental Navy: he was the product of aristocratic lineage and entitlement. Perhaps because of this, he had difficulty in getting along with his peers and was disliked by his subordinates. Born in New London, Connecticut, in 1738, Saltonstall was a descendant of Sir Richard Saltonstall, first associate of the Massachusetts Bay Colony and patentee of Connecticut. His pedigree included being the grandson of Gurdon Saltonstall, a clergyman, governor of Connecticut from 1707 to 1724, and a founder of the Collegiate School, a predecessor of Yale College. His father, Gurdon Jr., was deputy (roughly equivalent to mayor) for New London, a probate judge, a political activist, and generally a prominent citizen of the colony. Dudley Saltonstall's mother, Mary Winthrop, was a descendant of Governor John Winthrop of Massachusetts. No surviving portrait of Captain Saltonstall has been found, but on the back of his privateer's commission, issued on 21 May 1781 by Governor Jonathan Trumbull of Connecticut, Saltonstall in adulthood is described as "height 5 ft. 9 in. Sandy Colored hair, light complexion, light hazel eyes and thick set."[1]

In 1765 Dudley Saltonstall married Frances Babcock, the daughter of Dr. Joshua Babcock, Westerly, Rhode Island's first physician. The highly influential doctor served as the representative of the town in the Rhode Island General Assembly for nine years, was chief justice of the Supreme Court of Rhode Island for sixteen years, and during the Revolutionary War was appointed major general of the Rhode Island Militia. Saltonstall's brother-in-law was Silas Deane, a member of the Marine Committee, which administered the Continental Navy during the Revolutionary War. By colonial American standards, Saltonstall's pedigree and privileged position placed him in Connecticut's social upper class, a society that still judged people's worth by who their fathers were and whom they married. Eurocentric, American society was only beginning to value demonstrated merit and virtue in its appointed leaders.

In his formative years Dudley Saltonstall sailed on many mercantile voyages and served as a merchant captain during the French and Indian War, also known as the Seven Years' War in Europe. During this time he gained a reputation as being a competent sea captain. On 17 April 1762, at the age of twenty-four, he was given the command of the letter-of-marque brigantine *Britannia* and took the vessel on successful voyages to the West Indies and Europe.[2] When the American Revolution began, Saltonstall started his military career in the army as commander of a small artillery battery that protected New London harbor. Subsequently, according to John Adams, "At the solicitation of Mr. [Silas] Deane [of the Naval Committee of Connecticut] We appointed his brother in Law, Captain Saltonstall [as captain in the Continental Navy]."[3]

Many of the naval officers appointed during the Revolution achieved their rank by way of their position in society, others for accomplishment and demonstrated skill. In truth, necessity spawned the appointments via nepotism. The rebel government needed officers who could be depended on since loyalties to the Crown or the Revolution were difficult to discern. Thus Saltonstall's appointment as one of the five original captains in the Continental Navy was the product of family political influence. His first Continental Navy command was the 24-gun *Alfred,* a flagship of Rhode Island's Commodore Esek Hopkins.[4]

Saltonstall's first lieutenant and second in command of the *Alfred* was a young Scottish immigrant, John Paul Jones. Jones, an experienced captain from the British merchant fleet, was fastidious and intense and paid close attention to detail. While the *Alfred* was being converted to a warship, Saltonstall seldom appeared at the yard, leaving the tasks of refitting and crew training to Jones. When the captain boarded his ship from quayside, he often went directly to his cabin without words of recognition to Jones or his crew, thus demonstrating his imperious temperament, pomposity, and lack of empathy. He often appeared uncomfortable in the presence of those he considered to be his social inferiors. Jones, who loathed arrogance and snobbery, felt disdain for the Connecticut Brahmin during his service on the *Alfred* and throughout his naval career.

In time the 440-ton *Alfred* was successfully converted to a warship. The vessel sailed with a complement of 220 men and was armed with twenty 9-pounder cannons and ten 6-pounder smoothbore cannons. As the sun rose on 1 March 1776, Saltonstall ordered Jones to raise the Grand Union flag to the masthead of the *Alfred* as a signal for the *Andrea Doria* (sometimes called the *Andrew Doria* in American texts), *Cabot, Columbus, Providence, Fly, Wasp,* and *Hornet* (with a young Joshua Barney onboard) to set sail. Assembled by

Commodore Hopkins, this humble armada of eight small vessels sailed to New Providence (Nassau) in the Bahamas. A small fort protected the Bahamian port, but the town was deemed an easy prey and a source of much-needed arms and munitions.

The village of New Providence sprawled along the water's edge behind Hog Island. A civilian militia manned the two forts that guarded the harbor, with the towns of Montagu on the eastern shore and Nassau to the west. Most of the gunpowder was stored in Fort Nassau. The Royal Navy had been withdrawn except for a single armed schooner, the *St. John,* which was careened down on the docks for repairs at the time. The American fleet, now six vessels after the *Hornet* and the *Fly* were damaged by a collision in a storm en route, made sail for the eastern channel. A landing party of 250 marines marched to the rampart that protected Fort Montagu, and the British fired a few 18-pound shots but inflicted no damage. A militia officer came to the gate of the fort under a flag of truce to ask the commander of the marines their identity and intentions. The British officer decided that shedding blood served no purpose and surrendered, allowing the Americans to spend the night ashore within the fort.

Meanwhile, New Providence's governor Montfort Browne, aware of the American threat, ordered the captain of the merchant sloop *Mississippi Packet* to jettison his cargo of lumber. Under cover of darkness local militiamen loaded 162 barrels of Fort Nassau's gunpowder on board for shipment to St. Augustine. The British sloop crossed a treacherous sandbar and eluded capture by the American fleet. Meanwhile the Americans took Governor Browne and some officials prisoner. When Commodore Hopkins and the other ship captains came ashore on 4 March, they discovered that their expedition had been only partly successful. According to the log of the *Andrea Doria,* they seized "Large Quantitys of Shel & Shott, 16 Morters of different Sizes: 30 Cask of powder & some Provisions fifty two cannon Eighteens twenty fore & Thirty two pounders loaded with Foynd Shott Double headed & Grape & several other Articles."[5] This was an important confiscation of materiel for the war effort, but with additional planning it could have been better.

The New Providence raid was the first coordinated venture of the Continental Navy on foreign soil and the first time that American marines were put ashore in an amphibious landing to confront an enemy garrison. The element of surprise and the attack from a superior position made the excursion a rudimentary success, but the voyage proved costly in an unexpected manner. After the Americans sailed for home on 16 March 1776 with their prizes and three prisoners, Governor Browne and two local officials, an epidemic of smallpox ensued. The disease had been reported among the seamen before the fleet left the Delaware River. In two weeks the infectious disease began to reach epidemic proportions racing from ship to ship.

Captain Nicholas Biddle of the *Andrea Doria* had been a midshipman in the Royal Navy with Horatio Nelson.[6] Biddle ran a clean vessel, and some of his men had been variolated.[7] Apparently because of Biddle's attention to cleanliness and the possibility that the crew may have had immunity to smallpox, Hopkins decided to partly convert the *Andrea Doria* into a transportation vessel for the gravely ill.[8] The trip north along the Gulf Stream was largely uneventful, but the surgeon and his mate were taken sick with smallpox and were unable to care for the patients, thus causing additional suffering. The routine of sail changes was punctuated by sad commands of "heave to" so that the crew could perform periodic funeral services and burials at sea.[9]

Having accomplished this small but important victory in the West Indies, the flotilla sailed for home on 17 March. On 4 April, off Block Island, Hopkins's ships captured the schooner *Hawk,* belonging to the British fleet at Newport, and at dawn the next day they took the bomb-ship brig *Bolton.* At dusk, now off the eastern tip of Long Island, the Americans added both a New York–based brigantine and a sloop to their list of prizes. At about one o'clock in the morning on 6 April, the lookout on the *Andrea Doria* passed word to the deck officer of the approach of the 20-gun sloop *Glasgow,* under the command of Captain Tyringham Howe. The *Cabot,* being the nearest to the enemy, sailed within range of the *Glasgow,* but her broadsides had little effect on the British vessel. Soon the *Cabot* was obliged to change course and sail out of range of the *Glasgow*'s superior return fire. The flagship *Alfred* came up to replace the retreating *Cabot,* but after a short exchange of fire the steering mechanism of Saltonstall's vessel was damaged by the *Glasgow*'s cannon fire and became unmanageable. The *Andrea Doria* fired an ineffectual return broadside in an attempt to keep the *Glasgow* at bay.

Meanwhile the *Providence* appeared to hesitate by tacking back and forth. Its captain, John Hazard, seemed to show reluctance or an inability to join the fray. The *Columbus* did not get into the action at all, presumably because of light, inconsistent winds, although these did not seem to hamper the other nearby vessels. As daybreak parted the darkness, the outnumbered *Glasgow* spread all available sail and fled the area. Hopkins's vessels were deeply laden with the captured military stores and had dense sea growth on their bottoms from their Caribbean trip. The ships had become "dull sailors." In addition many men were lost to outbreaks of smallpox and yellow fever. Commodore Hopkins signaled to give up the chase as his fleet approached Newport harbor, the anchorage for a large British fleet that could, if it put to sea, overwhelm the American force. Hopkins's fleet arrived safely in New London on

8 April.[10] Shortly thereafter the British fleet left Narragansett Bay, and Commodore Hopkins had his squadron moved to Providence, where the much-needed supplies could easily be transported to General Washington.

After unloading the spoils of the Nassau raid, Hopkins was initially hailed as a hero, but he and Saltonstall were later summoned before Congress to answer for their failure to engage the Virginia and South Carolina British squadrons as ordered, as well as the inability of the fleet to defeat the single vessel *Glasgow*. The Marine Committee investigated the *Glasgow* incident and, on 11 July 1776, dropped all charges against Saltonstall as captain of the *Alfred* because the gunfire that had disabled the flagship was deemed a lucky shot—a chance misfortune of war.[11] Abraham Whipple of the *Columbus* was court-martialed on a charge of cowardice. The Rhode Islander was acquitted on the grounds that his plan of attack was an error of judgment rather than cowardice. John Hazard of the *Providence* was court-martialed for cowardice as well as for his conduct during the *Glasgow* affair and for a subsequent offense of embezzlement of stores. He was found guilty and lost his naval commission. John Adams mustered support for Esek Hopkins, his fellow New Englander, but the commodore was censured and eventually dismissed from the navy in January 1777.

The wellborn Saltonstall apparently suffered from bad luck along with a dash of ineptitude. On 5 September 1776 the 24-gun frigate *Trumbull* was launched at Chatham, the Middle Haddam section of East Hampton, Connecticut, about twenty-six miles up the Connecticut River. Again Silas Deane persuaded Congress to appoint Saltonstall as captain of the *Trumbull*. The following spring, on 4 April 1777, the Marine Committee in Philadelphia ordered three of its frigates to sea to intercept enemy transports reinforcing or supplying the British army in New York. Saltonstall took the newly fitted *Trumbull* down the Connecticut River. The vessel was fitted with cannons so that it could run a potential British blockade at the mouth of the Connecticut River. Because of the weight of the armament, the *Trumbull* drew so much water that it could not clear the Saybrook sandbar at the river's mouth. These cannons were removed and given to Captain John Manley so that he could put the *Hancock,* his frigate, to sea. Even with the armament removed, the *Trumbull* was trapped only yards from Long Island Sound, and Saltonstall was unable to carry out the orders of the Marine Committee.[12]

In addition to the boredom of being out of action, there were no prizes for Saltonstall and his crew. Being laid up was costly.[13] The New London naval captain had a challenge and appeared to be thwarted by it. The next summer Saltonstall repeatedly tried to meet the challenge of clearing the sandbar, but he was stymied again. He wrote to the Navy Board Eastern Department, recommending that camels be constructed to raise the *Trumbull* over the obstacle the following summer of 1778. Camels are large, watertight, rectangular, casklike structures that can be placed under or adjacent to a ship's hull. When flooded to a required depth, they are fastened to the ship's hull. The water can then be pumped out, and the camels, with a ship "on their back," are buoyant enough to float the vessel over shallow water.

Permission to build camels was denied because the Continental Congress imposed fiscal restraints. Therefore, the summer of 1778 was a repeat of 1777 with much effort and no success. In November the Marine Committee ordered Saltonstall to stop his attempt to get the *Trumbull* over the sandbar. The Navy Board reassigned the *Trumbull* to Captain Elisha Hinman. On the flood tide of 12 August 1779 the *Trumbull* passed over the bar and was subsequently freed from entrapment in the Connecticut River.

After Saltonstall left the still-stranded *Trumbull* frigate, he was appointed as commanding officer of the frigate *Warren* in Boston. Saltonstall's appointment to command the *Warren* came by default rather than merit. James Warren wrote to John Adams on 30 July 1779 as follows: "Capt. Hopkins of the *Warren,* and Captain Olney of the *Queen of France* are suspended, for breech of Orders [two of only three officers senior to Saltonstall on the Continental Navy list]: Capt. Saltonstall takes command of the former."[14]

By early 1779 New England privateers had begun to take a toll on British shipping sailing the New York–Halifax route. The harassment disrupted military supply lines and commerce, thus driving up insurance rates. As a defensive move, the British were forced to utilize a convoy system to protect their vulnerable vessels. In London, Henry Knox, undersecretary of state for the colonies, noted that the eastern province of Massachusetts Bay had a relatively small, isolated population who were not as ardent rebels as the Boston revolutionaries were. A naval installation in Maine would command the Bay of Fundy. This would prevent American excursions into what is now New Brunswick and also control the northern Maine coast, denying the rebels access to forests that furnished naval timber, building lumber, fuel, and a vital river highway into the north-central Maine lands. In the longer term the territory would become a new province, "New Ireland," for Tories fleeing the colonies and other refugees whom the British might wish to settle in an underpopulated area. It would cover northeastern Maine stretching from the Penobscot River to the St. Croix River. The establishment of a fort at the mouth of the Penobscot would give the British a short-term strategic advantage.[15]

The Penobscot River empties the vast watershed of central Maine, the former colonial eastern province of Massachusetts. Near the river's mouth lies an inverted-claw-hammer-like peninsula, only about a mile and a half wide and about three-quarters of a mile in length, that borders its eastern bank. The headland connects to the main peninsula to the north by a narrow salt-marsh neck. The peninsula's terrain slopes sharply upward from a small harbor on its southern edge. On the "hammerhead" western shore a steep bluff rises to a height of 220 feet, forming a dog-bone-shaped knob that descends to about 180 feet to the east. Most historians called this place Bagaduce, though it is now known as Castine.[16] Bagaduce changed hands among the French, British, Dutch, and Americans six times following its charting by Samuel de Champlain in 1612. The tiny, isolated Bagaduce peninsula became an important maritime focal point economically and politically.

Until the summer of 1779 the defense of the Massachusetts coast was mostly a local affair left to the seacoast merchant establishment, coastal traders and fishermen, and coastal militia artillery batteries. The policy of the Massachusetts Board of War was to use letter-of-marque privateers to interdict British warships and merchantmen. This policy was initially successful, but the American vessels cruising near the Massachusetts coast increasingly fell to the better-armed ships of the enemy. In April 1779 the Board of War changed its policy and concluded that the fleet might also be employed to defend the harbors and seacoasts, "which have been left in such an unguarded and defenceless Situation that where we have taken one Vessel of the Enemy. Their small privateers out of New York have taken ten from us."[17]

During the first half of 1779 British vessels were particularly destructive to New England trade and shipping. On 9 June the Admiralty's representative at Halifax ordered the occupation of Bagaduce.[18] On 12 June 1779 the British landed the Seventy-fourth and Eighty-second regiments, a total of 640 men under the command of Brigadier General Francis McLean. Their mission at the peninsula was to build a fort and gain the trust of nearby Loyalists. Captain Henry Mowat, who knew the coast of Maine well, was placed in command of two 14-gun vessels, the *Albany* and the *North,* and the 16-gun *Nautilus.* This naval contingent was stationed to protect the new fort during the battlement's construction.

The citizens of Boston learned about the British landings in a letter dated 18 June from the Reverend John Murray of Georgetown, Lincoln County, in the province of Maine. After confirmation that the British had landed a substantial force, other letters from concerned Maine citizens followed. Massachusetts had essentially ceased being a theater of land war since the British evacuated Boston in 1776. The General Court (legislative body) of Massachusetts considered this incursion a threat to the colony's agriculture, fisheries, coastal trade, and particularly to the vital source of tall pines that were essential for the construction of masts.[19]

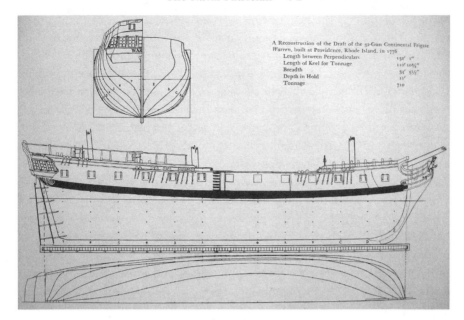

A Reconstruction of the Draft of the 32-Gun Continental Frigate
Warren, built at Providence, Rhode Island, in 1776
Length between Perpendiculars	132' 1"
Length of Keel for Tonnage	110' 10⅝"
Breadth	34' 5½"
Depth in Hold	11'
Tonnage	710

Line drawing of the hull of the USS Warren. *From John F. Miller,*
American Ships of the Colonial and Revolutionary Periods *(1978)*

As a response to this localized British hegemony over the northeastern territory, the General Court of Massachusetts ordered the formation of the Penobscot Expedition, the largest American naval and amphibious landing undertaking of the Revolutionary War. In late June the General Court ordered the Board of War to engage as many armed vessels as could be procured on short notice. If need be they would impress both vessels and sailors, promising fair compensation for all losses of whatever kind. Sensing the inadequacy of leadership in the state navy of Massachusetts or as a calculated hedge to shift blame in the case of failure, the usually independent General Court of Massachusetts appealed directly to the Eastern Department of the Continental Navy Board for assistance. The Navy Board responded by placing three Continental Navy ships, the 32-gun frigate *Warren,* the 12-gun sloop *Providence,* and the 14-gun brig *Diligent,* at the disposal of the state. Captain Dudley Saltonstall, on duty in Connecticut and then second in seniority on the list of Continental Navy captains, was to fly the broad pennant of commodore for the newly aggregated Massachusetts-based fleet.

Having commanded the Continental Navy vessels *Alfred, Trumbull,* and now the *Warren,* Captain Saltonstall seemed to have established his capability as a naval officer as the Penobscot Expedition to Maine was being assembled during late June 1779. In truth, the condescending Saltonstall had few accomplishments as the result of his own initiative; his ancestry was largely responsible for his lofty naval assignments. He was a product of nepotism, and Penobscot would be a test of his legitimacy as a leader. Although he was a Saltonstall, he represented the Connecticut rather than a Massachusetts branch. His orders were to command a complement of about one hundred untried crew members on his personal maiden cruise on the *Warren,* a ship that he had not tested in battle, and ferry ill-prepared and undermanned Massachusetts and, later, Maine militias to unfamiliar battlegrounds. He also had to protect an armada of Continental Navy ships, a state navy ship, privateers, and transport vessels that had never sailed together under a single commander.

The three Continental Navy vessels based in Boston were shorthanded by more than a hundred men. By contrast the Massachusetts privateers were far better manned because, although risky, this enterprise was also potentially profitable. To muster enough seamen for the three Continental ships and three Massachusetts state naval vessels, the Massachusetts authorities ordered a forty-day embargo on merchant shipping.[20] The embargo prevented seamen from securing other employment, making it easier to enlist sailors for the Continental fleet. Backed into a momentary economic corner, some privateer investors thought it prudent to reconsider and offered their ships to the state government. Ever speculating, other Bostonians bought shares in privateer vessels, assuming that the success of the expedition was assured and that they might receive a handsome return on their investment. In order to compensate for the interruption in the citizens' usual pursuit of a livelihood, the recruiters promised that the sailors' service would be brief, easy, and triumphant, an example of public patriotic zeal tempered with a measure of Yankee discretion. They discreetly had their vessels appraised and insured by the state to protect against the possibility of suffering a loss or the failure of the expedition.

In spite of appeals to patriotism, deal making, and clever speculation among the citizenry, the Massachusetts Navy Board was forced to impress the 20-gun *General Putnam,* the 20-gun *Hector,* the 20-gun *Black Prince,* and the 18-gun *Hunter* for a two-month "cruise" to the Penobscot.[21] Privateers were notorious for their independent behavior and lack of discipline, demeanor that would play a significant role in the upcoming expedition.

On 29 June 1779 the council of war informed New Hampshire governor Mesech Weare that the force was being raised, and the New Hampshire 20-gun privateer *Hampden* was contracted to join the task force when it sailed past Portsmouth. The fleet consisted of between sixteen and eighteen armed vessels and twenty-four transports carrying 314 to 344 guns. The numbers vary within the strict definition according to when the other vessels joined the

armada to sail northward, but it is sufficient to say that the size of the heavily
armed Penobscot Expedition was impressive.

The newly appointed Commodore Saltonstall's 13 July instructions from
the Continental Navy Board were to "Captivate, Kill or destroy the Enemies
whole Force both by Sea & Land, & the more effectually to answer that purpose, you are to Consult measures & preserve the greatest harmony with the
Commander of the Land Forces, that the navy & army may Cooperate &
assist each other."[22] Saltonstall had to overcome problems of leadership and
coordination so that he might accomplish the mission. An essential element
needed for military success is communication between the overall commander and his subordinate commanders. Unfortunately Saltonstall's haughty
manner negatively affected his leadership in this type of mission.

Saltonstall has been described as "egotistical, arrogant, irascible, obstinate, overbearing, a marginal officer, dictatorial, haughty, indefatigable, and
morose."[23] The maritime historian Samuel E. Morison has noted that, as "a
scion of . . . first families of New England, he [Saltonstall] seemed not to have
resembled the Saltonstalls who for generations have been noted for their
genial and democratic manners, but rather his mother's family, the Win-
throps, who were notorious for their condescending attitude toward social
inferiors. . . . Captain Nicholas Biddle described Saltonstall as 'a sensible indefatigable Morose man.' [John Paul Jones, who was his first lieutenant aboard
the *Alfred*] complained of his 'Rude unhappy Temper,' . . . Jones all his life
had been angered and humiliated by snobs . . . now he had to endure a New
England snob."[24]

In letters written to Joseph Hewes during May 1776, Jones stated, "in my
opinion a Captain of the Navy ought to be a man of Strong and well connected
Sense with a tolerable Education. A Gentleman as well as a Seaman both in
Theory and Practice, for, want of learning and rude Ungentle Manners are by
no means the Characteristick of an Officer. I have been led into this Subject
on feeling myself hurt as an Individual by the Censures that have been indiscriminately thrown out."[25] Saltonstall "behaved toward inferiours indiscriminately as tho' they were of a lower species;"[26] "[his] want of learning, [is]
rude [and] ungentle;"[27] "[the captain is] the sleepy gentleman;"[28] "[he is] Ill-
natured and narrow minded; [with] absence of refinement of character. . . . On
departing the *Alfred* Jones again wrote to his friend Hewes, "May he [Salton-
stall] soon become an affable, even disposition, and may he too find pleasure
in communicating happiness around him."[29]

Kenneth McCloud, an ambitious enlisted man who aspired to the rank of
quartermaster, the assistant to the master of a vessel usually charged with the

stowage and maintenance of the anchors and cable, also expressed little respect for Saltonstall. When offered the coveted position under John Paul Jones he said, "I would take the office of Quarter mastr if you Please But I am Content Ether Way for I am Determined to Stay By you So Long as I Recive the Same Good treatment as I always Have from you But Capt Saltison [Dudley Saltonstall] I will Not Saile with But you I Can Saile So Long is I Live."[30] In the same vein, a letter from Captain John Hazard to Commodore Esek Hopkins dated 12 May 1776 rebuked Saltonstall, the president of Hazard's court-martial board: "And as to Captain Saltonstall has Deprived me of many Priveledges which I ought to have had at my Tryal and as proof of his partialty towards me I Send you a Copy of an Original [defense] I intend for him the first convenient oppertunity which is the usage I did receive from him at my Tryal."[31] In summary, Connecticut's Dudley Saltonstall gave the appearance of being class-conscious, curt, and unfriendly. These personality traits were offensive to many colleagues and most of his subordinates.

The most important event of Dudley Saltonstall's naval career was the Penobscot Expedition, and his competence may be assessed through his actions or inactions during this expedition.[32] A chronology of events that involved the general planning for the land assault of the Penobscot Expedition is revealing.[33] On 24 June 1779 a directive was read in the Massachusetts House of Representatives ordering the formation of the expedition. General Solomon Lovell was appointed commander on 26 June, with Brigadier General Peleg Wadsworth as second in command. On 28 June, Colonel Nathaniel Jordan was sent to Bagaduce to spy on and assess the number of troops encamped and discover their deployment.[34] Saltonstall was formally appointed as commodore to direct the transport and naval aspect of the expedition on 2 July. Lieutenant Colonel Paul Revere was ordered to lead the artillery company on 8 July.[35] None of the ground commanders had participated in recent combat missions of any consequence.

Although assembled for departure on 14 July, Saltonstall's force left Boston's Nantasket Roads on 19 July. It was a daunting task to muster over forty vessels, eighteen of which were armed, and prepare troops and provisions for all these men and ships in a mere eighteen days. In fact, they fell short of the numerical requirements for men from the Boston area; therefore, the force was supplemented with additional militiamen from the Townsend area, now called Boothbay, Maine. Mostly farmers, loggers, or fishermen, these raw Maine militiamen were described as "boys, old men, and invalids. If they belonged to the Train Band or Alarm List they were soldiers, whether they could carry a gun, walk a mile without crutches, or only *compos mentis* sufficient to keep themselves out of fire and water."[36] This was the first time that the Maine militia units representing three different communities were to be joined under one command and likely to face combat. Only 433 men were cajoled into duty in Maine, making the expedition both shorthanded and inexperienced. Lovell's land force totaled 872 instead of the expected 1,500 men.

When the flotilla safely anchored in the harbor off Townsend, the first of many councils of war was called on board the *Warren* to discuss objectives and pass on vital information about the terrain and the enemy they were about to face. Revere's description of one council meeting colored these events darkly: "In the evening He [Lovell] called a Council of War, as it was an epitome of the whole campaigne. . . . there was nothing proposed and consequently nothing done: It was more like a meeting in a Coffee House than a Council of War. There was no President appointed, nor minutes taken; . . . after four hours consultation, they agreed upon nothing."[37]

Because of his rank and the importance of artillery to the success of the campaign, Revere was present at most of the general councils of war. Revere's recorded votes were mainly opposed to engaging the enemy. Before moving his fleet into Penobscot Bay, Saltonstall sent scouting parties to the area to determine the position of the British vessels. The expedition embarked from Boston on 19 July, arriving off Bagaduce on 25 July. Obviously keeping such a sizable undertaking secret was impossible.[38] When General Francis McLean heard of the expedition, he sent for reinforcements from New York and set about preparing his defenses, a four-foot-high rampart later to be known as Fort George. Secondary batteries were similarly established on the southern shore of the Bagaduce peninsula and on nearby Nautilus Island. Captain Henry Mowat moored his three armed sloops with a total of fifty-six guns close together at the western entrance to the harbor with small transports huddled behind.

Upon arrival Saltonstall deployed nine of his warships against the three small British ships that were moored. The Americans and the British exchanged ineffective cannon fire for more than an hour at a range that mostly was under half a mile. This gave the appearance that the commodore was reluctant to risk damage to his vessels. At dusk General Lovell attempted to establish a beachhead on Bagaduce.

In countering an amphibious operation the defenders are forced to spread their troops because an assault may come from any one of many directions. The attackers have an advantage because they can concentrate their forces at defensive weak points. On the one hand, ship-based supporting artillery can be advantageous in an attack because it is always harder to hit a moving target, particularly with no landmarks around it for gunnery corrective shifts. On the other hand, stationary cannons protected by earthen fort ramparts can

Dudley Saltonstall's hand-drawn map of Bagaduce on
the Penobscot River, Maine, 1779. Private collection

take more punishment than wooden bulwarks of ships. Nature, however, is always a wild card in war. As Lovell mounted his first assault, strong winds and tidal currents forced the general to call off the surprise landing because he feared that his men might be stranded on the beach.

On 26 July about 150 marines landed on Nautilus Island. Under cover of gunfire from their ships, they drove off the lightly entrenched British troops. Revere's artillery now commanded the British anchorage from the newly captured island. Reacting, Mowat moved his vessels about half a mile eastward into the harbor for protection, arraying them in a line across the mouth of the harbor on spring cables and enabling each of his ships to deliver destructive broadsides to any advancing ships. Therefore the British had a strong strategic position.

The Saltonstall papers indicate that he did not consider the option of converting some transports into fireships to harass Mowat's fleet in the small harbor. The prevailing summer winds in the area are westerly or southwesterly. The incoming tide, which can exceed ten feet, swiftly fills or empties the bay. The cool sea air frequently generates entrapping fogs during the humid late summer months. Vessels could easily have moved silently and quickly under these conditions, and once set ablaze, they could have been a great hazard to the anchored British ships. In addition, the burning materials on the fireships could have provided a smokescreen for the advancing American ships even if these ships did not ignite any British warship. Shore-based guns would have had difficulty finding their targets. A well-planned American naval assault might have quickly brought about the destruction or neutralization of the British ships.

Colonel John Brewer of the militia recalled telling the commodore that in his opinion the three British vessels could be silenced in a half-hour. Saltonstall was said to have curtly replied, "You seem to be damn knowing about this matter! I am not going to risk my shipping in that damn hole!"[39] Most historians have interpreted this often-quoted comment as evidence of Saltonstall's cowardice. Brewer recalled the commodore's words long after the battle, so their accuracy may be questionable. Even if the quote is true, it is likely that Saltonstall, the seaman, meant something more pragmatic. If the commodore got into the harbor, his ships would have had restricted maneuvering room because of shifting winds, aberrant tidal and river currents, and inherent difficulties in handling eighteenth-century square-rigged vessels. It takes both significant headway and maneuvering room to turn a square-rigged vessel, let alone complicating the tactic while sailing among a group of vessels in close quarters. Saltonstall's chart did not show details of shoals and sandbars. Some sailing vessels of the era could have been rowed by sweeps from their decks if the tides and/or currents permitted, and one can presume that some of Saltonstall's fleet had this capability. Viewed practically, however, it was difficult to operate the long sweep oars and successfully man guns on the same limited deck space. Saltonstall would have been at an untenable disadvantage sailing into a "damn hole," a place with limited exits that would enable him to save ships and men. Therefore the comment may have reflected prudence, the child of experience.

The privateer captains agreed with Brewer, but perhaps for another reason. Privateers were seagoing mercenaries whose revenue depended on the capture of enemy ships. This expedition was a forced diversion from the profitable endeavors of privateering. Naval tactics were Commodore Saltonstall's problem, not theirs. The privateer role was likely to have been supportive of the three Continental naval ships that would lead the spearhead. Therefore the privateer captains were probably not as concerned about getting into harm's way as was Saltonstall.

On 27 July 1779 thirty-two lieutenants and masters of several privateer vessels, none of whom was a Continental officer, appealed to Saltonstall to engage the enemy before the British could fortify and strengthen their positions.[40] Saltonstall said, "What advantage would it be to go and take the Enemy's Shipping?"[41] Because of his background as captain of a privateer, the commodore's answer appeared reasonable. Privateers generally tried to avoid conflict by using bluff and bluster to subdue and preserve the prize. This may have accounted for Saltonstall's hesitancy, but he yielded to his fellow officers' entreaty.

A small party had reconnoitered the British position to locate weaknesses in their defenses. On 28 July an amphibious assault was launched on Bagaduce under cover of a naval bombardment. Fort George was at an approximate elevation of 160 feet and inland about 1,000 yards. The relatively flat trajectory of most naval cannons on ships about a mile from their target would have made it difficult to provide effective artillery support for ground troops, perhaps accounting for Saltonstall's limited naval artillery support. Mortars fired from bomb ships would have been useful, but there is no evidence that they were part of the expeditionary force. Revere's two howitzers, mounted on field carriages, had relatively high trajectories and might have been effective against the fort or troops under cover.

The battery on Nautilus Island dueled with Mowat's warships anchored in the harbor, causing little harm. Firing slackened, and the transports carrying three divisions of Yankee militia and marines nosed up to the beach. The marines met the stiffest resistance but fought their way up the steep western bluff while British defenders fired down on them. Despite heavy casualties, the Americans managed to scale the heights and drive the defenders back from their outlying positions to the safety of their fort. This engagement was the only significant American victory of the expedition.

At what should have been the critical point, the cooperation between the American land and sea forces collapsed. Lovell's men had fought to within six hundred yards of the British defenses, but Lovell refused to order a second assault. He insisted that Saltonstall's fleet deal with the enemy's ships before the American militia troops attacked the bastion. With the British protected by their entrenchment, Lovell felt that his exhausted force was insufficient to take the enemy stronghold if Mowat's warships supported the nearby fort.

Revere would later disagree, commenting that the British, "not knowing our strength, and we being flush with victory, I have no doubt they would have lain down their arms."[42] Saltonstall refused to attack the British ships even though he enjoyed overwhelming naval superiority. He argued that if Fort George was taken and the British ships were isolated, then he would move against Mowat.

At ten o'clock in the morning of 29 July the commodore engaged Mowat's ships with the *Warren* and three other American vessels. An unfavorable wind made maneuvering difficult, so the naval battle was fought as long-range cannon exchanges. Many of the *Warren*'s men were new to their ship as well as to naval gunnery; therefore, it was not surprising that the British guns found their mark more often than did those of the Americans. The *Warren* suffered damage to her mainmast, bowsprit, and forestay rigging. This unfortunate encounter apparently influenced Saltonstall, and for the sake of prudence or cowardice, he never again placed the *Warren* in harm's way.

As the Penobscot Expedition continued, arguments between the navy and militia officers seesawed back and forth. No one seemed to be in charge. As days stretched into weeks of stalemate, Fort George grew into a more formidable structure. The privateers, largely participating for financial gain, became disenchanted as they sensed that victory was slipping away. Their time could be more profitably spent hunting quarry. Similarly the tired, disillusioned militiamen wanted to return to their farms and businesses. Mass desertions were a constant threat. "Six Capt's of the Armed vessels said, their men were so uneasy, and deserted so fast that if we staid 3 days longer, they should not have men enough to work their vessels."[43]

Some American captains, worried about the threat of a British squadron appearing from Halifax or New York, pleaded with Saltonstall to launch an immediate attack. A battle plan was formulated by Captain Hoysted (or Hoysteed or Hoystead) Hacker of the Continental sloop *Providence* and accepted by most of the expedition leaders. The increasingly deliberate Saltonstall remained reluctant to risk his ships to protect a land assault, realizing that he would be personally blamed for the loss of any vessel.[44]

On 11 August 1779 General Lovell made a detailed, forceful appeal to Saltonstall for naval cooperation for an assault on the British fortifications.[45] Paradoxically, in a council of war on that same day, Lovell stated that "the great want of Discipline & Subordination of many of the Officers being so exceedingly slack in their Duty, the Soldiers so averse to the Service & the wood in which we are encamped so very thick that on an alarm or any special occasion nearly one fourth part of the Army are skulked out of the way and conceal'd."[46]

News of Commodore Saltonstall's inaction reached Boston. On 12 August the Navy Board sent him a steely rebuke: "We have for sometime been at a loss to know why the enemy's ships have not been attacked. . . . It is agreed on all hands that they are at all times in your power. . . . It is therefore our orders that as soon as you receive this you take the most effectual measures for the capture or destruction of the enemy's ships."[47] The American naval and militia officers eventually agreed to mount a combined coordinated assault on14 August.

Just before sunset on 13 August two American vessels patrolling the mouth of Penobscot Bay sighted a British naval force that had come to reinforce the besieged British garrison. Commodore Sir George Collier had left New York on 3 August on board the 64-gun *Raisonable* in company with the 32-gun *Blonde* and *Virginia* plus the 28-gun *Greyhound*, the 20-gun *Galatea*, the 20-gun *Camilla*, and the 14-gun *Otter*. Counting Mowat's three vessels, the British now had a naval armament of 266 guns, many of which threw more weight of metal than did those of the Americans.

The siege was about to be lifted as Saltonstall and Lovell evidently recognized that interdependency was necessary for the completion of their mission. Unfortunately the decision to act came too late. A fog rolled up the river's mouth at the onset of darkness, slowing the progress of the British ships and giving American troops time to organize an orderly withdrawal onto the transports. However, Revere noted:

> When a Reinforcement to the Enemy appeared, it being near Night, we returned to the woods and Retreated on board the Transports before daylight and brought off every thing. Next morning when the tide made, we were ordered up the River, the Ships drew in a line to wait the Enemy. The Transports came to Anchor being no wind and tide against them. About one oClock the wind began to blow from the South. All our Armed vessels got under way and stood up the River. When we found that the Transports got under sail, but the ships soon catched them and left them in the rear. They ran on shore & sett them on fire. Then the men took to the woods. The Gen' got on board the *Warren* and went up the River.[48]

The demoralized American militiamen abandoned what equipment they had brought ashore and, in panic, raced for the safety of the transports. During a frantic meeting on the *Warren*, some determined officers argued that the fleet could make a stand. The river channel funneled northward from the bay, making it necessary for the enemy to approach in a line-ahead maneuver. Because of this it was impossible for the British to fire their heavy guns mounted along the sides of their ships. If the American ships drew up in a crescent, they could rake the approaching British men-of-war with broadsides. By firing grape and canister shot into the rigging and bows of the approaching British men-of-war, enough damage might be done to allow some of the American ships to escape. Saltonstall initially appeared to agree, but the incoming tide and a southwesterly wind favored the British; he demurred.[49] About noon on 14 August, Saltonstall signaled his captains to retreat and deny the ships to the enemy. He ordered every man to be responsible for himself. Fighting against what he believed to be an overwhelming, superior British force would bring only losses of American lives, ships, and arms. Unfortunately discipline quickly disintegrated, and a rush for safety resulted. All of the American armed ships and most of the transports sailed up the Penobscot River with Collier's vessels in pursuit.

Saltonstall attempted to exonerate himself by describing the closing events of the expedition to a board of enquiry:

> [I was] totally not acquainted with the river, [and] the counsel of
> Massachusetts Bay refused upon Application to be at the expense of
> obtaining the necessary Information of the Nature and Situation of
> the country. . . . I did not suffer her [the *Warren*] to be destroyed till
> every hope of preserving her to ourselves was vanished—. . . when I
> reached the other ships [I] found their men in an ungovernable state
> swearing that as the Militia had deserted them they would be held-no
> longer. I was [told by two captains] that they could not pacify their
> men or keep them together any other way than by assuring them
> that the ships should be burned the next day. . . . the land force
> were scattered and gone home and there were no entrenching tools
> provided. . . . with every Effort we had scarcely time enough to escape
> falling into the Enemies possession. . . . a Number of our Ships abreast
> were then proceeding up the river with all the sail they could crowd
> and had the *Warren* had fired her stern Chasers, it might have thrown
> the whole into confusion and given the enemy an eminent Advantage
> in the pursuit.[50]

With the order to evacuate, Revere sent one of the ship's boats to Grant's Mill to find and reorganize his men. General Lovell passed him in another transport and ordered the colonel to bring up his artillery to make a stand against the British. Revere obeyed but was unable to locate enough of his militia to reconstitute an effective unit. General Wadsworth ordered Revere to give up the vessel so that the crew of a schooner that was drifting toward the advancing enemy could be evacuated. Revere initially refused the request and argued with Wadsworth, an act of overt insubordination. The colonel later recanted and gave up his boat. Revere then left the retreating forces without orders and went about a mile into the woods with two of his officers and eight men, not telling his commanders where he was going. By 16 August, Revere had trekked the grueling trail to Fort Western in Augusta, Maine, with whomever he could muster. By 26 August he had returned to Boston, probably by way of the Kennebeck River and then by sea.[51]

During a one-sided melee the 20-gun American warships *Hampden* and *Hunter* tried to run through the British line and were captured. Most other vessels were run aground. Before the seamen and soldiers fled into the surrounding woods, the Americans set fire to as many of their ships as they could to keep them from falling into enemy hands. By nightfall the chaos was complete. Lovell wrote in his journal, "To attempt to give a description of this terrible Day is out of my Power. . . . Transports on fire. Men of war blowing up . . . and as much confusion as can possibly be conceived."[52]

A disorganized rabble of dispirited soldiers, sailors, and marines trudged through the Maine wilderness toward scattered townships in Maine, southern New Hampshire, and the Boston area. The Americans lost 474 men killed or taken prisoner, while only 70 British were killed during the assaults. All of the armed American ships were forfeited, a total of forty-three in all. Forty-six American vessels of various kinds had taken part in the expedition, but the 14-gun brig *Pallas,* on patrol duty at Blue Hill Bay when the British fleet arrived, escaped. The privateers, the 6-gun *Charming Polly,* and the 14-gun *Renown* had left the scene after completing convoy duty. All of the British vessels at Penobscot survived without significant damage. The American cost was tallied at £1,041,760 in the colonial currency of the time, but it was noted that "All of the monies the public could raise, the General Court promise[s] to make provision for all payments of said debit as soon as the state treasury would permit."[53]

The Penobscot Expedition had sailed before the fair winds of great expectations, but the results were an enormous loss of vessels, dispirited soldiers and sailors, a host of sore feet, a growing population of disgruntled citizens, and two potentially ruined military reputations. The Massachusetts House of Representatives reported the debacle as follows:

> This failure has occasioned universal uneasiness and the public in general will expect that a thorough enquiry will be made into the causes of it; . . . We also earnestly recommend, that speedy and effectual provision be made for the payment of those persons who have cheerfully engaged their vessels in the service, or have furnished to the government with such supplies of provisions and other articles as were necessary for carrying on this expedition. . . . the public credit will be

greatly affected, and the public spirited exertions in the future, it is
to be feared, will be greatly discouraged, if there should be any delay
in this matter. . . . the board of war [is] to furnish . . . an estimate
of what may be due to the several creditors of the government upon
this account.[54]

Financial responsibility, although mentioned last, was clearly an important
issue to the legislators. The officers of the militia blamed the navy and privateer fleet for the failure of the expedition, while the sea captains blamed the
leaders of the militia. Failings lay on both sides, caused by hasty preparations,
an inadequately trained fleet and militia, and poorly conceived battle plans
coupled with weak leadership made worse by lack of cooperation.

In order to establish a claim against the Continental Congress so that the
cost of the expedition might be recovered, the General Court of Massachusetts blamed Saltonstall's lack of aggressive spirit and energy for the debacle
that resulted.[55] In a deposition on 25 September 1779 for a General Assembly committee chaired by General Artemas Ward, Captain John Williams of
the 10-gun brig *Hazard* said, "it is [my] opinion that it was in the power of
Our Fleet to have taken or destroyed the enemy's Shipping at any time before
the arrival of their reinforcement."[56]

General Wadsworth, in a similar deposition of 29 September, said, "Uniform Backwardness of the Commander of the Fleet appear'd in several Councils of War at which I was present; Where he always held up the Idea that the
Damage that his ships would receive in attempting the enemys Shiping would
more than counterbalance the Advantage of Destroying them."[57] Wadsworth
argued that if Saltonstall had supported their land attack by suppressing
Mowat's ships, they would have been successful in their mission. He con-
curred with Captain Williams's testimony, saying, "I believe that the Enemys
Ships might have been destroy'd at any time during the Siege."[58] The aristocrat Saltonstall, who should have proved his competency as a naval officer in
the expedition, ultimately led one of the sorriest episodes in American naval
history.

The Penobscot Expedition has been the subject of historical debate and
criticism for many years. In 1845 the naval historian and novelist James Fenimore Cooper was generally sympathetic toward Saltonstall, writing: "Captain
Saltonstall was . . . justly censured . . . though . . . more from . . . publicity . . .
than from any other cause. Had a due regard been paid to secrecy, time might
have been gained . . . before a sufficient force could be collected to go against
the assailants. In a military sense, the principal faults appear to have been a
miscalculation of means, at the commencement, and a neglect to raise such

batteries as might have protected the shipping against the heavy vessels of the enemy. It could not surely have been thought that privateers, armed with light guns, were able to resist [British] two deckers."[59]

One hundred twenty years after the expedition, Richard Saltonstall compiled a comprehensive genealogy of his family, in which Dudley Saltonstall was a minor figure. The author, however, defended his ancestor's conduct before and after the Bagaduce battle along a variety of lines. He noted that the Board of War tried to assemble the expedition and prepare the armed Continental Navy, state navy, and privateer armada in less than two weeks. In addition Lovell was a farmer, an amateur general who had little command experience and lacked familiarity with amphibious assault operations (although he did have some success at Bagaduce). He was given command of a Massachusetts militia that was ill trained, inexpert, and insufficient in number. The Massachusetts Board of War did not consult with the Continental Army's General Horatio Gates in Rhode Island about offering troops or advice about strategy and tactics. A proposal had been introduced in the Massachusetts House of Representatives calling for aid from Continental troops but was rejected out of hubris. Some members felt that if only a small contingent was involved, the Continental Army would take full credit for an expedition that promised to be an easy victory.[60]

Richard Saltonstall also argued that there was state nepotism in assessing blame. The high-ranking state officers were all exonerated and praised. If culpability could be shifted to the naval officer in charge, the Continental Congress would be liable for any losses. In fact, evidence of the "insurance" preparation of the expedition indicated that this was the intent of the General Court. Richard Saltonstall finally stated that the commodore could have mounted an appeal concerning his dismissal by "an address to Congress . . . though he never made application in person. . . . He appears to have been treated shamefully and cruelly sacrificed."[61] Essentially Richard Saltonstall agreed with Cooper's assessment that Dudley Saltonstall was chosen as a scapegoat for a military humiliation and logically a reason for national government economic recompense.[62]

There appears to be some support for this argument in a reexamination of Commodore Saltonstall's actions during the expedition. Lovell, Wadsworth, and other leaders of the Massachusetts militia defended their own actions at Bagaduce before a sympathetic Massachusetts investigatory commission. It was clearly in their interest to shift blame, making their records appear competent. Critical examination of depositions taken during the investigation reveals some minor inconsistencies in individual recollections of events, but it is not unusual for witnesses to recall the details of an event differently. Still it is unlikely that all of these men colluded to blame the defeat on Saltonstall. A conspiracy involving so many men, particularly with such strong egos, is improbable.

Saltonstall had personal shortcomings, but the captain also faced many problems. He had been given command of the *Warren,* a "new" vessel with which he was unfamiliar, that was manned by an undertrained crew, and that was asked to fight in the restrictive, dangerous confines of the Penobscot and Bagaduce rivers. Little is recorded about Saltonstall's court-martial defense. Existing records of the Penobscot Expedition are one-sided, but an examination of naval tactics employed and the limitations of seamanship suggest that Saltonstall may not have been as inept as he has been portrayed. In the face of what he assessed as probable defeat, he denied the enemy American supplies, powder, and cannons and tried to save his men to fight another day. This was an accepted military strategy repeatedly employed by the Continental Army during the Revolutionary War. His vilification may have largely been sacrificial, an opportunity for the Massachusetts investors to win at least partial compensation for the expedition from the Continental Congress.

Legally Massachusetts could not try Saltonstall because he was under orders from the Continental Congress and therefore not subject to the state's jurisdiction. Although the record of his court-martial is lost, the account of the charges against him survives.[63] He was tried in Boston on 28 September 1779 on board the 32-gun frigate *Deane,* the ship named for his brother-in-law. He was found guilty and placed in a reserve status called "out of actual service." Subsequently he was dismissed from the navy.[64] The commodore did face many problems and occasionally voiced reasonable military and seamanlike responses. Therefore the verdict and penalty for a defeat of such magnitude appear both justifiable and compassionate. To paraphrase an often-repeated maxim, victory spawns many fathers; defeat is an illegitimate orphan.

When Saltonstall returned to Connecticut, he asked Adam Babcock of New Haven, kin to his wife, Frances, if Babcock might be willing to convert and arm a merchant ship into a privateer. His proposition was approved; on 21 May 1781 Saltonstall went to sea once again as captain of a Connecticut brigantine, the 16-gun *Minerva.* Serving once again as a Connecticut privateer, he was quite successful.[65] He captured the 10-gun *Arbuthnot* with a cargo of tobacco on 24 June and the next week the 16-gun *Hannah,* whose general cargo was worth approximately eighty thousand pounds. The vessel was the most valuable prize taken by a Connecticut ship during the war. In another ironic twist, Revere purchased shares in Saltonstall's Connecticut privateer venture.[66] Later Saltonstall dabbled for a time in the slave trade, transporting slaves from the West Indies to Charleston, South Carolina.[67] In 1796 he died of unknown causes in the West Indies tropics.

Dudley Saltonstall was contentious and irascible but in a different way from other Continental Navy captains. He had what is now euphemistically called "an attitude problem." He considered himself a patrician with considerable political influence and could be manipulative if it was to his advantage. Saltonstall lacked empathy; he was a scornful snob to those whom he considered beneath his social rank. At times his command style of firm resolve bordered on stubbornness. Because of these unpleasant traits, his leadership was often ineffectual.

Saltonstall's defeat at Bagaduce—its cost in deaths, injuries, ruined reputations, ships, and treasure—was an immense waste. Had the Americans prevailed, the British doubtless could have recaptured Fort George if they had desired. Being small and isolated, Bagaduce was an ideal site for siege warfare, perhaps one more organized than that mounted by the Americans. The British had vastly superior sea power, a seasoned army, and marine troops to accomplish the mission. A better-planned and led American Penobscot Expedition might have produced a victory, but it was likely to have been temporary. The wisdom of the entire venture could be questioned. One definition of "leadership" is the application of prudence, the ability to assess information patterns in any situation and recognize what goes together and what is irrelevant. In the complexities of battle situations a leader quickly makes these assessments and acts decisively to achieve a desired outcome. It took an ignominious defeat for the Continental Congress to realize that Dudley Saltonstall did not possess the desired characteristics of a naval leader.

The Lieutenant Commodore

Joshua Barney

Perhaps the most colorful man who sought and earned an officer's commission in the Continental Navy was Joshua Barney. He had little formal education or military experience but was a mariner who had natural gifts of seamanship, leadership, and courage. Barney took part in thirty-five Revolutionary War naval engagements and lost five of these encounters. As a result he suffered imprisonment three times but escaped twice by using clever disguises. He was also shipwrecked twice and put down a mutiny. Barney's impressive sea victories, frustrating defeats, and cleverness as a prisoner of war constitute a remarkable series of events, and yet at times he was hot tempered and vengeful.

Joshua Barney was born on 6 July 1759 near Baltimore, Maryland, then a village of only a few hundred people. The seaports along Chesapeake Bay had just begun to rise to prominence, and shipbuilding emerged as an important industry. Barney's social status was that of the upper middle class of Maryland society, and his parents had each inherited considerable farmland holdings.

Barney, one of fourteen children of William and Frances Barney, was raised not far from Bear Creek on Patapsco Neck, Maryland. The family's farmhouse was near one of the many inlets for the small boats plying the Patapsco River, and early on he was exposed to life on the water. However, his prosperous farmer father, William Barney, considered the career of a seaman beneath his aspirations for his son. Therefore he arranged for Joshua to be apprenticed to a Baltimore merchant banker. Young Barney worked at the job for about a year but decided not to return to the countinghouse. He desperately wanted to go to sea instead, and with his father's reluctant permission, Barney signed on as a hand aboard a pilot schooner that plied the Chesapeake in 1771. This was where he would learn the rudiments of seamanship.

After eight months as a pilot schooner hand, Joshua Barney crossed the North Atlantic to Liverpool as a seaman apprentice on a small brig captained

Joshua Barney.
From the author's
Harper's Weekly
print collection

by Thomas Drysdale, the husband of Barney's older sister. Barney's father died suddenly in a farming accident while he and Drysdale were at sea, and thus Barney became more dependent on his brother-in-law. On their return to Baltimore, Drysdale was given the command of a larger merchant brig, the *Sidney.* When Barney reached fifteen, Drysdale appointed him as apprentice second mate with the responsible jobs of cargo and deck officer. Just prior to embarking on their first trip, the first mate got into an argument with Drysdale and left the ship. Barney, with little experience, was then promoted to the position of first mate on short notice. On 22 December 1774 the *Sidney* left Baltimore bound for Nice, France, with a cargo of wheat. This perilous winter trip in the diminutive brig proved to be a turning point in Joshua Barney's life at sea.

A few weeks into the Atlantic passage Drysdale became ill with a fever, and tragically he died in his bunk. The *Sidney,* under the command of the teenaged Joshua with an inexperienced crew and a perishable cargo, now started to leak in the middle of the frigid North Atlantic. Sensibly, Barney should have returned to Baltimore to salvage what he could, but the callow skipper resolved to complete the voyage to Nice and deliver the wheat to the consignees. A violent nor'easter gale that arose in the eastern Atlantic almost shook the ship apart at its seams. The brig limped into Gibraltar harbor after an exhausting round-the-clock effort by its crew at the bilge pumps. When the *Sidney* dropped anchor, her decks just shy of awash, crewmen from other ships rowed to her assistance to keep her afloat and stabilized.

The Gibraltar shipwrights and the *Sidney*'s crew refitted the ship in three months. Determined to deliver his cargo, Barney sailed for Nice, a city then renowned as one of the most difficult northern Mediterranean mercantile ports in which to do business. As the grain was being unloaded, the merchants became conscious of the fact that the captain of the *Sidney* was a minor. By international maritime law, Barney's signature on a receipt for the delivery of the cargo would be meaningless. Fearing future legal entanglements or more likely seeing a chance to cheat the young American, the merchants informed him that they would not pay for the wheat. In response, the young shipmaster ordered his crew to seal the deck hatches. A confrontation was at hand. A local armed force of infantry arrived at quayside, challenged Barney's unarmed crew, and took command of the vessel.

Barney decided to make an appeal to Sir William Lynch, the British ambassador to the court of Sardinia in Milan. The fifteen-year-old shipmaster vehemently protested his treatment. He told how he had been intimidated, his British-flagged merchant ship and its cargo confiscated, and—most important to the Crown's ambassador—how British sovereignty had been insulted by an armed foreign contingent. Impressed by the young man's mettle, Lynch wrote a strong letter of protest to the king of Sardinia. When Barney returned to Nice, the provincial governor effusively apologized, ordered payment for the grain, and offered the solicitude of his city. Aware of the turn of events, the captains of the other British ships anchored in Nice's harbor made much of the young Barney, inviting him to many dinners and bestowing other maritime honors on him. Perhaps he was embarrassed, but more likely he enjoyed both the obvious irony and his temporary celebrity.

Now that the *Sidney*'s hold was empty, additional profit for the voyage lay in finding a cargo for his spring 1775 return trip to North America. Barney decided to sail to Alicante, Spain, and upon his arrival was surprised to find the harbor crowded with frigates, schooners, brigs, sloops, supply ships, and a collection of small craft. As the *Sidney* dropped anchor, small boats scampered between the myriad of vessels like frenzied water bugs. Barney and his crew had never seen such a concentration of warships, transports, and support ships.

The hurried activity was, in fact, the formation of an expedition against the dey of Algiers, a leader of the Barbary corsairs who plagued the Mediterranean and its Atlantic approaches during much of the eighteenth century. Every ship that chanced into Alicante was "asked" to provide transport for the troops and arms. Barney was offered a generous lease for use of the *Sidney*, with effectively no choice of refusal. The king of Spain impressed the British-flagged merchant vessel into his service.

On 1 July 1775, a few days before Barney's sixteenth birthday and three months after the events at Lexington and Concord, which were not known to the young Americans, the fleet of ships sailed from Spain and anchored in the Bay of Algiers. When the armada assembled offshore, it took a week of wrangling for the flag officers to finalize their invasion plan, a common problem in amphibious operations of the time. The Moors used this time to organize thousands of troops and to set their defenses to prevent the landing. When the attack finally took place, the well-dug-in Moors won an easy victory. The bloody rout had a lasting psychological effect on Barney. Upon returning to Alicante unscathed, Barney and the *Sidney* crew received a profitable but unrecorded cargo of Spanish goods for their cooperation and trouble.

As the *Sidney* reached the American shores of the Chesapeake on 1 October 1775, the British sloop-of-war *Kingfisher* intercepted her. An armed boarding party impounded the *Sidney*'s scant firearms, thoroughly searched the ship, and carefully examined the ship's papers. Barney boldly and perhaps unwisely questioned the British navy's reason for what he considered a breach of maritime courtesy. He was then informed about the Massachusetts battles of Lexington and Concord that had taken place in April and the more recent battle in June on Bunker Hill at Charlestown. There was an emerging state of war between Britain and her North American colonies, and the Royal Navy was on alert.

After tying up to the wharf in front of Baltimore's familiar brick houses, Barney walked to the office of John Smith, owner of the *Sidney*. The merchant had heard nothing from the ship after she sailed the previous December under the command of Thomas Drysdale. Now, ten months later, before him stood a lad of sixteen who had delivered his cargo in Nice and brought his ship home with another cargo, one that should bring a tidy profit. The shipowner must have been pleased with Barney's accomplishments.

Barney, no longer an apprentice seaman, thought of joining the rebellion. He hoped to become a junior officer in the Continental Navy, a more glamorous occupation than carrying cargo along familiar shipping lanes. This required Barney to travel north to Philadelphia, the capital of the new nation and headquarters of the Continental Navy recently authorized by the Continental Congress.

Lacking the political contacts needed to obtain an officer's commission, he explored the opportunities for a billet on the Delaware River waterfront. Impressed by Barney's experience and enterprise, Captain William Stone, a Bermuda native, asked him to be his master's mate for the newly converted 10-gun sloop *Hornet*. Barney accepted the position, and the sixteen-year-old lad was given the critical job of recruiting a crew, preferably in Baltimore. Salty master's mate Joshua Barney was the very symbol of a rebel leader—a handsome, self-assured, enthusiastic recruiter standing in front of a Baltimore waterfront public house with the new American banner, spreading the exhilarating idea of revolution.

Barney recruited a full crew of former packet men, coastal sailors, and fishermen for the *Hornet*.[1] Commodore Esek Hopkins had assembled a humble armada, including the *Andrea Doria, Cabot, Columbus, Providence, Fly, Wasp,* and Barney's *Hornet*. On 1 March 1776 Lieutenant John Paul Jones raised the red-and-white-striped "Don't Tread on Me" flag on the flagpole of the taffrail of the *Alfred,* under the command of Captain Dudley Saltonstall. With the *Alfred* in the lead, the ships set sail for Chesapeake Bay with the mission to engage British shipping along the Carolina coast and ultimately to sail to New Providence (Nassau) in the Bahamas to capture much-needed arms and munitions for the Revolution. During a storm they weathered en route, the tender *Fly* collided with the *Hornet,* carrying away the *Hornet*'s masthead and boom. At daybreak the *Hornet,* unable to keep up with the rest of the American squadron, sailed for the Carolina coast and safety, arriving off the Cape of Delaware on 1 April 1776. Therefore, Barney missed taking part in the New Providence raid, a venture that became the cause of some of the earliest internecine conflicts in the new Continental Navy.

Barney had grave doubts about Captain Stone's courage. A slow decision-maker and deeply religious, Stone frequently sang hymns to himself or prayed. These suspicions were tested after a pilot informed the captain that the British frigate *Roebuck* was anchored in the roads of Delaware Bay. One of the *Roebuck*'s tenders cruised near the capes (May and Henlopen) taking lesser-armed merchant ships as prizes, but this tender was now vulnerable because it had fewer men and cannons than the *Hornet*. The watchman on the king's tender noticed that an American merchant sloop was entering the bay, and the tender promptly closed to engage with the intention of plundering her. With her guns run inboard because of recent foul weather, the *Hornet* looked like easy prey, the harmless merchant sloop she had once been.

Barney, functioning as the mate in charge of the deck, kept a few crewmen visible at the bulwarks to deceive the British and hid the rest next to their gun tackles. As the British came within cannon range, Barney ordered the guns run out and the matches lit so that the cannons would discharge on command, but Stone ordered him not to fire. In a rage, Barney hurled a lighted match on its iron stick at Stone's head, but the flaming missile missed him. This was early evidence of Barney's ardor and temper. Apparently fearing bloodshed, Stone fled to his cabin and remained there for the rest of the voyage. The officer on the British tender quickly realized that the sloop was not as innocent as she appeared and tacked out of harm's way.

Barney now assumed de facto command of the little 10-gun *Hornet* as she headed up Delaware Bay bound for home. Once the anchor was set in the mud underlying Philadelphia's harbor, the pious Captain Stone emerged from his cabin and left the ship with his hymnal in hand. Barney strongly felt that the captain was a coward and lacked leadership in the face of hostility, but he still hoped to obtain a lieutenant's commission in the naval service. He did not openly discuss his feelings about the cowardly Stone, criticism that might damage his career. Barney requested to be transferred to the schooner *Wasp*, commanded by Charles Alexander, a Scotsman with a reputation as a courageous seaman and gentleman.

After a brief mission escorting a merchant ship bound for Europe out into the Atlantic, the *Wasp* returned to Delaware Bay to discover that two British frigates, the *Roebuck* and the *Liverpool*, had entered the bay behind her. The *Liverpool* gave chase, and in order to elude the powerful enemy, Captain Alexander sailed the *Wasp* close to the shore of the shoal-ridden bay. Shortly thereafter the *Liverpool* struck a sandbar and had to wait for the next tide to float free. The *Wasp* then sailed for the safety of the Cape May channel and was joined by two American warships, the brig *Lexington*, under the command of John Barry, and the ship *Surprise*, under Captain Lambert Wickes. Thus the *Wasp* avoided a likely mismatch against the remaining British frigate *Roebuck*.

About a month later the *Wasp* became trapped in one of the many tributaries to Delaware Bay. Nearby some shallow-draft, open-decked galleys with limited armaments took to harassing the British. These vessels, built on the Delaware River shores, were used to keep the deep-draft British frigates out in the channels of the bay. After some initial success in their mission, the galleys started to receive unacceptable losses to their crews and armaments. Barney asked Captain Alexander permission to take a gun crew from the *Wasp* and man a galley so that he could attack the vulnerable British. The American captain agreed, and Barney's galley intermittently harassed the frigates with thrusts and retreats in a two-day battle. The British men-of-war had to quit the blockade of the small river because of the bold, aggressive behavior of Barney and the other American commanders in small boats.

The triumphant flotilla of galleys rowed and sailed all the way to Philadelphia. There Captain Alexander made special mention of the meritorious conduct of master's mate Barney in his report of the conflict to Congress and
urged that Barney be promoted to lieutenant. Shortly thereafter the sixteen-
year-old, newly commissioned junior officer was transferred to the 10-gun
sloop *Sachem* to supervise her refitting for naval duty.

On board the sloop *Sachem*, commanded by Captain Isaiah Robinson,
Lieutenant Barney received his first opportunity to serve as an executive officer. The *Sachem* had served as a tender in the Royal Navy before her capture
by Captain John Barry. After being taken into the Continental Navy and refitted, she was ordered to sea patrol on 2 July 1776, four days before Barney's
seventeenth birthday. A few days out of port the *Sachem* met the armed
British merchant brig *Two Friends*, carrying sugar and rum. The two evenly
matched ships traded cannon fire for over two hours. During the skirmish
Robinson was wounded, but the more badly mauled *Two Friends* was forced
to surrender. The British brig's cargo of rum was put to good use lessening
the pain of the wounded on both sides of the action. The stricken Robinson
placed Barney in command of the *Sachem* and her prize as they sailed back
to Philadelphia. When they returned on 7 September, Robinson and Barney
were rewarded for their efforts with a transfer to a larger naval warship, the
soon to be renowned brigantine *Andrea Doria*.[2]

The seventy-five-foot *Andrea Doria*, with Barney as its first lieutenant, had
a crew of 130 and was armed with fourteen 4-pound guns plus swivel guns
mounted on deck. Flying the red-and-white-striped Grand Union flag with the
British Union Jack in its upper left canton at her masthead, she sailed for the
West Indian Dutch island of St. Eustatius in late October 1776.[3] The Dutch
were good businessmen, and though officially neutral at the time of the American Revolution, the *Andrea Doria* had orders to transport a shipment of arms
for the Continental Army. A profitable sale from a remote colonial island to a
trading partner was not considered a serious violation of neutrality in Holland.

The *Andrea Doria* entered the harbor of St. Eustatius on 16 November
1776, backing her topsails to slow her headway. As the ship prepared to drop
anchor, Captain Robinson decided to make a noticeable port entry. He dipped
the Grand Union flag and fired an eleven-gun salute with her four-pound guns.
Abraham Ravené, the commander of the fort, after consultation with the
island governor Johannes de Graaff, answered the salute of the American ship
of war. The booming cannon volley tacitly meant that the Dutch St. Eustatius,
a prominent European nation, had formally recognized the independence of
the United States, an important gesture that was more than a footnote in history.[4]

While returning from the West Indies the *Andrea Doria* encountered the brig *Racehorse,* part of the British fleet assigned to protect British commerce in the Caribbean. The two vessels were evenly matched in firepower and men, but the gun crew on the American vessel was faster at reloading cannons. When they closed to within range of each other's cannons, they swapped thunderous broadsides. The *Andrea Doria*'s shots splintered the spars, damaged the rigging, breached the hull of the *Racehorse,* and mortally wounded Lieutenant William Jones, the *Racehorse*'s commander. The *Andrea Doria* suffered minor casualties and superficial damage, and her guns remained operational. Thus the British brig struck her colors, giving Captain Robinson a prize to take to Philadelphia.

En route to Philadelphia the *Andrea Doria* captured the small merchantman *Thomas.* With two prizes to bring into port, Robinson made Barney captain of the prize *Thomas,* which encountered a violent storm off the North Carolina coast and foundered. The crew of the *Thomas* was subsequently rescued as well as captured by the British 24-gun *Perseus,* with Captain George Keith Elphinstone, an officer of the chivalrous school of warfare, in command. Elphinstone granted Barney a parole on Barney's word of honor that the young lieutenant would not bear arms against the king until an officer of like rank was exchanged for him at some future time. Barney agreed. The two shook hands and doffed their caps in the eighteenth-century naval salute of officers and gentlemen.

Barney was put ashore at the nearest port, Charleston, and eventually found transport back to his home in Philadelphia. On 20 October 1777 a letter reached Barney from Elphinstone stating that an exchange had been arranged and Barney was officially released from his parole obligations. He could now return to naval duty, and fortunately the *Andrea Doria* was nearby.

Meanwhile, General William Howe's forces had attacked Philadelphia by moving overland from troop landings on the Chesapeake, but the Americans retained control of the Delaware River just south of the city.[5] The British needed to link their troops in Philadelphia with those on both banks of the Delaware River. As part of their strategic plan the British started a bombardment of the American defenses on 2 October 1777. The American naval flotilla guarding the forts south of Philadelphia consisted of four Pennsylvania State Navy vessels, the frigate *Montgomery,* two lateen-rigged xebecs, thirteen row galleys, twenty-six half galleys, and two bargelike floating batteries. The Continental Navy also provided seven vessels—the frigate *Delaware,* the *Hornet,* the *Wasp,* the *Andrea Doria,* the *Surprise,* the *Fly,* and the *Racehorse*—plus fire rafts and small galleys.[6]

On the shore and on river islands the Americans made their defense from Fort Mifflin, on Mud Island at the mouth of the Schuylkill River, and Fort Mercer, at Red Bank on the New Jersey shore just southwest of the city. Fort Mifflin was manned by a Continental Army regiment from Rhode Island that included an artillery officer, Major Silas Talbot, with whom Barney would clash in a decade and a half. The local militias set up channel obstructions near the forts, making navigation hazardous for the British vessels. Unwary ships might become impaled, or in attempting to avoid these obstructions a few might come within range of the American shore batteries.

Lieutenant Barney was pleased to rejoin his comrades on the *Andrea Doria* off Mud Island. He and his shipmates were busily employed in harassing skirmishes and bombardments. The British mounted a coordinated naval attack from the deep channels of the river combined with mass artillery from the shore to overwhelm the ill-fated American forts and their protective cover of ships. On 20 November 1777 the Continental Army commanders surrendered Forts Mifflin and Mercer and ordered that all the American navy vessels, including the *Andrea Doria*, be burned to keep them out of British hands. Coincidentally the three ships on which Barney started his naval career, the *Hornet, Wasp,* and *Andrea Doria,* were destroyed at about the same time, in the same way, and in the same place.

With the Philadelphia-based Continental Navy fleet largely destroyed, the Marine Committee reassigned Barney to the 28-gun frigate *Virginia* under Captain James Nicholson, which was to sail out of Baltimore. On 31 March 1778 strong spring winds blew the larger British vessels off their stations in Chesapeake Bay, giving the *Virginia* the opportunity to slip by their blockade. The unlucky *Virginia* ran aground on Middle Ground Shoal just as three British frigates appeared about two leagues to windward at dawn's light.

Joshua Barney would remember the next incident for the rest of his life. With capture inevitable, Nicholson ran from his cabin, ordered his personal boat into the water, and rowed himself to shore, leaving his papers and other possessions behind. This abruptly left Lieutenant Barney in command of three hundred frightened men who were about to be taken as prisoners. Although possessing authority, Barney was only seventeen and had only recently reported to the grounded *Virginia*. The discipline and morale of the crew disappeared following Nicholson's desertion, and the crew broke into the purser's liquor locker. The British boarders took possession of the *Virginia* and subdued its largely inebriated ship's company without a struggle. Barney considered this one of the worst disgraces of his naval career. He was now a prisoner of the British for the second time in only six months.

A second insult to Barney's pride occurred midmorning on 2 April when Nicholson rowed out to the frigate under a flag of truce to recover his personal effects. Barney's temper welled up, and he risked a possible court-martial by sparing few words to tell Nicholson, in front of the British captors, what he thought of the captain's actions. The *Rules and Regulations of the Navy of the United Colonies* state that any officer, seaman, or marine who cites or joins in any mutiny or promotes sedition in the vessel to which he belongs shall be court-martialed. Although he placed himself at needless risk, Lieutenant Barney's verbal abuses were met by a silent stare. Nicholson simply gathered his belongings and rowed back to shore.

Barney was held captive for a time on the British frigate *Emerald* and was treated with kindness and respect. In May 1778 Barney and part of the *Virginia*'s crew were put ashore in British-held New York. There they were interned in a hulk, a ship taken out of naval service or a floating captured prize not worth repairing but sufficient to be used as a prison. It was especially miserable to be confined among the sick and dispirited on board one of these barely floating wrecks.

The city of New York had recently received a new naval commander, Vice Admiral John "Foul Weather Jack" Byron. After inspecting the hulks, Byron became disgusted with the conditions on board the vessels and immediately ordered the crowding relieved. He appointed medical personnel to tend to the sick and wounded and instituted a prisoner military hierarchy to look after the complaints and needs of the inmates. In addition Byron transferred all American naval officers from the hulks, thus improving Barney's life as a prisoner. A prisoner exchange was arranged later, and after fifteen months of captivity Barney was a free man.

After only a little over two years of war, the Continental Navy had been devastated by the greatest sea power in the world. There were few American ships in service and therefore few officer billets available. Thus Barney was given ample leave to recuperate from his confinement in Baltimore. One morning while walking with comrades on a quay, he encountered Isaiah Robinson, his former captain on the *Andrea Doria*. Robinson was looking for a first lieutenant and recruiting a crew for a ship based in Alexandria, Virginia. He invited Barney to join him in a new career as a privateer. Barney accepted with delight, pleased to have the opportunity to work again with a mariner whom he respected. In November 1779 Joshua Barney entered the privateer's world for the first time. He became the first lieutenant of the letter-of-marque *General Mercer* in a venture that turned out to be lucrative. Barney's share of the prize money was substantially greater than his salary as a junior Continental Navy officer, and it presented him with the opportunity for his next big milestone in life.

Joshua Barney had matured into a vigorous, handsome bachelor; he was five feet, eight inches tall and had black hair, a dark complexion, and sparkling eyes. His radiant smile and his self-confident manner made him popular with the ladies, and now, as a man of relative means, he was considered an extremely "good catch" in the eyes of many Philadelphia women. He courted Anne Bedford, a comely young lady from a prominent family, and soon "struck his colors" by proposing marriage. The lieutenant had a strong sense of responsibility and decided to invest his fortune of a few thousand dollars of Continental script in a shore-based business enterprise in Baltimore. On his way to deliver the cash, he was robbed. With his fortune lost, Barney returned to the more steady and prudent income provided by the Continental Navy in order to support his new wife. A billet became open, and in July 1780 he received orders to the 18-gun sloop of war *Saratoga* as first lieutenant under Captain James Young.

The *Saratoga* had a successful cruise, and among the prizes was the merchantman *Charming Molly*. Barney was appointed prize captain and sailed for Alexandria. On 11 October 1780, a few miles off the mouth of the Chesapeake, the British ship of the line *Intrepid* together with the frigate *Raleigh* spied the *Charming Molly* and gave chase. With only a small, lightly armed prize crew, Barney realized there was no purpose in fighting against two heavily armed foes, and on 15 November 1780 he became a prisoner of the British for the third time. Captured as a naval officer, he was transported to a naval prison in England. From the devastating voyage Barney, like the other prisoners, emerged hollow-eyed, wan, and emaciated. Barney was tried and sentenced to Old Mill Prison near Plymouth, where he joined hundreds of Americans already in custody. Among the prisoners at the Old Mill were Silas Talbot, the former Rhode Island artillery officer who had fought to defend Fort Mifflin in 1777, and John Manley.

The Old Mill prison complex consisted of several stoutly constructed gray stone buildings surrounded by double walls about twenty feet apart. The only access was through two eight-foot-tall iron gates. Sentries patrolled the gates as well as the two walls that overlooked the prison yards and the road to the prison. Escape attempts from this prison were common, and Barney worked out his own plan to elude his captors. The cunning Barney disguised himself as a British naval officer, gained access to the formidable walls, and made a daring escape. After making his way to a safe house in Plymouth run by an American sympathizer, Barney purchased a fishing smack with the help of two fellow Marylanders and their servant. The motley band of four Americans tried to escape to France across the treacherous English Channel, but a British privateer intercepted them. They were returned to England, but Barney avoided prison in a second audacious escape. This time he was successful, making his way to Belgium. In nearby Amsterdam he contacted John Adams, who arranged for his passage home.

By the spring of 1782 the American navy was decimated. It was down to only two frigates, the *Deane* and the *Alliance,* and half a dozen smaller vessels. The *Saratoga* had been lost at sea. The *Confederacy* had surrendered without a struggle to the *Iris,* and during the previous summer the *General Monk* had captured the new American frigate *Trumbull,* formerly under the command of Dudley Saltonstall. The latter capture was particularly humiliating because the *Iris* had been John Manley's *Hancock* before being renamed after its capture. Similarly the *General Monk* was the refitted former Rhode Island privateer *General Washington,* which Silas Talbot had surrendered almost two years earlier.

Barney now assessed the prospects for his career in the Continental Navy. The list of unassigned naval officers numbered twenty-two captains and thirty-nine lieutenants; therefore, the likelihood of finding a billet appeared slim. Fortunately Daniel Smith, secretary to the Pennsylvania commissioners for the defense of the Delaware waterway, was aware of Barney's availability and offered him the commission of captain in the Pennsylvania State Navy and a ship of his own. A Pennsylvania commission, though not a Continental Navy rank, might prove to be an effective route to the desired Continental Navy captaincy that he sought.

The Pennsylvania State Navy purchased and armed the one-hundred-ton merchantman *Hyder-Ally,* and the twenty-two-year-old Barney assumed direction of her conversion into a warship.[7] The elapsed time from his appointment as captain of the Pennsylvania warship, the recruiting and rudimentary training of the approximately one-hundred-man crew, and the ship's refitting was an astonishing fourteen days, a testament to Barney's leadership abilities. He cast off on 7 April 1782 to await any enemy who might appear in the Delaware Bay.[8]

The Marine Committee of Pennsylvania ordered Barney to escort a convoy of seven merchant ships to the mouth of the Delaware and out to sea. At sundown the wind died and the convoy was forced to anchor in sheltered water inside Capes May and Henlopen. Out in the Atlantic the British frigate *Quebec,* the sloop of war *General Monk,* and the brig *Fair American* cruised between the capes at the mouth of the Delaware, with the *Quebec* patrolling a few miles out to sea beyond the capes in order to interdict any escaping American shipping.

The next morning Barney's lookout noticed that three ships were approaching the *Hyder-Ally* and the convoy. Barney ordered all vessels to weigh anchor, return up the channel, and stay as close to the shore as possible. The British warships were unlikely to follow in shallow, poorly charted water. The *Hyder-Ally* would act as their rearguard protector. The tight throng of American ships weighed their anchors and set sail. In its haste, the merchantman *Charming Sally* ran aground on Overfalls Shoal and became a potential British prize. The *General Greene,* armed with twelve guns, disobeyed Barney's order to leave and opted to fight alongside the *Hyder-Ally.* The usually obstinate Barney did not object, reasoning that the battle would now be even—two Americans ships battling two British vessels. Barney had his crew throw overboard any heavy, unneeded equipment in order to lighten the *Hyder-Ally.* The two American vessels tacked back and forth in order to present a tempting target for the approaching enemy in shoal water while covering for the remainder of the departing merchant fleet.

The British privateer *Fair American* led the *General Monk* into the engagement with the Americans. The *General Greene* abruptly changed course to avoid disadvantageous contact, but the quarters were too tight and she ran aground off Cape May Point. The *Fair American* sailed past the stranded *General Greene* to pursue the fleeing convoy of potentially even richer prizes; the *General Greene* could be dealt with later. Now Barney's defensive strategy of sailing close to the shore worked. The *Fair American* buried its keel in the muddy flats, taking her out of action. The maritime battle that had yet to begin now had one British and two American vessels aground on various shallows near the mouth of Delaware Bay.

The 18-gun *General Monk* and the 16-gun *Hyder-Ally* initially exchanged ineffectual shots from afar. Then they maneuvered alongside each other to trade damaging broadside for destructive broadside. During the thunderous exchange of fire, the two ships drifted closer to within earshot of each other. Barney then told his helmsman to follow his next orders, but by "the rule of the contrary," that is, to do the opposite of the command that is given. Patiently watching for the right moment when the *Hyder-Ally* had about a third of a boat-length lead on the *General Monk,* Barney bellowed a command to his helmsman at the top of his lungs. This purposeful order was easily heard on the *Monk,* and her captain ordered the helmsman to cover this tack. The *Hyder-Ally,* however, abruptly turned to starboard as the *Monk* turned to port, and the jibboom of the latter became tangled in the *Hyder-Ally*'s rigging.

As the battle progressed, Barney climbed upon the wooden binnacle to direct the fighting through his speaking trumpet. In a shower of splinters, the binnacle was shot away from under him, but Barney escaped serious injury.

The privateer Hyder-Ally *in combat with HMS* General Monk.
From John Frost, The Lives of the Commodores *(1845)*

Barney then ordered deckhands to secure the British ship's jib spar to the American ship's rigging, preventing the *Monk* from backing away. Barney commanded his gunners to fire a broadside of preloaded grapeshot in order to wound as many of the British gun crews as they could. The grapeshot also caused British canvas, rigging, and yards to fall heavily onto the *Monk*'s deck. Barney's men then boarded and fought through the debris of cordage and broken spars. After about twenty-six minutes the one-sided conflict ended. Barney had seized the *General Monk*. With the recapture of Talbot's former vessel, the lives of these two men indirectly crossed again.

Barney had to anticipate engaging the *Quebec,* which was only about a league away. The *Hyder-Ally* was damaged but could still be sailed under control. To deceive the *Quebec,* Barney ordered the British ensign to run up on both ships. A crewman found a copy of the British signal book in the *Monk*'s cabin. Barney cunningly signaled a battle success and was able to correctly answer any signals from the distant *Quebec*. To continue the ruse, Barney had the *Hyder-Ally* tied to the stern of the *General Monk,* much like the British would have expected for a prize ship. The captain of the *Quebec* evidently assumed that the *Monk* was going to apprehend any stragglers in the American merchant ship convoy and elected to stay on his blockade station at the mouth of the Delaware River.

Before the day ended, Barney started for home and overtook six members of his convoy now safely anchored farther up the bay. Leaving the smaller *Hyder-Ally* anchored among his mostly intact merchantmen convoy off Chester, Barney sailed his prize, the *General Monk,* back to the port of Philadelphia. A thirteen-gun salute and a swelling crowd of well-wishers gathered at the dock announced his arrival.[9]

This late Revolutionary War battle was one of the few decisive American naval victories against a stronger foe, both in number of vessels and in weight of cannon shot. It gave the United States a sorely needed act of heroism in which to display military pride. The state of Pennsylvania awarded Barney a presentation sword as an expression of gratitude for valor, which became a great source of personal pride.[10] Perhaps because this incident occurred subsequent to the more historic Battle of Yorktown and it was a state victory rather than a Continental Navy victory, it is not well remembered today.

The Pennsylvania State Navy repaired the *General Monk* and changed her name back to *General Washington.* Joshua Barney was ordered to use the ship for the defense of the Delaware waterway as a letter-of-marque 18-gun warship of 250-ton burden and carrying 120 men.

During the summer of 1782, the war wound down, and raids on the Delaware were less of a problem. The Pennsylvania Commission, in need of money, sold the *General Washington* to the Continental Navy for use as a dispatch vessel. Barney returned to Continental Navy service as her commander, still holding the rank of lieutenant.[11]

Barney was ordered to France to ferry French and American personnel and documents needed for the impending end to hostilities. By chance Barney carried to Philadelphia the news that the provisional peace treaty had been signed on 30 November 1782, information that had taken about two months to cross the Atlantic. On 16 April 1783 Admiral Count d'Estaing reported the official signing of the Treaty of Paris to the general population in Philadelphia.

The war was over, but the American government was in dire financial difficulty trying to meet its debts to its soldiers, sailors, and creditors. One apparent drain on the economy of the new nation was its tiny navy. Therefore it was recommended that the *General Washington* be put up for sale. Before her sale, however, the *General Washington* was given one final mission: to transport Captain John Paul Jones to France to collect money owed for his prizes taken to European ports during the war and to return some distinguished French officers home after the war. Setting sail for Europe on 10 November 1783, the gregarious, well-composed, aristocratic Frenchmen prepared for their triumphal return as victorious warriors. By contrast the

reserved, serious, and often somber Scottish immigrant Jones hardly inter-
acted with the other passengers. His manner was sometimes foreboding, other
times almost melancholy, but seldom companionable.[12]

Barney and Jones had much in common but perhaps more in contrast.
Barney was a dozen years Jones's junior and was at the time still only a lieutenant in the Continental Navy. He was charming and good-looking, with a
youthful vigor that made it easy to make friends. Dissimilarly Jones was a difficult loner and introspective. They did, however, share a dislike for incompetent, pompous politicians who ran their military lives as well as some naval
officers whom they deemed cowardly. They also shared the traits of bravery
and excessive egotism, manifested as pride and a sense of the prerogatives of
naval rank and privilege, vestiges of the British model of naval command. During the transatlantic voyage the two men became close and spent many hours
striding the deck, the younger Barney respectfully listening to Jones's views
on naval warfare.

Barney had orders to land Jones in Europe at the place of his choosing.
The place Jones requested was in England, where he was accused of being a
pirate and also had been vilified in the press. Barney advised Jones against
the plan. The possibility of his financial reward lay in France, but in England
lay the probability of imprisonment or even death. In spite of the danger, the
dogged Jones was adamant in his decision to deliver dispatches to an un-
named person in England. Jones said, "The packet boat [*Washington*] was
forced by contrary winds to enter at Plymouth, and I was entrusted public dispatches of importance. I immediately took the mail carriage for London and
was so diligent that five days after my departure from Plymouth I reached
Paris and delivered my dispatches."[13]

The *General Washington* sailed on to Le Havre in mid-December. After
about three weeks Jones informed Barney by letter of his safe arrival in Paris.
Barney returned to Philadelphia on the *General Washington,* but the vessel
had been badly battered and damaged by storms at sea. On 11 May 1784 Barney received a copy of the resolution of Congress directing the sale of the
General Washington at Baltimore. With the sale of the vessel, Barney would
automatically be retired from active naval service. In a touching letter received by Barney about this time, the patriot Henry Laurens wrote, "Your discharge from the service of the public, an act of necessity and with your own
approbation, cannot obliterate the honor you acquired, nor wither the laurels
which you gained in that service. The ploughshare now is preferable to the
spear. You are on shore making a better *provision* for your progeny. . . . I am
persuaded that you could not remain a day unemployed."[14]

Joshua Barney had spent thirteen years at sea, most of them in service to his country, but now the treacherous shoals of business and politics awaited onshore. In the fall of 1784 he became a Baltimore businessman with shipping and commerce interests in the West Indies. Barney was an opportunist and, if the profit were right, would deal with a former enemy. During this time he became entangled once again with British sea power and the British legal system.

In the aftermath of the French Revolution, the new republic of France once again declared war on Britain. The British government reinvoked the "Rule of 1756" against nations trading with an enemy in time of war. In 1792 Barney purchased a three-hundred-ton merchant ship, the *Sampson,* in order to participate in the lucrative West Indies trade. In the course of a voyage to the then French colony of Haiti, Barney and his crew were taken captive by three British privateers under this reinstated "Rule of 1756." Although the United States was neutral, Barney traded with a French colonial government of an enemy and was thus vulnerable.

After he was placed in custody, an argument ensued among the three privateers about the distribution of prize money that the seized vessel and its cargo might bring. During the five days of arguments while he was a captive at sea, Barney and his men were badly maltreated. In a brazen act he and three of his crew successfully regained command of the *Sampson* using arms they had secreted away on the ship. When the hapless Americans returned to Baltimore, Barney demanded redress from the British government for what he deemed a personal insult. The British, in turn, considered his actions against bearers of letters of marque from King George III as piracy.

Some months later the 32-gun British frigate *Penelope* recaptured the *Sampson* in Caribbean waters. Barney was subsequently tried for piracy in the Admiralty Court in Kingston, Jamaica. The court acquitted him of the charge of piracy but confiscated the *Sampson* and its cargo, and he was remanded to prison. This episode led to yet another dramatic rescue from custody. Barney, like John Paul Jones, was unjustly accused of being a pirate. He felt that he had committed an act of self-defense reclaiming his vessel, the *Sampson,* which had been forcibly taken from him by the crew of the *Penelope.* After this episode, Barney changed his attitude from dislike to forthright contempt of the British and enhanced his loathing for the royal system of justice.[15]

When America was a British colony, the most powerful navy in the world protected its colonial citizens, but the protection ceased with American independence. By 1794 Britain and France were once again at war, both sides seizing American ships suspected of trading with the enemy. As the United States grew into an important commercial nation, English and French vessels increasingly searched for military contraband, and both European powers occasionally impressed American seamen into their navies. At the same time the Barbary States of North Africa had a policy of generally maintaining a state of war with at least one nation, thus giving them an excuse to seize the ships of their "enemy" to extract tributes, a common national extortion scheme.

Seizures of men and cargos, as well as detentions of merchant ships by foreign states, had reached alarming heights and became a serious threat to America's ability to engage in international trade. The United States Congress, after much argument, passed the Navy Act of 1794, which gave birth to the United States Navy by authorizing the purchase or construction of six frigates. On 5 June 1794 Joshua Barney received a letter from Secretary of War Henry Knox appointing him as one of the first six captains in the newly constituted Unites States Navy. He was flattered until he noted the seniority ranking of the new captains: John Barry, Samuel Nicholson, Silas Talbot, Joshua Barney, Richard Dale, and Thomas Truxtun. Furious at being listed after Silas Talbot in seniority, Barney contended that Talbot had served as a Continental Army lieutenant colonel during the Revolutionary War but never as a naval officer, let alone as a captain. Also, because Talbot was serving as a congressman from New York at the time, he suspected that the appointment might have been political. Barney's statement about Talbot's military service was incorrect and unjust.

Talbot, a true hero of the Revolutionary War, was wounded six times in a series of land and sea battles. Talbot was the former captain of the *General Washington,* and since its recapture was Barney's proudest victory, it is likely that the Marylander knew this fact. The two officers were fellow prisoners in the hulks anchored in New York harbor and later were interned together at Old Mill Prison. Shortly after his release from the Old Mill, Talbot was commissioned as a captain in the Continental Navy, a rank that Barney did not quite achieve while serving during the Revolutionary War. It is true that Talbot never had his own Continental Navy vessel to command, but that was because few ships were available at the time. Therefore, Barney was technically correct about this aspect of Talbot's service record, but it is difficult to explain why he should have so bitterly complained about the seniority ranking.[16]

Barney's strong objection to the seniority ranking reached the War Department. Secretary Knox responded, "Since the nominations to the Senate have been known, it has been said that you would not accept the appointment on the ground that Capt. Talbot was junior in rank to you during the late war. That the reverse of this is the case, will fully appear by the enclosed resolve of Congress creating Col. Talbot a captain in the navy on 19 September 1779; whereas it appears from the list that you continued as lieutenant to the end of the war. Respect to the justice of the President of the United States requires that this circumstance should be mentioned."[17] Barney did not reply to Knox's letter of explanation or to the implication that he had lied about Talbot. Perhaps overcome by shattered pride, Barney refused to accept a captain's commission in the navy. It appears that the services of one of the most capable naval officers in the nation were lost over vanity, envy, and spite. Ironically, as discussed in chapter 4, a dispute over seniority in rank marked Talbot's career as well.

During America's Quasi-War with France from 1798 through 1800, Barney succeeded in having his self-esteem reinflated by accepting a position in the French navy as capitaine de vaisseau du premier. He did not consider it traitorous to accept a position in the navy that had been our staunch ally only a decade before, during the Revolutionary War. The French Admiralty traditionally favored men of noble blood to become naval officers. In the bloodbath that followed the French Revolution, many competent men met unfortunate ends, and the new French government was in need of proven naval commanders. The valiant yet vain Barney was susceptible to the flattery of high rank and its trappings, which included the elaborate French uniforms accorded officers of high naval rank.

Unfortunately his acceptance of this position in the French navy at this politically inopportune time in the United States branded him as a renegade in many quarters at home. One of the French naval vessels assigned to Barney's command was the *L'Insurgente*. In September 1798 navy secretary Benjamin Stoddert's intelligence said that a force of three British ships at Le Cap François blockaded Barney. Stoddert wrote Captain Thomas Truxtun that "a frigate . . . I understand, was launched about the Time of the Western Insurrection first broke out, and in Honor to those Scoundrels, it is said she is called *L' Insurgente,* and afterward put under the Command of Commodore Barney. If this be the case, she should be the first taken."[18] When the 38-gun *Constellation* captured the 40-gun *L'Insurgente* on 9 February 1799, without Barney on board, a Federalist newspaper wrote, "it is to be regretted that the renegade Barney who behaved so insolently in Chesapeake Bay in '97 was not in command [of the *L'Insurgente*]."[19] Barney's well-deserved image as an American hero was tainted. This new persona became difficult to live down, as he found out when he returned. Barney lost two bids for election to Congress from Maryland, perhaps in a vain attempt at following in the political footsteps of Silas Talbot.

After the Quasi-War with France, Barney returned to Maryland and went into business as a partner in a merchantman out of Baltimore. The Haitian Revolution had begun, and Barney had many contacts on both sides. Ever an opportunist, he became involved in running supplies to both the French and the rebels. At one point a minor French bureaucrat took offense at one of Barney's actions. He challenged him to a duel—another instance of an officer being coerced into a duel—which ended in a harmless exchange of shots to assuage honor. Though Barney prospered as a businessman, his wife, Anne, died on 25 July 1808. After only nine months of mourning, he married Harriet Coale of Anne Arundel County, Maryland, who subsequently added more children to the family. He did not regain national recognition until he became a highly successful privateer and a heroic naval commodore during the War of 1812.

When Barney was asked to assume command of the Chesapeake flotilla in 1814, a delusional Baltimore merchant, Lemuel Taylor, wrote to navy secretary William Jones in protest. Taylor called Barney "a most abandoned rascal both as to politics and morals and that he is despised by $^{9}/_{10}$ of all [those who take] an active part in the defense of Balto [Baltimore]."[20] This led to yet another duel, in which this time Barney wounded his opponent. Taylor recovered, evidently recanted, and went on to participate in Baltimore's defense. Barney's recklessness in preservation of his pride was evident once again. Although appearing needless by current standards, dueling was not an unusual code of behavior among gentlemen at the time.

During the Battle of Bladensburg, an American defensive position designed to thwart the invasion of the capital, Washington, Barney's sailors fought bravely behind five of their naval cannons hauled overland from their scuttled galleys. Sadly units of the Maryland militia supplemented with some regular troops that were assigned to protect his flanks deserted him in battle, running in all directions before the disciplined, advancing British army. Barney, left virtually unprotected, rallied his sailors. Unfortunately the commodore was badly wounded by a musket ball that entered his thigh. After the war and up until his death Barney became extremely vindictive toward what he considered the cowardly Maryland militia.

After the burning of Washington and the defense of Baltimore, a recovered Barney resumed command of what was left of his flotilla. His officers and seamen had lost most of their personal effects when, as a prelude to both the battle of Bladensburg and the defense of Baltimore, they had been ordered to blow up their vessels to prevent their use by the British. Barney petitioned Congress for financial compensation for his men, but to no avail. As the first winter frosts coated the Maryland countryside, the men of the flotilla, who were poorly clothed, became desperate.

General Samuel Smith, the commander of the military forces of the city of Baltimore, saw this as an opportunity for exploitation. He suggested to Baltimore's Committee of Safety and Defense, heavily influenced by the wealthy Smith, that Barney's men should be employed at raising scuttled ships in the Baltimore channels and harbor and that perhaps the committee could find some additional funds for their extra work. (This was for the general's personal benefit since many of the sunken vessels belonged to Smith.) The committee, to no one's surprise, rejected the supplementary pay and allowance provision but nevertheless ordered the flotilla men to toil at the arduous task of raising ships in the freezing harbor's waters.

Incensed, Barney told his men to ignore the command. A personality, rank, and authority struggle followed between Smith and Barney. Smith then played a trump card. He went well over Barney's head by having the order to raise the vessels come from the office of the secretary of war in Washington. In a fit of rage at Smith's political chicanery, Barney wrote a scathing letter of protest to Congress and threatened to resign his naval commission. Barney's display of temper may have been justified, but it was one more example of his contentious behavior and contempt for a superior. Congress did, in fact, honor his valiant service by presenting him with a specially wrought, ornate sword. Barney was flattered, but again he vociferously complained that the federal government held money and supplies due him and his men. He repeatedly dipped his pen into the caustic ink of vitriol to little avail.

In 1818 the British ball that Barney carried in his leg took his life. Barney was one of the most captivating of the contentious sons of the brine. He fought bravely against the British in war and tenaciously in his disputes with the American governmental hierarchy concerning the expected rewards for his service. The colorful, yet sometimes cantankerous mariner rests near the banks of the Allegheny River far from his Maryland home.

Captain Paul

John Paul Jones

John Paul Jones has become the most famous among the first American naval officers. His competence, courage, and creativity as a naval commander have been well documented, but there were many instances of conflict with his officer brethren during his long career. Most historians have acknowledged, but not emphasized, this side of his leadership. Although Jones emerged as the greatest naval hero of the Revolutionary War, he was also one of the most quarrelsome, repeatedly clashing with other Continental Navy officers.

John Paul was born on 6 July 1747 at Arbigland, Scotland, Kirkbean Parish, in the county of Kirkcudbright. His father, John Paul senior, was a gardener, a common laborer of the servant class. Within the strict hierarchical society of household staff he had some status as the chief gardener of the estate of the wealthy landowner William Craik. His position was roughly the outdoor equivalent of head butler. Young John Paul's formal education remained rudimentary and ended at the tender age of twelve in the parish school. Few children of the working class went much further. His home on the north shore of rocky, windswept Solway Firth gave Paul early exposure to a seafaring life at the nearby port of Carsethorn.

Because Solway Firth was difficult for deep-draft ships to navigate, cargoes were usually off-loaded at Carsethorn. One of the most common cargoes taken from the holds was American tobacco. Therefore, while socializing in the busy port, Paul had the opportunity to converse with mariners from the colonies who were volubly discontented with the Crown. He likely sympathized with the growing anti-British sentiment uttered by the Americans. The Scots had similar feelings after the British brutally defeated them at Culloden in 1746, a year before Paul's birth.

During the summer of 1759 a merchant-ship owner, James Younger, signed on the hale twelve-year-old Paul as an apprentice seaman on the eighty-foot, approximately two-hundred-ton merchantman *Friendship*, which was

Bust of John Paul Jones
by Jean-Antoine Houdon.
From John Paul Jones:
Commemoration at Annapolis
24 April 1906 *(1907)*

under the command of Robert Benson. Paul quickly learned the practical nautical arts of the sailor and evolved into a fastidious seaman who paid close attention to detail while developing a commanding bearing—two traits that would foretell his successful maritime career. Paul's first trip to America took him to a small port on the Rappahannock River in Virginia, not far from where his older brother William had immigrated, settled, and married. This site, where Paul first set foot on American soil, would later also become his home.

In 1764 Paul logged many crossings of the Atlantic on board the *Friendship,* but hard economic times in Scotland forced Younger to sell the vessel. Released from his apprenticeship, Paul moved up in rank to the position of third mate on a slave ship, the *King George,* and then signed on as first mate on another slaver, the *Two Friends.*[1] By 1767 he decided that three years of the dreadful slave trade was all he could tolerate. After the *Two Friends* delivered its human cargo of slaves in Jamaica, Paul took his wages and arranged for passage from Kingston to his home in Scotland on board the Kirkcudbright brig *John,* under Captain Samuel McAdam. On the North Atlantic passage, both McAdam and the first mate became ill and died of a tropical fever. Although a passenger, Paul was the only man on board who knew navigation, and he brought the brig safely home. In the summer of 1768, the delighted owners of the *John* rewarded him with the command of the sixty-foot, 180-ton *John* with a crew of six. Paul had made the transition from seaman apprentice to ship's master in just over eight years.

Captain John Paul, who had recently turned twenty-one, demanded that his ship be maintained and sailed according to the strictest rules of seamanship. When either did not meet his standards, he was known to display his unchecked youthful temper. During his second transatlantic voyage as captain of the *John,* he had an altercation with carpenter's mate Mungo Maxwell, son of a prominent family of Kirkcudbright and a man who was very conscious of his social station. Maxwell did not want to take orders from the son of a mere gardener, so Paul had him flogged for disobedience.

The punishment of flogging was common on naval ships and almost never was contestable, but on merchant ships a beating at sea occurred less frequently and could lead to a charge of assault and unjust abuse in a court of law. Maxwell brought these charges against Paul in 1770 in a Tobago court, the site of their first landfall after the incident. A surgeon examined Maxwell and found that the wounds were not particularly dangerous or disfiguring. The local judge then determined that the flogging was within the captain's right in the case of flagrant disobedience and dismissed the case. Maxwell had now been humiliated before his shipmates. The sulking Maxwell left the *John* to find passage to Scotland on another vessel.

Some months later, when Paul sailed the *John* back to Kirkcudbright Bay, he was astonished to learn that Maxwell had inexplicably died on his voyage home. The rumor in town was that Paul had brutalized him and was the real cause of his death. Maxwell's father, Robert, a member of the powerful local clan of Nithsdale, used his influence to have John Paul arrested. Paul obtained bail, returned to Tobago, and within months sailed to Scotland with copies of Caribbean court documents showing that he had been exonerated of charges of cruelty. Furthermore the documents indicated that Maxwell had left Tobago in apparent good health. In an attempt to trump Robert Maxwell's influence on the court, Paul's father's employer, the respected landowner Mr. Craik, certified young Paul's moral character. The judge, after considering the evidence, agreed that Mungo Maxwell had deserved the stripes for his disobedience and that his subsequent death, although regrettable, appeared to be coincidental. Still, in the small, inbred Scottish community the close-knit people were unforgiving, and the Maxwell incident made Paul a local social outcast.

While Paul was obtaining the exonerating evidence for his trial in Tobago, the *John* had been sold to raise some much-needed cash. The ship's former owners, however, gave Paul good recommendations, and he became master of the three-hundred-ton ship *Betsy* out of London. This would lead to a political epiphany for the young Scot. While sailing from the busy naval port of London in 1772, Paul had his first extended encounters with British naval officers. He tried to win their acceptance as maritime colleagues but was uneasy in their presence and sensed attitudes of condescension. Naval officers generally looked down on merchant captains as mere traders. As one tersely expressed it, "The habit of buying and selling goods must have a tendency to detach an officer's thought from those high and delicate refinements which constitute the distinction between the art of war and the art of [financial] gain."[2] Certainly merchant captain Paul, the product of a working-class Scottish family, could hardly be considered their peer. This blow to his fragile self-esteem festered and grew to an unconcealed disdain for the British naval hierarchy.

By the summer of 1773 Paul, working as captain of the merchant ship *Betsy,* had amassed a nest egg of twenty-five hundred pounds sterling—enough to buy land and a house in Virginia near his brother and lead the life of a gentleman farmer. Unfortunately, on a trip from London to the Caribbean, his luck turned. The *Betsy*'s aged frame started to fail. While the ship was laid up and repaired in Ireland, Paul became ill with a severe fever that badly weakened him. When the mended vessel was able to complete its trip to Tobago around Christmas, the young captain got into a dispute with a discontented crewman over what the sailor considered unfair compensation. After the costly repairs to his ship Paul had invested the money he had left over to purchase a cargo that could be sold at a profit for the return trip. He had no funds available to assuage the man, and a fight ensued.

Paul, defending himself against the crewman, who was wildly swinging a bludgeon, allegedly accidentally ran the man through with his sword. There were no witnesses to the fight, and in the face of such danger Paul thought that he had a right to defend himself. Regardless, the death of a sailor under such circumstances meant a second trial in the Admiralty Court in Tobago. This time, however, the charges could have led to a murder conviction and death by hanging. Since the malcontent lived on Tobago and the jury would be constituted from the white men who also lived on the island, Paul decided that the odds of an acquittal were unfavorable. The safest option was to leave Tobago and the British merchant trade as soon as possible.

Paul fled to Virginia in the winter of 1774 with only fifty pounds sterling in his sea chest, but he was determined to achieve the status of gentleman in the new American society. Because of the unanswered charges, his first act was to change his name, not unlike many immigrants before and perhaps more that followed. He now called himself John Paul Jones and became more widely known in maritime circles as Paul Jones.[3]

Now in America, Jones intended to withdraw from the vicissitudes of maritime life and earn a living in more predictable pursuits onshore as a farmer. He believed that he had many of the agricultural gifts of his gardener father. As a resident of colonial Virginia he was becoming more and more aware of the political turbulence that was infecting his new home region and the rest of the colonies. The dissatisfaction of the colonists deepened, and the possibility of breaking all connections with the parent country became a frequent topic in the local taverns.

The dynamic Jones was becoming discontent with his new, mundane life as a squire. On 14 June 1775 the Continental Congress decided that it would be necessary to have some sort of a naval force to assist in America's defense should it declare independence. Congress appointed a provisional Naval Committee to organize one. A search was made to find qualified officers and seamen who were also devotees to the rebel political cause. John Hancock, having heard of Jones's reputation as a competent sea captain, formally asked him to advise and assist the committee in the formation of a navy on 24 June 1775. Jones not only gave his advice but also volunteered to become an officer in the newly formed navy of his adopted country. Thus Hancock granted him the first American naval officer commission and personally awarded it to him. Ironically, throughout much of Jones's life, he scorned people who achieved rank through influence, but he apparently received his Continental Navy commission through his political connection with Hancock.

The squire made arrangements for a prolonged absence from his estate. At twenty-nine, Jones, full of vigor and verve, was convinced that his nautical skills would be a great asset to the navy even though he had no military experience. The first naval officer list of December 1775 named five captains, five first lieutenants, and eight junior lieutenants. Jones was assigned to be the senior first lieutenant and second officer of the 24-gun *Alfred,* a converted light frigate and the flagship of the Continental Navy. The other vessels, the 24-gun ship *Columbus,* the 14-gun brigs *Cabot* and *Andrea Doria,* the 12-gun sloop *Providence,* and the 10-gun sloop *Hornet,* were all converted merchantmen assigned to the original American naval fleet, which also included the 8-gun *Wasp* and the 6-gun *Fly,* both schooners.

Modesty was not a prominent personality trait of John Paul Jones. Because of his many years as a British merchant captain, he considered himself among the most qualified of the first group of American naval officers. Unhappily he found himself under two men whom he would later disparage: Esek Hopkins, the commodore of the fleet; and Dudley Saltonstall, captain of the *Alfred*. Both were experienced mariners but had gained rank through political connections. Hopkins was the brother of Stephen Hopkins, colonial governor of Rhode Island, a political leader in the American Revolution, and a signer of the Declaration of Independence. As a young man Esek Hopkins had commanded merchant vessels, and during the French and Indian War he became a successful privateer. The well-bred Saltonstall, also a successful merchant captain, had the reputation of being a highly condescending officer, a character flaw that Jones found offensive but of which he became accused later in life.

During the winter, while being fitted for a cruise, the flotilla of American vessels became frozen in the Delaware River at Philadelphia. Commodore Hopkins finally got his flagship, the 24-gun *Alfred,* and his small fleet to open water in the river on 17 February 1776. Making their way out to sea, they sailed on a southerly course. Their quest was to capture military stores on the island of New Providence (Nassau) and to seek and destroy Virginia governor Lord Dunsmore's vessels off the coasts of Virginia south to South Carolina. Hopkins disregarded the latter "seek and destroy" order and avoided all contact because he felt that his untested fleet was no match for experienced British naval ships.

During the cruise a sudden squall arose, and the *Hornet* and the *Fly* collided. The two small schooners had to leave the squadron for repairs, leaving five vessels to sail off the Florida coast. The fleet arrived at New Providence (Nassau) on 2 March and the next day put ashore a raiding party of hundreds of marines, who captured the fort and its supplies. This was the first use of American marines in an amphibious landing in naval history. The raid, although not entirely successful, did take possession of arms and gunpowder, a main objective of the mission.

On their return voyage Hopkins's squadron encountered Captain Tyringham Howe's 20-gun brig *Glasgow* off Block Island. Saltonstall brought the *Alfred* into action, but the vessel was hit by a lucky gunshot—a chance misfortune of war—which damaged the steering gear and disabled her. In addition, a combination of dense sea growth on her hull from the passage along the Gulf Stream and the weight of the extra cannons from the New Providence foray affected the *Alfred*'s sailing abilities. The other vessels in the armada proved ineffective, and the *Glasgow* was able to escape the Americans.

Embarrassed that the British could escape from the apparent overwhelming force, the Marine Committee investigated the *Glasgow* incident looking for a scapegoat. Some of the captains, including Saltonstall, were charged with what amounted to dereliction of duty. On 11 July 1776 the committee dropped most charges against the captains, but Commodore Hopkins was reprimanded. Although influential through political connections, he never regained prominence in the Continental Navy.[4]

When asked about his view of the events surrounding the escape of the *Glasgow*, Jones had prudently decided not to offend an establishment with which he would have to deal in the future. He wrote, "I wish to avoid censuring any individual . . . and leave wiser heads the privilege of determining their propriety. . . . I have the pleasure of assuring you that the commander in chief [Hopkins] is respected through the fleet and I verily believe that the officers and men in general would . . . execute his orders."[5] In spite of this public declaration, Jones continued to question Hopkins's competency, but the old Rhode Island commodore stayed on for a time as captain of the new frigate *Warren*, which would become the Continental Navy vessel commanded by Saltonstall during his abortive Penobscot Expedition. Jones was promised a small fleet to harass British bases in the Caribbean, but the aged Hopkins could not find enough ships in ready repair or not bottled up in harbors behind British blockades. Jones's impatience led him to say, "The navy would be far better without a head than a bad one."[6]

Jones's feelings about the imperious Saltonstall were similarly uncharitable. In describing the aristocratic Connecticut captain's relationship to his subordinates he said, "It is certainly for the interest of the service that a cordial interchange of civilities should subsist between superior and inferior officers—and therefore it is bad policy in superiors to behave towards their inferiors indiscriminately as though they were a lower species."[7] Saltonstall's haughtiness rankled the thin-skinned Jones, who went on to say, "Such conduct will damp the ardour of any man. . . . Men of liberal minds . . . can ill brook being used thus. . . . The rude ungentle treatment . . . ought [not] ever be the characteristic of an officer."[8] He later added in his 19 May 1776 letter to Joseph Hewes that the failure for not taking the *Glasgow* was no one officer's fault, but he once again castigated the "rude unhappy temper" of Saltonstall. When Jones left the *Alfred* to command the *Providence*, he and Saltonstall had improved their relationship, and Jones managed to obtain a "blessing at parting" from the Connecticut Yankee Brahmin.[9]

Although multiple courts-martial resulted from the *Glasgow*'s escape, it was a relatively minor naval incident, a small blunder in a strategically important foray. Nature had intervened by slowing the American ships with sea growth and the loss or incapacity of many men to disease. Unfortunately it appears to have set a precedent for some of the antagonistic accusations and counteraccusations among many American captains.

Tactically the Nassau engagement was beneficial, giving the American rebels a much-needed store of artillery and munitions for General Washington's poorly supplied soldiers. The cruise and coordinated attack also provided training for inexperienced naval officers and the American crews. Furthermore, since the raid on Nassau brought the war to the West Indies, it caught the attention of the Crown because of British trade concerns and conflicts with the French. The concern for losing hegemony over the West Indies, which was vital to British trade, deflected English interests and kept military assets away from the war in America. This seemingly unimportant raid resonated loudly in the halls of the British Admiralty and Parliament and drew a threatening tone affecting later English decisions. Therefore, Hopkins's venture, which at the time appeared as a minor military footnote, had far-reaching strategic implications.

After the raid on Nassau the Marine Committee revised and augmented its seniority list of officers. At the top of the list came James Nicholson, about whom Jones seemed to have no overt opinion, although Nicholson had seen no naval combat action. Next was John Manley, whose service went back to 1775 as an army captain and then as a commodore of Washington's fleet that harassed shipping into Massachusetts Bay. Once commissioned as a Continental Navy captain, Manley made it his primary mission to supervise the building and arming of his 32-gun frigate *Hancock*. Manley's reputation among some vainglorious naval-officer peers was one of competence, but they shared a measure of disbelief that this semiliterate fisherman could have become a successful naval officer—an unfortunate expression of social preconception. Because Manley had served in the British navy as an enlisted man, Jones considered him an overrated, simple man who had merely served as a boatswain's mate. This attitude was ironic since it mirrored Jones's own history. This was evidence of the snobbery that Jones possessed but found so repugnant in others. Fourth on the list was Dudley Saltonstall, whom Jones considered both arrogant and inept.

Jones's name appeared near the bottom of the list as number eighteen, a blow to the Scot's pride. He was scornful of those above him, such as Thomas Thompson of New Hampshire, whom Jones described as "a dull inactive genius more fit to be a ship's carpenter than a captain."[10] The only man he openly respected was his crony Hector McNeill, the antagonist of John Manley. Jones always felt that favoritism played a prominent role in the makeup of the seniority list. This idea seemed to fester in him and likely became a driving force in his effort to prove his worth to the Marine Committee.

On 10 May 1776 Jones was given command of the *Providence* and sailed to New York, returning about one hundred Continental Army soldiers to George Washington, who had lent them to Hopkins to help in the New Providence raid. A month later Jones successfully intervened when a brigantine that was bringing munitions to the rebels from Hispaniola was fired on by the British frigate *Cerberus.* The *Providence* left the Delaware capes on 21 August to begin an independent cruise and shortly thereafter took the brigantine whaler *Britannia,* sending her into Philadelphia as a prize.

John Paul Jones possessed an unusual blend of confidence and brashness. He enjoyed a naval combat of parries and blows, of anticipating his foes' maneuvers and then running, feinting, and striking, much like a lithe boxer. On 1 September, Jones used daring seamanship to escape from the British frigate *Solebay,* which was far more heavily armed than the *Providence.* Two days later he captured the *Sea Nymph,* carrying sugar, rum, ginger, and oil. On 6 September the *Providence* caught the brigantine *Favourite,* but the British man-of-war *Galatea* recaptured the prize before Jones's prize crew could reach an American port. The *Providence* took a few more small prizes on 8 October during her return to Narragansett Bay.

During October 1776 Jones succeeded Saltonstall as captain of the *Alfred,* and Hoysted Hacker was given command of the *Providence.* The two ships hunted the sea-lanes together, getting under way on 11 November. After less than a fortnight they took the brigantine *Active* and the armed transport *Mellish,* carrying winter uniforms and military supplies for the British army. On 16 November they captured the snow *Kitty.*[11] The next night the *Providence,* troubled by leaks that had developed during bad weather on the cruise, headed back to Rhode Island, and Jones later returned to Boston. In essence, Jones and his crew on the small sloop *Providence* effectively harassed the British off the North American coast for less than a year.

Jones received a letter from Commodore Hopkins, dated 14 January 1777, informing him that Captain Elisha Hinman had been given command of the *Alfred,* a position Jones coveted. In a long memorial to the chairman of the Marine Committee in Philadelphia, Jones partly stated his objections as follows: "As I am unconscious of any neglect of duty, or misconduct, since my appointment at the first as eldest lieutenant of the navy, I can not suppose that you can have intended to set me aside in favour of any man who did not at time bear a captain's commission, unless in deed that man, by exerting his superior abilities, hath rendered or can render more important services to America. Those who stepped forth at the first, in ships altogether unfit for war, were generally considered rather frantic than as wise men; for it must be remembered, that almost every thing then made against them." Jones then wrote, "I was myself superseded by thirteen men, not one of whom did . . . take the sea against the British flag at first; . . . and none of them since been very happy in proving their superior abilities. Among these thirteen there are individuals who can neither pretend to parts nor education, and with whom, as a private gentleman, I would disdain to associate. I leave your Excellency and the Congress to judge how this affect a man of honour and sensibility." This letter vividly shows Jones's sensitivity along with his hostility toward his peers.[12]

Still, the Marine Committee was impressed by John Paul Jones's successes and reasoned that he might be even more effective with a newer and more powerful vessel. He was ordered to take possession of the frigate *Indien*, which was being built in Holland for the Continental Congress. On 1 November 1777 Jones sailed for France in what he thought would be his temporary new command of the 20-gun *Ranger*, built in Portsmouth, New Hampshire, and largely crewed by men from that colony. While the vessel was top-heavy and unruly in foul weather, she was considered a comely looking ship. During the thirty-two-day passage he added to his inventory of prizes by capturing two brigantines.

When he arrived in France, he was disappointed to learn that the promised *Indien* had been sold and that he would have to search for another warship. For the time being, Jones had to make do with the warship *Ranger*. Once, while sailing in Quiberon Bay, he succeeded in having a French naval vessel give a patronizing nine-gun response to his honoring thirteen-gun salute. Thus the *Ranger* became the first ship flying the Stars and Stripes ensign that received a traditional cannon recognition salute by a European power.[13] This episode became one of Jones's most memorable wartime moments.

Emboldened and even more bellicose, Jones now decided to take the war to the British home waters, but he was not alone in this endeavor. Three American Continental Navy captains, Lambert Wickes, Gustavus Conyngham, and John Paul Jones, carried the war into the European theater. They attempted to breach the famed wooden wall that was the British navy in its own waters. Each man had his own independent agenda in bringing the war to the enemy by raiding within sight of the British coasts. Sometimes these agendas overlapped.

Wickes used French ports as bases for raids. He primarily devised practical ways around legal and bureaucratic obstacles and developed a model for disposing of captured ships and their cargoes. Wickes also had a strategic goal, to embroil France and Great Britain in diplomatic disputes in the hope of instigating another war between them. Conyngham focused on disrupting British commerce in the nearby home ports, forcing the British Admiralty to assign additional Royal Navy vessels to convoy duty. This lessened the number of vessels available to blockade the North American coast. Also the loss of ships to these raids increased merchant ship insurance costs and raised the desire for peace in the influential British merchant community.

Jones was not interested in raiding commercial ships per se but saw these prizes as a way of obtaining the funds needed to underwrite his warring operations. An important by-product of prize taking was the acquisition of British prisoners, "human currency" that could be used in exchange for captive American sailors. Jones sought to get into the British psyche, to make the British feel irritated and angry about the North American war they were forced to support so far from their own shores. Therefore, John Paul Jones was the most troublesome of the three because he attacked British shipping close to shore, raiding their harbors and occasionally their homes. This strategy was particularly vexing to the British establishment. Lord Sandwich (John Montagu) had written to Lord Frederick North on 3 August 1777: "I lay down a maxim that England ought for her own security to have a superior force readiness at home to anything that France and Spain have in readiness on their side."[14] Obviously he had not counted on a voracious American force.

On 10 April 1778 the *Ranger* sailed from Brest to take on the British off their coasts. A strong westerly gale forced her into the Irish Sea. On 20 April, Jones learned from some local fishermen that the 20-gun man-of-war *Drake* was guarding Carrickfergus in Belfast Lough. Jones boldly attempted to capture the unsuspecting *Drake* while she was at anchor, but the boarding was botched even though the ship's company was taken by surprise. Undaunted, Jones had other ideas and crossed the Irish Sea to the English west coast in search of further prey.

On 22 April the *Ranger* sailed within sight of Whitehaven in Cumberland, a town near the mouth of Solway Firth. Jones was elated to learn that hundreds of vessels of every description lay at anchor in the harbor, some exceeding 250 tons of burden. Jones decided that if the crew of the *Ranger* could take advantage of the ebb tide, they might be able to set many of them on fire and easily escape in the ensuing confusion. In American democratic fashion, his lieutenants were consulted in a mini war council, but most objected to his plan. In frustration Jones took the initiative and commanded the raiding party himself.

At close to midnight thirty volunteers in two small boats rowed toward the harbor with muffled oars. The raiders misjudged the distance to the anchored ships in the dark, and the strong Scottish tide turned against them, making it difficult to reach their objectives. Then, before they could land, it became daybreak. Concerned that his plan might fail, Jones sent one boat to the northern side of the harbor to set fire to as many vessels as possible, while he led his men to capture a fort at the harbor's entrance. The small garrison was taken without much of a fight, and the Americans spiked the British cannons. Looking over the ramparts of the fort, Jones was astonished to see only one burning vessel on the northern side of the harbor. He could just distinguish his second boat, backlit by the fire, apparently returning without accomplishing its objective.

Meanwhile, the smoke from the anchored burning vessel and the shrill sounds of alarm emanating from the fort produced a growing crowd onshore. Jones and his party wisely retired to the safety of the *Ranger*. The one British vessel that the Americans had set afire was seriously scorched but not sunk. When accounting for his crew, Jones found that one man had not returned to the ship. It was assumed that a crewman, an expatriate British subject, had deserted his American comrades, raised the alarm, and subverted their mission.

After the abortive Whitehaven raid Jones sailed across the firth to his birthplace, Kirkcudbright, in the hope of taking the Earl of Selkirk, the town's most prominent citizen, prisoner and holding him hostage. When the *Ranger* entered the mouth of the river, it was mistaken for a British man-of-war that was presumably bent on impressing able-bodied men for the British navy. Many of the younger men hid as the local population quickly dispersed. Jones landed with a boatload of armed men and demanded to know the whereabouts of Lord Selkirk. He learned that the earl was away in London but that Lady Selkirk and her children were at home in the castle. Jones's men broke into the castle and, although courteous, demanded the Selkirk family silver tea service as booty, including a much-prized teapot still warm from the morning breakfast.

Absconding with the silver was Jones's way of demonstrating to the British that the Americans were unstoppable yet civil and would not inflict bodily harm. Unfortunately for Jones, the actions of his men had unintended consequences. The attack on British vessels in their home waters, and later raids ashore with the taking of private property, made the Scottish expatriate appear even more as a pirate in the eyes of the Admiralty and the Crown's court of law.

On 24 April 1778 Jones returned to Carrickfergus in the hope of reengaging the *Drake*, and this time the captain of the *Drake* was only marginally better prepared for an attack. When the *Ranger* sailed within cannon shot, a small boat called a pinnace was lowered from the *Drake* to reconnoiter the unidentified vessel. Jones masked his guns, hid the crew below, and gave the *Ranger* the appearance of a harmless merchantman. The midshipman in command of the pinnace and his British crew were deceived and, when invited on board the *Ranger*, were taken prisoner. The newly buoyed Americans gave up their *ruse de guerre* and prepared for battle.

Now that the Americans' intent was evident, the *Drake* weighed anchor and came out to engage the *Ranger*. Strangely the British ship was attended by several yachts and pleasure boats that hoped to watch the impending melee. When the action started, however, they retired to a respectful distance. Then the battle between the *Ranger* and the *Drake* took place at a close range. After an hour and five minutes it produced much carnage—mostly to the British. Both the captain and the first lieutenant of the *Drake* were mortally wounded, and forty-five officers and men were either killed or wounded. The *Ranger*'s tally was two killed and six wounded. With the decks of the *Drake* covered with blood and debris, the English ensign was struck, and Jones took possession of the man-of-war.[15]

Returning with the *Drake* and another valuable ship taken along the way as prizes, Jones sailed to Brest after twenty-eight days of active service. With the dramatic crushing of the *Drake* in British home waters and the interruption of their domestic shipping, Jones had created a critical political by-product for the American war effort. He had succeeded in agitating the populations of the coasts of Scotland and Ireland, fanning the flames of the Scottish and Irish volunteers who were already hostile to the English. In response, the British were forced to expend considerable scarce resources to fortify their many harbors.

All, however, was not cheerful on board the *Ranger*. Jones's first lieutenant, Thomas Simpson of New Hampshire, felt that he deserved more credit for his part in the defeat of the *Drake*. He also resented the ways of the "Scottish foreigner" and seemed to encourage discontent among the largely New Hampshire crew members. In a letter to John Adams, Simpson attempted to make the case that perhaps Jones had, in fact, taken too much credit for his victory over the *Drake*. Adams responded, "The true source of dispute aboard the Ranger, I suppose, was the same that produces most quarrels among Naval officers, the division of Glory."[16] Adams had succinctly identified the problem. The few Continental Navy victories at sea, all too often the result of vexatious captains, became an issue that plagued many American naval officers. By contrast, victory had almost become a tradition for the Royal Navy. Of course, there were glory seekers among the British officers, but generally they were content to achieve their fame as a result of duty well performed.

The *Ranger* served Jones well, much as had the *Providence* before her, but the vessel had many shortcomings. Jones now demanded a faster and more formidable warship in France. He wrote many memorials to the Continental Congress and ultimately obtained command of the French 40-gun *Duc de Duras*. He changed the name to *Le Bon-Homme Richard* (*Bonhomme Richard*) in honor of Benjamin Franklin's *Poor Richard's Almanack,* or in French, *Les Maximes du Bonhomme Richard.* He admired the spirit of one of *Poor Richard*'s sayings, "If you would have your business done, come yourself."[17] The *Richard,* as she became known, was the flagship of Commodore Jones's potent American squadron. This included the 36-gun frigate *Alliance,* the 32-gun converted merchantman *Pallas,* the 18-gun cutter *Cerf,* and the 12-gun brigantine *Vengeance,* in addition to two privateer vessels whose commanders had agreed to join the fight for a share of the money that the prizes would bring.

When Jones left the *Ranger,* some of the ship's company appeared pleased to see him go. One petition by noncommissioned officers in his command reads, "His government arbitrary his Temper & Treatment insufferable, for the most trivial matters threatening to shoot the Person or Persons whom he, in sallies of Passion, chose to call Ignorant and disobedient."[18] Jones had a quick, violent temper and, like many naval officers, had no tolerance for what he discerned as laziness or insubordination. He held high standards for the running of his ship and was not above publicly berating a man or kicking him in his rear end if he thought that would get his attention. To many subordinates, Jones's leadership came as a perquisite of his rank rather than through the admiration of his men.

One of his officers was Pierre Landais, a French merchantman lieutenant, who had smuggled arms to America for the well-known playwright and entrepreneur Pierre Augustin Caron de Beaumarchais.[19] Beaumarchais created a profitable fictitious trading enterprise called Hortalez et Cie. He successfully channeled French arms, with the cooperation of Spain's King Charles II, to the Americans via colonial West Indian entrepôts and then sold them to American agents. After Landais retired from the smuggling trade, he was awarded honorary citizenship in Massachusetts and subsequently was appointed to command the American ship *Alliance* on 18 June 1778.[20]

Jones's initial impression was that Landais was "a sensible and well-informed man."[21] During Landais's first voyage as captain of the *Alliance,* however, a mutiny occurred. A court-martial took place. John Adams now became disillusioned with the French immigrant, noting that Landais "is jealous of every Thing. Jealous of every Body . . . he knows not how to treat his officers, nor his passengers, nor any Body else. . . . There is in this man an Inactivity and an Indecisiveness that will ruin him. He is bewildered . . . an embarrassed Mind."[22] These character faults and other personality traits would make Landais and Jones adversaries when mutual support would have been of joint benefit.

On 14 August 1779 Jones sailed the *Richard* and his squadron in search of English ships. This was about the time that Dudley Saltonstall was leading his Penobscot Expedition to Bagaduce, with the subsequent loss of more than forty American vessels. When word of this disastrous defeat reached Jones some months later, Jones put up "a great hue and cry" for all who would listen. This confirmed his evaluation of Saltonstall as an incompetent naval officer.[23]

On 25 August, Landais had his first of what would be many open disagreements with Jones. Jones was deeply troubled because he had lost some of the squadron's small boats in the dense fog that plagued the Irish coast. Landais, always aggressive in his hunt for enemy vessels, wanted to chase a prize into treacherous waters, but Jones, fearing that he might lose the badly needed *Alliance,* ordered him to stay with the fleet. Landais argued that he had the right to follow his own "opinion in chasing when and where he thought proper and in every other matter."[24] Jones tried to placate Landais, saying that he was concerned about the *Alliance.* The fog and turbulent seas in the area were unpredictable, as was evident from the recent small boats tragedy. Landais said that the loss of the small boats was due to Jones's incompetence. The volatile Jones, in fury, responded that Landais was guilty of calumny.

This enmity produced an affront to the honor of each according to the code of eighteenth-century gentlemanly behavior. The piqued Landais took immediate offense and challenged Jones to a duel—but with swords. The choice of the sword as the dueling weapon would give Landais, raised in the French tradition of swordsmanship, a distinct advantage.[25] Jones was also outraged, but he managed to subordinate his ego and vanity to a higher virtue— the sense of duty when on a mission. Even though both tempers were elevated, Jones sensibly suspended the duel until they were on land. Jones stated in his memoir, "Captain Landais, a man of the most unhappy temper, not only behaved with disrespect to the commander, but soon assumed to act as he pleased, and as an independent commander, refusing to obey the signals of the Commodore, giving chase where or how he thought fit, and availing himself of any pretext to leave the squadron which he finally did."[26]

Crews of most ships of the time were international. There were many neutral ports around the North Atlantic, and prizes captured at sea were frequently taken to the nearest port as a *guerre de course.* Once a ship had been disposed of, members of the prize crew could be left to fend for themselves, and they signed on to whatever available ship might take them to a more desirable port. In this way, a burgeoning population of maritime nomads with little sense of morality and allegiance grew on the high seas. Therefore, the multinational crew of the *Richard* was difficult to control because of divided loyalties. "They were generally so mean that the only expedient I could find that allowed me to command was to divide them into two parties and let one group of rogues guard the other."[27] The most dissident were sailors whom Jones had pressed into service from French prisons. Among some of their prior crimes had been mutiny, and before long these men plotted a mutiny on the *Richard*. However, Jones broke up the plot and severely punished the ring-leader, thus putting the crew on notice that he was in charge.

On one mission the squadron sailed in search of the British in the Bay of Biscay. The *Richard* and the *Alliance*, blinded by a squall, emerged from the turbulent weather on a collision course. Landais, hearing shouts from the *Richard*'s bow watch, assumed that some of the *Richard*'s ex-British sailors had become mutinous. Rather than ordering a change in course, Landais descended into his cabin to arm himself. The predicted collision occurred with a loud crack as the bowsprit of the *Richard* tore into the *Alliance*'s rigging and damaged her mizzenmast. Jones, who had been off watch asleep in his cabin, relieved Lieutenant Robert Robinson, the officer of the deck of the *Richard* at the time of the accident. Although this unfortunate incident was unintentional, it aggravated the tension between the two captains.

By 15 September 1779 Jones's squadron had worked its way up the Firth of Fourth, seizing occasional prizes along the way. When the *Richard* sailed near the coast of Fife, the vessel was mistaken for the 50-gun British warship *Romney*. A cutter was sent from shore to warn the ship's master that the "pirate Jones" had been seen in these waters and that he should be vigilant. Jones thanked the local men for the intelligence and asked to borrow the cutter's pilot to help him navigate the treacherous shores. The pilot complied and in passing asked if Jones could spare some powder and shot for their shore defenses against the American buccaneer. Jones then identified himself as the very "pirate" the man feared. The stunned pilot pleaded that his life be spared. Amused, Jones released the frightened pilot unharmed and sent him off with a small barrel of powder, apologizing that he had no shot to spare. This illustrates another aspect of Jones's character, his humor and audacity. He appeared to enjoy taunting his opponents. This was particularly true in a potentially overmatched sea battle situation. He would start to close with the enemy and then would sail out of harm's way in order to frustrate them, displaying his mischievous and contemptuous nature even in dangerous situations.

On 23 September 1779, in the North Sea off Flamborough Head, England, the American squadron came across the 44-gun *Serapis*, her consort the *Countess of Scarborough*, and a convoy of forty-four small merchant vessels that were carrying naval stores. The *Serapis*, rated as a 44-gun vessel, actually carried fifty guns (twenty 18-pounders, twenty 9-pounders, and ten 6-pounders). The poorly armed merchantmen, seeing the approaching Americans, hastily crowded on sail and swiftly headed for the nearest British port. The two British escort warships steered into the path of the American challengers to assure the escape of the convoy. After a short battle the *Countess of Scarborough* struck her colors to the *Pallas,* an American converted mer-chantman.

As evening approached, a bright full moon rose from the sea. Jones made a lantern signal to the *Alliance* to join the *Richard* in the battle so that they would have a numerical advantage, but Landais stayed his course, ignoring Jones's order. The *Serapis* opened fire first, blasting the *Richard* in the ini-tial broadside. The *Serapis* fired her formidable 50-gun armament against the *Richard*'s forty guns (six 18-pounders, twenty-eight 12-pounders, and six 9-pounders). The *Serapis*'s greater weight of shot did a great deal of damage wounding or killing members of the *Richard*'s gun crews, thereby taking away much of the *Richard*'s firepower. In addition, the *Richard*'s hull was breached in several places and her rudder badly damaged.

Now that the moon was higher in the night's sky, brilliantly illuminating the battle scene, the *Alliance* sailed into the fray, rounding the stern of the *Richard* and the bow of the *Serapis.* The *Alliance* cut loose a broadside of grapeshot that hit both vessels, but most of its damage was done to the *Richard.* The *Alliance* then changed course, returned to the two stricken ships, and fired another grapeshot broadside into the bow of the *Richard,* wounding many Americans on deck or in the rigging. James Fenimore Cooper later described the scene: "As the Moon had been up for some time, it was impossible not to distinguish between the two vessels. The *Richard* being all black while the *Serapis* had yellow sides; and the impression seems to have been . . . that the [*Richard*] was attacked intentionally."[28]

In desperation Jones ordered the commodore's identity signal lanterns to be hoisted aloft in the hope that the *Alliance* would not fire again—presum-ably in error. In spite of the *Richard*'s highly visible lanterns, at around ten o'clock the *Alliance* closed once again to engage the two ships that were locked in combat, and Landais ordered another grapeshot broadside to be indiscriminately fired. "After the battle Landais confided to one of the French colonels that his intention was to help *Serapis* sink the *Richard,* to capture and board the British frigate and emerge victor of the battle. Later he had the impudence to claim that his broadsides forced [the *Serapis*] to strike."[29]

The commander of the *Serapis,* Captain Richard Pearson, was appalled at the slaughter on board the American vessel and knew that the *Richard* was in danger of sinking. He called out to Jones through his speaking trumpet to ask if he was ready to strike his colors and surrender. Legend has it that Jones replied, "I have not yet begun to fight," now an American naval aphorism and inspiring motto. More likely his response was, "No sir, I have not yet thought of it, but am determined to make you strike."[30] In battle, the line between bravado and desperation can be thin. With the two ships literally locked

Bon Homme Richard *and HMS* Serapis, *by Julian O. Davidson, circa 1885. From the author's* Harper's Weekly *print collection*

together in combat, sharp-shooting marines fired from the *Richard*'s fighting tops, raking the *Serapis* with gunfire. The result was devastation to the vulnerable British sailors on deck. Jones and his crew continued to fight tenaciously, even as their ship appeared to be sinking beneath them. It was Pearson who eventually capitulated by ordering the British Union Jack of the *Serapis* struck.

When the sun rose the next morning, the American ensign could be seen flying from both the *Richard* and the vanquished *Serapis*. As the *Alliance*, *Vengeance*, and *Pallas* rejoined Jones, they likely heard a few choice remarks about what had transpired during the battle. From the bloodstained deck of the *Serapis*, the survivors of the American and British vessels watched the waves gently engulf the *Richard*. On 25 September a tranquil sea claimed the mortally wounded hulk of the once proud *Bonhomme Richard*. When the

Americans reached the safety of Holland, arrangements were made to exchange the British prisoners for American prisoners of war.[31]

Once ashore Jones wasted little time in accusing Pierre Landais of incompetence for his haphazard firing of grapeshot that struck the crews of both contesting vessels. Lieutenant Richard Dale of the *Richard* noted, "If Landais was guilty . . . his is no solitary instance of such a disgraceful perfidy on the part of French seamen. After the battle of Trafalgar, it is notorious that the flying French ships, as they escaped, pored broadsides into the Spanish vessels. . . . The indignation of the Spaniards at this detestable cruelty from their allies, for whom they had fought so bravely and profusely bled, may well be conceived."[32]

Landais was unrepentant and almost pathologically unapologetic for his errors of judgment. Later, at a chance meeting with Jones in an Amsterdam tavern, Landais reminded the commodore that they had agreed to a duel once they were onshore. Jones avoided the challenge once again by saying that their differences would be appropriately settled in a court-martial in the United States. Meanwhile, Jones had Landais relieved of command of the *Alliance,* assuming command of his antagonist's ship. The loss of command of the *Alliance* further infuriated Landais. Jones continued to humiliate Landais by writing that "the [*Alliance*] in so bad a condition. Epidemical disorders raged among the crew; the officers were always drinking grog. And there was a total want of subordination, and negligence."[33]

King Louis XVI of France, impressed by Jones's exploits over their common British enemy, honored the commodore with the title of Chevalier de l'Ordre du Mérite militaire, an honor also coveted by Landais. Jones, who seemingly had a low tolerance for elitism, lobbied to obtain special authorization, prior to the ratification of the Articles of Confederation, to be allowed to use the distinguished title in public. Under Chevalier Jones the *Alliance* was ordered to sail to L'Orient, France, to take on a cargo of war supplies. Meanwhile, Landais became obsessed with forcing a duel with Jones and pursued him on the streets of L'Orient, often with his sword drawn and ready. This was more annoying than provocative.

In another move, a calculated effort to aggravate Jones, Landais tried to rally his former officers and crew of the *Alliance* in an attempt to regain his lost command and sail back to America. Some of the men of the *Alliance* were loyal to Landais, but others were loyal to Jones. Benjamin Franklin, the American minister to France, intervened between the contending factions. He used raillery with the men devoted to Landais by saying, "Captain Jones loved close fighting, [but] Captain Landais was skillful at keeping out of harm's way, and that therefore you thought yourselves safer with the latter."[34] Franklin also warned Jones that Landais would likely continue to be troublesome as long as they were in the same place. However, Jones was cautious, stating, "The general conduct of Landais was that of a malignant madman, as much incited by the prevailing influence of frenzy as actuated by deliberate villainy."[35]

On 9 June 1780 the scapegrace Landais strutted purposefully on board the *Alliance* when Jones was ashore and claimed command of his former vessel. The covert loyalties of the crew quickly became evident and were divided between the two captains. When Jones returned, a captain of marines loyal to Landais blocked his entry to the *Alliance*. Jones now considered Landais to be mad and impossible to reason with. He avoided still another confrontation by going to Paris to receive official written orders placing him in command of the *Alliance*. Along with the official transfer of command orders, King Louis authorized French naval forces to be placed at the disposal of Jones to prevent the *Alliance* from sailing from L'Orient under Landais's command. Landais, who seemed always prepared to duel, was more timid when faced with unfavorable odds in a naval battle. Jones had maneuvered himself into an advantageous position. In a decision that appears out of character, he decided to allow Landais to sail the *Alliance* to America without a challenge and perhaps out of his life forever.[36]

Landais's return voyage to America was fraught with problems. A mutiny was threatened because of continual abuse from the captain. He had publicly dressed down his first officer, J. A. Degge, before his junior officers and the crew. After members of the crew tossed in a few fishing lines as they crossed the shallow water of the Grand Banks of Newfoundland, Landais furiously ordered all fish thrown overboard even though the men were running low on fresh provisions. Landais then secluded himself in his cabin until the ship reached Boston. When the *Alliance* docked in Boston on 19 August 1780, Landais was ordered to leave his ship and turn over his cabin and furniture to Captain John Barry, who was to relieve him. He refused the order and threatened a captain of the marines with a pistol. The captain, a sergeant, and two men eventually arrested Landais and dragged him off the vessel to stand trial.

Since Jones had allowed the *Alliance* to leave, he was now forced to find another vessel to transport arms and uniforms for Washington's men back to the United States, and this became a long, slow process. Jones became frustrated with the French Admiralty and complained bitterly to Franklin about its lack of cooperation. Franklin lost patience and reprimanded the impetuous Jones, writing, "If you should observe on occasion to give your officers and friends a little more praise than is their due, and confess more fault than you can justly be charged with, you will only be sooner for it, a great captain. Criticizing and censuring almost everyone you have to do with, will diminish friends, increase enemies, and thereby hurt your affairs."[37] These caustic words from one of the few men whom Jones greatly admired must have stung, especially in light of the enemies he had made among his fellow officers and some superiors. If only Jones had heeded this advice given by a well-liked leader. In his records, letters, and memorials there is scant approbation for Jones's brother officers. He was quick to rebuke but slow to acclaim, a leadership flaw likely based on an inflated ego. Jones's biographer Samuel Eliot Morison states, "He could never have fought successfully without the help of brave and competent lieutenants, petty officers and seamen; but very seldom does he mention any by name."[38]

Jones brooded but at the same time set out on a campaign to recover payment for himself and his crew on the *Bonhomme Richard* for their prize vessels. By October 1780 he and the vital war supplies found passage to America on the French frigate *Ariel*. Upon his arrival on 18 February 1781 Jones was summoned to Congress for a public investigation of charges of deformation of character and slander brought against him by Landais. The charges were subsequently found to be without merit and dropped. Instead, in an added insult to the disgraced Landais, Congress presented Jones with a gold sword. It was inscribed, "for his zeal and, prudence and intrepidity with which he had sustained the honour of the American flag, . . . and in general for the good conduct and eminent services by which he had added luster to his character."[39] Although Jones was pleased with his honors, what he coveted most was the title of admiral, the next goal that the proud sea captain would pursue.

Jones vigorously lobbied the agent of marine Robert Morris and Congress for a new vessel. On 23 June 1781 he was given command of the *America*, the largest ship authorized by Congress for the Continental Navy. Being captain of this warship, Jones thought, should be the stepping-stone to the flag rank he so desired. At this time, however, Captain James Nicholson displayed the bitterness that plagued many of the earliest group of American naval captains. He worked behind the scenes to see that Jones was denied the unprecedented promotion. After Nicholson's appointment as senior captain of the navy, he had lost the frigate *Virginia* in what the young, impressionable Joshua Barney considered a cowardly act.[40] Nicholson had heard that Congress was seriously considering the approval of Jones's promotion to the rank of rear admiral. Not to be upstaged by Jones, he and Captain Thomas Read lobbied Congress that the promotion of Jones was an injustice to those who were senior to him. In addition Nicholson said that there were "many things pretty severe of the *Chevalier*'s private as well as Public Carrector too odiuos [*sic*] to mention and yet unnoticed."[41] Thus Nicholson and Read were successful in persuading Congress to withhold the title of admiral from Jones. No

American captain would receive the admiral rank until David Farragut was so honored during the Civil War eighty years later.

When the war was concluded, Congress authorized a special gold medal to be struck with the appropriate legends and devices to honor Jones for his valor and service. Now in semiretirement, Jones gave a great deal of thought to how the American navy might be prepared for future conflicts. He suggested to Robert Morris that a proper corps of junior officers should be trained on each naval ship to learn tactics, seamanship, mathematics, and mechanics. Each of these would be "a little academy on [ship]board."[42] John Paul Jones was still proud of having a foreign title. At times he signed his formal letters "Chevalier Jones," but he realized that an impressive title did not bring riches.

On 10 November 1784, still in need of funds owed to him, Jones sailed to Paris on the *General Washington,* a former state warship that had been converted to a packet ship and was now under the command of Joshua Barney. The two men had briefly served on different vessels in the squadron that Esek Hopkins took to Nassau in 1776. Barney had great respect for Jones and befriended him during their journey across the Atlantic, their only recorded meeting. Barney granted Jones's wish to be put ashore near Plymouth, England, but he worried that if Jones were recognized, he might be arrested. Jones convinced Barney that he was willing to take that risk and made a secret rendezvous in Britain. During this time he also returned the silver tea service that he had confiscated from Lord Selkirk. The earl had earlier refused the silver but this time graciously accepted Jones's courteous action, and Jones had a story written about the event for the London newspapers. He was not above a little self-promotion. Perhaps public knowledge of this act would help get him absolved of the accusations of piracy. Being thought a common criminal in Britain greatly disturbed him. Jones ultimately found his way to Paris to petition Louis XVI for payments owed to him and his men for captured prizes. He received some compensation, but not the amount that he felt was due to him.

Because three of Jones's prize vessels had wound up in Danish ports, Jones was forced to go to Denmark in 1787 to recover some of the prize money owed to the captain and crew of the *Bonhomme Richard.* While in Copenhagen he met with the Russian ambassador to the Danish court. Catherine the Great had heard of the American's exploits and, in need of experienced naval officers, asked her ambassador to offer Jones the title of supreme commander of the empress's Black Sea Fleet. The adulation from a crowned head of state, the opportunity to go to sea to engage in battle again, and perhaps most of all, the offer of an exalted rank were unexpected. Jones's

*John Paul Jones. From the
author's* Harper's Weekly
print collection

vanity came to the fore once again. He seriously considered this opportunity as a reward to balancing the many frustrations he had suffered of late. It was even said that Jones was fond of the dashing white summer uniforms of the Russian flag officers. Being a pragmatist, though, he felt that his financial interests were in America and Western Europe; he decided to decline the offer. In refusing the position he felt duty-bound to thank the czarina in person.

Jones set out for St. Petersburg by way of Sweden. At Greshelham he learned that the passage through the Gulf of Bothnia was blocked by ice. He tried an alternate route via Finnish islands but had no success. In frustration, he hired a boatman to sail in a thirty-foot open boat together with a small tender through the pack ice back to Greshelham. When they were nearly opposite Stockholm, the boatman refused to go on, so Jones forced the boatman at pistol point to complete the route that he devised across the Gulf of Finland. The temperature dropped, and they found themselves locked in the frozen grip of sea ice. Using a pocket compass and a carriage light to see during the short late November days, Jones navigated their way over ice and patches of open ocean to Revel, Livonia. This minor episode was another example of Jones's dogged perseverance and use of armed force to get his way.

Exhausted by what he would later describe as the most difficult trip of his life, Jones arrived at the court of the czarina. There he was greeted with overwhelming courtesy and this time was offered the rank of rear admiral of the Imperial Navy. The exhausted but flattered American chevalier accepted, putting aside his previous hesitation and qualms. He did, however, make one request—that he "should never be condemned unheard."[43]

Jones took command of the Russian fleet on his flagship *Vladimir*, stationed at Liman near the mouth of the Dneiper River, on 26 May 1788. His opponent was an Algerian, Ghazi Hassan, Captain Pasha of the Turkish Fleet. The *Vladimir* was built to house sixty-six guns, but because of the vessel's deep draft and the shallow water in the area, the ship carried only twenty-four guns. Jones's squadron was supported by a flotilla under Charles Nassau-Siegan, Prince of Nassau, and supported by land forces commanded by Prince Grigory Alexandrovich Potemkin. Two separate battles ensued in the Black Sea, affording Jones opportunities to display his intrepidity and seafaring skills.

In irritation, Jones found his naval tactics second-guessed and not fully supported by his comrades-in-arms. The American unsuccessfully tongue-lashed his fellow naval officers for their lack of bravery and cooperation. Jealousy on the part of Nassau-Siegan plus a series of court cabals largely orchestrated by Potemkin deprived Jones of well-deserved military honors for his valor. The Russian navy needed him, but Jones lacked the ability to navigate the convoluted shoals of imperial court politics. This put him at an intractable disadvantage. His bluntness and lack of diplomacy made him many new enemies, particularly Nassau-Siegan and Potemkin, both of whom had substantial influence with Czarina Catherine. In an act of kindness but perhaps more akin to tokenism, Jones was invested with the Order of St. Anne as an acknowledgment of his fidelity to the Russian Crown.

Shortly after he returned to St. Petersburg, however, Jones found himself falsely accused of sexual impropriety. He was infuriated at not being able to adequately defend himself against these charges in the foreign closed society. The charges of immorality crushed the sensitive Jones. Disgusted by the unremitting intrigues of the inner circle at the court, he left Russia in August 1789, never to return.

Jones spent the remainder of his days in the Netherlands and France. He collected documents in an attempt to prove that additional funds were due to him. He also devoted a great deal of time to arranging his personal affairs and preparing papers for posterity that would attest to his character and services to America.

On 1 June 1792 President Washington commissioned Jones to negotiate a treaty with the dey of Algiers to release captive American sailors from Algeria. The next day Washington formally extended the commission by appointing Jones as American consul for Algeria. Jones had a history of being sympathetic to captured sailors and was particularly appalled at the treatment they had received from the Barbary pirates. This diplomatic venture likely would have pleased Jones, a fitting honor to cap his career. Washington's commission, countersigned by Thomas Jefferson, was given to Thomas Pinckney, who was the newly designated American minister to Britain. Pinckney departed for London in mid-July. John Paul Jones died on 18 July unaware of the final request of and appointment from his American government.

Jones had become debilitated from pneumonia, coupled with probable congestive heart failure and kidney dysfunction. His death in Paris came shortly after his forty-fifth birthday. Jones died in relative poverty. In spite of the consul commission from the United States government at the time of his death, the bold Revolutionary War captain lingered in relative obscurity in a French grave. About a hundred years passed before he would be recognized as America's greatest naval hero of the Revolutionary War and the man who set the standard for courage and resourcefulness for the American navy. John Paul Jones also was arguably one of the more querulous of the nation's first naval officers. He was a complex man: calculating, courageous, and plucky; pensive, depressed, and despondent; vain, confrontational, and insulting. To rephrase a lyric line of W. S. Gilbert from *Pirates of Penzance,* he may well have been the very model of a Continental Navy "Captain Contentious."

Issues of Leadership, Personality, and Psychology

Exactly what is leadership? This is a timeless and, in the context of *Captains Contentious,* a topical question. The answer may be general or specific, abstract or tangible. Like the search for the definition of "pornography," as Supreme Court justice Potter Stewart noted, it is difficult to define but obvious when witnessed. The oldest written listing of the attributes of leadership is found in Sun Tzu's fifth- or fourth-century B.C.E. work *The Art of War.*[1] In his first chapter he lists them as the virtues of wisdom (*zhi*), trustworthiness (*xin*), benevolence (*ren*), courage (*yong*), and discipline (*yan*). The intervening centuries have provided some philosophical notes about leadership. These are well expressed in quotes on elemental leadership traits from five twentieth-century leaders three generals, an admiral, and a university president. They are succinctly delineated as follows:

Leadership is the capacity and will to rally men and women to a common purpose and the character that inspires confidence. (Bernard Law Montgomery)
Leadership [in the military] means firmness, not harshness; understanding, not weakness; justice, not license; humaneness, not intolerance; generosity, not selfishness; pride, not egotism. (Omar N. Bradley)
Leadership is the art of getting someone else to do something you want done because he wants to do it. (Dwight D. Eisenhower)
Leadership is a two-way street, loyalty up and loyalty down. Respect for one's superiors; care for one's crew (Admiral Grace Hopper)
The very essence of leadership is vision. You can't blow an uncertain trumpet. (Theodore Hesburgh)

Thus leadership is difficult to characterize and can have different meanings to a range of people. But how were these qualities perceived, if at all, in the selection of men for command? Presumably each captain of a Continental Navy ship was chosen for command because of demonstrated competency and particularly for these elusive traits of leadership. Unfortunately, during the later part of the eighteenth century military commanders were generally persons who rose to power within a hierarchical system, more often through an accident of birth as opposed to ability, a transparent example of nepotism. These leaders could at times be compassionless and ruthless in their expression of determination—determination tempered by a sense of duty. They led by the privilege of rank. Their authority was asserted unwaveringly on subordinates, regardless of their abilities, with rapport largely considered unnecessary. Those sailors who served under this system intuitively showed deference to their superiors, regardless of whether these officers were tyrants or saints. Previous chapters presented evidence that some naval officers had many conflicts with fellow officers, and these quarrels affected both their leadership and their performance. Was this a trait unique to these Continental Navy officers, or was it ubiquitous among all military officers, and if so, why?

Contentiousness and occasional guileless calumny were not exclusive to the Continental Navy. During the Revolutionary War, these attributes were also found among some of America's most esteemed leaders, the so-called founding fathers. For example John Adams denigrated Thomas Jefferson and Benjamin Franklin; Alexander Hamilton was at odds with Jefferson and Aaron Burr; George Washington did not like Horatio Gates and found Edmund Randolph devious. In fact contentiousness was rampant and in a sense may have defined that time in America. It must be remembered that at the onset of the Revolution about a third of the American population was in favor of the rebellion to bring independence from the British; a third was loyal to the Crown; and the rest were relatively content to survive either way.

The Articles of Confederation and Perpetual Union was the first governing document of the United Colonies of America setting the rules for operations of the government, but one weakness was that it gave a great deal of independence to each of the states within the federation.[2] The individual states bickered and looked after their own interests rather than those of the whole burgeoning country as a body. The quarrels between some Continental Navy officers appeared to have been in a similar vein. Concerned with their own interests, their clashes related to the division of glory, vanity, and, most important, leadership deficiencies.

The hostility that was present among this admittedly small sample of Continental naval officers also existed among their British adversaries, but arguably to a lesser extent. The animus among the American officers may have been the result of misapplications of basic doctrines of leadership. Formal leadership training was not part of the curriculum of officer education until the first part of the nineteenth century. Few if any doctrines concerning the elements of good naval leadership were published. The intellectual and authority tools of a leader were intuitive, and their use and availability varied greatly. For example, a strong personality was a driving force for leading men.

A widely accepted principle of eighteenth-century leadership was that of deference, the acceptance of the fabled "pecking order." In a social, economic, political, and military hierarchy, some men occupied a prominent position by accident of birth, election, or elevation, and others were obligated to be subservient to them. Deference was adherence to the chain of command, a powers structure that provided an orderly society, whether on shipboard or shore. This was leadership from the top down. The judicial use of punishment for poor performance or well-considered incentives such as rewards captured subordinates' attention. Men needed a multiplicity of motivational factors when faced with the rigors of naval shipboard life, being away from family for indefinite periods, and the imminence of sporadic combat.

The simplest application of leadership was Sun Tzu's ancient principle of discipline. This was a proved method for governing men—a skill that could best be learned through years of practice. For many novice officers, leadership and discipline were synonymous. They were a way to maintain authority within a command. Gaining this authority, whether innate or learned, became the essential tool for motivating men under one's command. Discipline effectively controlled the behavioral state of men under arms, even in the frightening face of certain death. This was an essential means for making men respond to orders in a reflexive manner. Command directives had to be obeyed. Discipline had to sustain a standard and yet be an evolving process.

An officer set standards and goals for his men but then wisely provided a form of recognition when his objectives were achieved. Acknowledgment often proved to be vital for the sailor's self-respect and the esteem of his comrades-in-arms. An important morale boaster for the sailor was being able to be identified with a renowned captain, a famous ship, and/or an elite unit—the essence of esprit de corps. This met an almost intrinsic need for being on the winning side so as to bask in the light of reflected glory. (This is commonly expressed today in people taking pleasure in supporting and identifying with a winning athletic team.) In contrast, a leader can use the threat of humiliation to coerce. All mariners dreaded being publicly exposed as cowards and suffering castigation from their peers. Even when beaten under the lash while being tied to a grate on deck, a sailor tried to show toughness by taking his punishment without flinching or at least without crying out before his shipmates.

Setting and upholding an exceptional example for one's men could successfully infuse discipline. Officers had to be seen as heedful of their own orders, obedient to their superiors, but displaying fairness to their subordinates. When commanders assumed their leadership role, they also assumed several responsibilities: for the safety of their men, for the availability of their equipment, for their training, and for reasonable support to the accomplishment of their missions. At the same time, discipline meant that sailors who refused to do their duties understood that they alone would be held accountable.

Officers also accepted broader responsibilities, somewhat like those of surrogate parents, to many of their charges. They tried to learn the names of the crew or at least their posts on board. They had to assure that the crew members were kept in good physical health, clothed, fed, and had a work environment as clean and safe as possible. This was relative to what many sailors endured ashore. In addition officers directed the crew's moral health, usually by discouraging gambling, profanity, and petty squabbles. As succinctly expressed in a roughly contemporary historic naval regulation, "[the officers] will recollect that the crew are confident to their care and that in no circumstances can warrant a breach of this important duty."[3]

Unfortunately, providing this "care" was difficult. Life on board eighteenth-century sailing warships consisted of terrible discomforts for the seamen, and it was the commanders who controlled this untoward environment. One graphic description states: "The men slept in hammocks some fourteen inches apart . . . [to] lay there in his soaking wet cloths in cold and darkness—no fires were permitted below—and the darkness dripped, because all wooden ships . . . continually leaked. There was a stench compounded of the reeking water in the bilge, of accumulation of rotting refuse . . . of wet, close packed men, lousy and flea-infested, who practically never changed there cloths, who seldom washed . . . compounded by the decaying carcasses of drowned rats and other vermin below."[4] It is a wonder that many sailors lasted through their enlistment. An often-quoted remark of Samuel Johnson comes to mind: "No man will be a sailor who has contrivance enough to get himself into a jail; for being in a ship is being in a jail, with the chance of being drowned. . . . A man in jail has more room, better food, and commonly better company."[5] Therefore, providing care as advocated in the naval regulations and being a leader under these conditions was an onerous task. It required a variety of skills, some learned but more often innate.

Differences in the application of leadership strategies by naval officers, whether Royal or Continental, likely contributed to individual successes in battle. American and British officers shared the attributes of the military trinity: the pursuit of glory, fame, and honor. These were gained through intelligence, foresight, resolve, self-confidence, and imperturbability (and a measure of luck)—particularly when faced with a crisis. Spontaneity, courage, and

Below decks with crew's hammocks in place.
From Charles J. Peterson, American Navy *(1858)*

prudence supplemented these qualities. Decisiveness in action coupled with an ability to realistically reassess volatile changing situations were necessary ingredients in any conflict. The five Continental Navy officers profiled in this book possessed these vital character qualities in variable degrees, but they displayed them irregularly. At the same time, these men also shared some critical leadership failings that account for their sporadic episodes of rancor. It has been said that analysis of historical events or figures "can no more reveal its causes than dissection of a suicide's body can reveal his despair."[6] Still, our five contentious naval captains were historical figures and left ample records of their interactions with others.

All these navy officers possessed behavioral traits, complex masks that one sees as personality that can be analyzed through the tools of psychology. One trait that was common to all five of the contentious officers was that of narcissism, a form of egotism that gave them the self-confidence to think that they were strong leaders.[7] They also had a second trait that psychologists call "perfectionism." Good naval officers desire excellence and strive for perfection in their men and particularly in themselves. A third shared personality attribute was the assertion of power through aggression. Controlled by good judgment, aggressiveness is an essential ingredient needed to win battles.

Narcissism can be multifaceted and often manifests itself as exaggerated self-confidence darkly shaded with feelings of superiority and a willingness to exploit others without much empathy. It also can be a compensatory trait to hide a sense of emotional detachment, low self-esteem, self-hatred, or problems in forming meaningful relationships. The mythical character Narcissus, who gave his name to this trait, fell in love with his own image reflected in a pool of water. Like Narcissus's reflected likeness, a narcissist's image can be easily dispelled, and therefore he can feel vulnerable. The ego of a narcissist needs maintenance, and this need often takes the form of boasting or chest thumping to gain adoration from others. Obvious expressions of narcissism exasperate subordinates and cause followers to withdraw their support, crushing the narcissist's ego and making him seek vengeance in return.

Narcissism can manifest itself in some military officers as a trait that historians and laymen have seen as "color." Associated with the trait is a stereotypical need for colorful self-adornment, such as the desire for fancy or special uniforms, excessive display of military decorations, or a quest for personal recognition or public laudation. A poignant and arguably undeserved theatrical example can be seen in the opening scene of the motion picture *Patton*. George C. Scott plays the grandiose General George Patton, resplendent in his highly decorated uniform, delivered an inspiring speech, but at the same time portraying narcissism and self-adulation coupled with pomposity and pretension. Patton's film image had some basis in reality. The general firmly believed that a leader should be distinct on the battlefield in order to inspire his men and bring fear to the enemy. Therefore, he wore his gleaming white, ivory-handled pistols prominently positioned on his hips in battle and tried to be visible even under fire. A similar vainglorious attitude may have prevailed in the British navy. Narcissism was partly responsible for the death of Horatio Nelson, who insisted on wearing his easily identifiable naval admiral's uniform on the deck of the HMS *Victory* while engaged in battle. He was easily identified and subsequently mortally wounded by an enemy sharpshooter.

Another illustration of narcissistic behavior is found in a letter from John Adams to James Warren. The sometimes sardonic Adams, founder of the Continental Navy, portrays an unidentified person, putatively Benjamin Franklin:: "A Man must be his own Trumpeter—he must write or dictate Paragraphs of Praise in Newspapers; he must dress, have a Retinue and Equipage; he must ostentatiously publish to the World his own Writings with his Name. . . . he must get his Picture drawn, his state made, and must hire all Artists in his Turn to set about Works to spread his Name, make the Mob stare and gape, and perpetuate his Fame."[8] To varying degrees the trait of narcissism can be seen in the five naval officers whose biographical sketches appear in this book, but none exceeds this presumed image of Franklin by Adams.

Images made of eighteenth-century military figures often portrayed them in heroic poses suggesting boldness and rugged masculinity. John Paul Jones vainly sought titles, and many busts and oil portraits show his likeness. Jones was fond of using his honorary title chevalier. In addition, although the title was considered a mark of pretentiousness in eighteenth-century American society, he appeared to take great pleasure in his role as celebrity and later in life was very taken with his elegant white Russian navy rear admiral's uniform.

Joshua Barney commissioned many portraits, the most ostentatious being one he had painted while holding flag rank in the French navy. The ostentatious capitaine de vaisseau du premier appears bedecked in plumage, braid, and lace. Barney's most satisfying accomplishment was his victory over the *General Monk*. He commissioned a painting, made in France, using his own description of his heroism during the battle. That painting now hangs prominently over a portal in the museum of the United States Naval Academy. Barney was awarded two swords for valor, one of which was stolen while he was in Paris. The capitaine was despondent until he was able to replace it with another.

There are no surviving portraits of Dudley Saltonstall, but historical evidence suggests that he was especially interested in naval officer uniforms and served as chairman of the committee that designed the first Continental Navy officers' uniforms.[9] One formal portrait of Silas Talbot seen in the G. W. Blunt-White Library of the Mystic Seaport Museum shows him as an almost Nelson-like officer looking proud of wearing a navy uniform that displays his Cincinnati insignia. In Talbot's defense, it was fashionable in the late eighteenth century to have personal portraits made for one's family. Because painted portraits were a costly luxury and highly regarded social status symbol, appearing at a sitting in an ornately decorated uniform showed one's status for the family generations to come.

John Manley appears to have been the least narcissistic of this quintet. His most telling instance of indiscretion was his petition to Washington for a better vessel and a sympathetic ear for payment of his men. Conversely one could argue that Manley's "imprudence" was a demonstration of good leadership. Certainly a better vessel would enable him to accomplish his mission better, and a good leader shows concern for the well-being of his men. His actions, however, became self-serving. When Manley did not hear from Washington in a timely fashion, in frustration he sent a letter resigning his army commission. Because the resignation letter had not been received by

Washington in a timely fashion, however, this irritation from lack of approbation became a nonissue once he learned that his grievances were satisfactorily addressed.

Narcissistic leaders can be highly competitive in their pursuit of recognition, to the point of arrogance. This almost obsessive drive to take on challenges has been called "situational narcissism"; the focus of an event in which such a person participates is on the individual proving himself rather than on necessarily moving toward the completion of an assigned task. This may have been part of the motivation of John Paul Jones and his raids on the British coast. He strove to show the British that they were vulnerable in their own country and perchance demonstrate to them the capability of an expatriate Scot. The downside is that this narcissistic trait in a leader can make him vulnerable to adulation, the flattery of sycophantic parasites. These people are suspicious of the sincerity of their friends, leading to feelings of paranoia.

One common narcissistic personality trait is the craving to be the center of attention, always wanting to be in the limelight. This trait, which may seem relatively harmless, can be self-destructive in a military leader. Such a person may be compelled to perform courageous acts, showing bravery in the presence of others to set an example. Barney, Manley, and Jones repeatedly put themselves in harm's way. All suffered wounds and musket balls piercing their clothing. Certainly the burns Talbot suffered in the fireship incident with the *Asia* and his plucky capture of the *Pigot* are other examples of well-observed courageous acts. But on the downside, recall the death of Nelson from a French sniper aloft in the crosstrees while the admiral strolled on his ship's deck resplendent in his uniquely ornate uniform. To their credit, such leaders' conspicuous bravery inspired their men. If they had chosen to avoid being at the center of a conflict, their leadership roles would have been greatly diminished or negative.

Dueling played a tragic role in American history and accounted for the untimely, wasteful death of great Americans, such as Alexander Hamilton and Stephen Decatur. Since many of our American "contentious captains" faced challenges of honor, a review of the chronicle of settling disputes by means of duels seems in order. Settling the defense of one's honor by a duel had its roots well back in the haze of history.

In 1777, shortly after the beginning of the Revolution, a code of honor published as the *Code Duello* was formalized in Ireland. This elaborately detailed ritual or code consisted of twenty-six rules of behavior and ceremony, including the proper steps to take for obtaining an apology and the etiquette of behavior while an apology was sought, accepted, or rejected.[10] The rules also covered the selection of weapons and a suitable site, time, and date negotiated by the principals, the seconds, and often friends of both parties. Additionally, and perhaps most important, the code outlined what constituted the end of a duel. Discussions between the protagonists and their seconds could go on for weeks or months, and the passage of time often abated some tempers. The result was that the duel might not be carried out, swords not drawn in anger, shots not fired or shots deliberately missed—by mutual consent. Dueling was frequently far more often bluster than blast.

The grounds for issuing a challenge to a duel were almost limitless. They ranged from a disdainful look, to an expression of disrespect or perceived slight, to an accusation of cowardice or "giving to lie," to insulting a person's integrity, to a dishonor of one's lady. Being a part of the cultural institution of the aristocracy, duels were generally fought between men of equal social status and were inappropriate for persons grossly differing in rank. In 1806 the U.S. Congress passed a law prohibiting dueling among army officers, but this was not applicable to naval officers. The rationale for the disparity was that if a duel took place overseas, which was more likely for naval personnel, it was out of American jurisdiction. In fact, the United States Navy (the navy that replaced the Continental Navy) included the rules of the *Code Duello* in the midshipman's handbook until dueling by naval officers was banned in 1862—fifty-six years after its banning by the army. Thus the *Code Duello*, being an established part of the nascent navy's ethos, likely played a role, arguably a historic role, in wardroom contentiousness.

By what may appear as ironic contrast, some narcissists can be reluctant to risk their lives in private acts of courage such as a duel. An example of this behavior would be John Paul Jones and his disinclination to take up the challenge repeatedly made by his nemesis Pierre Landais. Barney and Talbot each had duel encounters with their subordinates or fellow officers, and although they escaped unharmed, they did not embarrass themselves. Manley offered a dual challenge while in prison, but he was rebuffed. Historically defense of honor by use of arms was an aristocratic concept, keeping a positive reputation among one's fellow gentlemen. The only Continental Navy captain who could be considered an aristocrat was Dudley Saltonstall. There is no record of his challenging or being challenged to a duel.

Most perceived personal offenses precipitated anger, but a defensive rage might arise if a narcissist were seriously criticized or frustrated. In essence, the officer could feel that he was the only one who had truly accomplished the goals of his superiors. At various times this was the case with Manley, Saltonstall, Talbot, Barney, and Jones during their careers. Alternately, some would withdraw, perhaps thinking that if they were not appreciated, they would resign. Jones's bitter memorial to the Marine Committee after Elisha Hinman was appointed to command the *Alfred* in 1777 exemplifies this behavior. Manley, Jones, Talbot, and Barney acted similarly when they felt underappreciated. In their overt acts of self-glorification they jeopardized the respect of colleagues and subordinates, becoming prisoners of their own inflated egos. Another sign of one's ego interfering with leadership was the incapacity of some officers to recognize and/or praise their subordinates. This was especially true of Jones and Saltonstall and likely accounted for the occasional discords with their peers.

Narcissism can be pernicious, expressed as selfishness, and sometimes coupled with a dash of cruelty. One revered British naval officer demonstrated multifaceted narcissistic behavior that led to events with consequences on the outcome and/or conclusion of the Revolutionary War. The colonial Dutch Caribbean island of St. Eustatius was the site of a lucrative arms trade with the Americans during the Revolutionary War. It proved so lucrative that agents from all over Europe were located there, ironically including a handful of British merchants. (Profit often trumps patriotism in time of war.)

After a series of unresolved, troublesome diplomatic events between the Dutch and the British, His Majesty's Parliament decided to declare war on Holland. Admiral Sir George Brydges Rodney was dispatched to attack St. Eustatius and cut off the important source of arms for the American forces. The island was virtually defenseless, and the colonial government quickly surrendered. Rodney, who had accrued a large personal debt during his naval career, confiscated all merchandise stored in the island's warehouses and seized approximately 150 ships and smaller vessels along with their valuable cargoes. As Rodney's men plundered St. Eustatius, the Dutch flag flew over the island as a *ruse de guerre* to entice additional, unsuspecting ships to enter the British snare and thus add to Rodney's treasures. The European merchants' properties were seized, and they were ordered to return to their respective countries or to nearby Caribbean colonial islands.

Rodney's wholesale pillage of St. Eustatius violated part of the mannerly eighteenth-century rules of war toward fellow Europeans. After conquest, civilian noncombatants typically were allowed to retain their property and become subjects of the victorious state. Rodney, however, considered the Dutch Jews, a significant part of the merchant class that conducted business on the island, to be stateless and not subject to this chivalrous policy. They were isolated and stripped in order to locate any valuables that might have been concealed in their clothing. The Jewish men were then separated from their families and denied access to their homes. On 5 February 1781 the adult male Jewish population of St. Eustatius was scattered into exile, their families left behind and all their property confiscated.[11] This was a pitiless but profitable anti-Semitic act, calculated to add significantly to Rodney's spoils.

The admiral was so preoccupied with conveying booty back to England to relieve his debt that he largely neglected his Caribbean fleet command, and the men remained on St. Eustatius until late July 1781.[12] Rodney's narcissistic avarice allowed French admiral François-Joseph-Paul Compte de Grasse time to assemble his fleet and sail from the West Indies to arrive off Hampton Roads in early October 1781. The presence of de Grasse's armada at the mouth of Chesapeake Bay prevented the British from reinforcing and supporting Lord Charles Cornwallis's troops at Yorktown, Virginia. Cornwallis was then forced to surrender on 19 October 1781. Had Rodney not been so self-absorbed with his debit and newly acquired booty while neglecting his military duty, perhaps Americans might have lost at Yorktown and the outcome of the Revolutionary War would have taken an entirely different course.

Oddly enough, narcissism can be a positive attribute. It can act as a dominant engine that drives leaders to achieve their great successes. Perennial optimism and charisma often attract others to help accomplish goals. Leaders possessing these traits can appear to be inspirational, imaginative visionaries. Although John Paul Jones seemed rarely endearing, his imagination and courage brought the Revolutionary War to British shores, making the conflict unpopular in England. Joshua Barney apparently exuded charismatic charm. His popularity in the French Royal Court and later during the postrevolution formation of the French Republic facilitated his rise to the rank of capitaine de vaisseau du premier. Barney's integrity in battle was demonstrated repeatedly. It likely contributed to the high esteem with which his men held him. Even up to his death Barney fought to have what he considered just compensation for his subordinates' efforts in defense of their country.

The trait of perfectionism is usually associated with ambition and obsession, with repetition and compulsive maintenance of order. These are common leadership traits that officers strive to instill in their subordinates. The navy considers striving for perfection to be a building block that leads to disciplined sailors who, when faced with urgency, will reflexively be able to save their ships and hopefully their lives. Still, like all desirable qualities, perfectionism can be carried to excess. Many take pleasure in military ceremonies or ostentatious displays of a commander's lofty place in the military hierarchy. This can be an expression of both perfectionism and narcissism, but these once again are not exclusively American traits. British admiral John

Jervis was known for insisting on having elaborate ceremonies staged on his flagship every morning. This muster consisted of a dress parade of his Royal marines with all hands assembled in formal ranks and the playing or singing of "God Save the King." Certainly formal military ceremonies promote a sense of continuity of history, patriotism, and arguably esprit de corps, but taken to an extreme, they can be interpreted as expressions of narcissism.

Behavioral traits are typically a complex blend that is perceived as personality. Some leaders' personalities can appear stubborn and uncompromising, not unlike Dudley Saltonstall's intransigence at the Penobscot Expedition. Such people purposely create a persona of confidence, a self-assured "presence," or a poised military demeanor to project an authoritative image to their subordinates. The downside is that this must be balanced with a modicum of modesty or they may be perceived as being imperious. In fact, captious leaders have been known to provoke their subordinates through vanity, exploitation, and even on occasion malicious threats. Those traits being accepted, it should be remembered that naval eighteenth-century commanders lived in an atypical society that regularly required them to place men in harm's way. Discipline, discerned as bravery in the face of mayhem and violent death, was the currency and the gold standard of their military profession. It took character and confidence to lead others into mayhem and perhaps death.

Of the three traits under discussion (narcissism, perfectionism, and aggression) aggression is perhaps the most obvious and observable. For that reason it requires little space for discussion. An aggressive individual continually competes with others in order to assert dominance. Placed in a positive context, striving for power is ambition. All five of the "contentious captains" showed instances of ambition too numerous to reiterate. Their successes in battle were functions of disciplined and measured aggression, with the possible exception of Dudley Saltonstall at the Penobscot Expedition. However, according to the historical record, even this hesitant Connecticut Yankee had his moments of aggression followed by military achievement.

The American "contentious captains" described in this book shared two other behavioral traits, irritability and quarrelsomeness. These attributes produce people who are likely to be contrary, moody, and quick to find fault. They can be hypersensitive, argumentative, pessimistic, grumbling, obstructive, critical, and scornful of authority, and they frequently show resentment toward peers who succeed.[13] They appear to resent conformity, and yet military service is in many ways a profession based on conformity. Their disgruntlement is manifested by feelings of being misunderstood, mistreated, underappreciated, or perpetually victimized. Paradoxically a commander, like many well-publicized athletic coaches, can be truculent and unpredictably explosive but alternately may quickly display warmth and charm. These people fluctuate between the poles of defiance and deference, aggressive negativism and obedience, cynicism and certainty.[14] They may exhibit paranoia, distrust, and trepidation, and yet they are able to control or countermand these impulsive traits with boldness in stressful situations.

People who are subject to attitude oscillations employ defense mechanisms or strategies of recompense. This trait in a leader can be subtly expressed but is dangerous both socially and politically.[15] In the Manley/McNeill, Barney/Talbot, Talbot/Truxtun, Saltonstall/Lovell, and Jones/Landais/Saltonstall conflicts, each used defense mechanisms and yet expressed independence by challenging authority, each sought authority's favor, and each was rebellious at times while making sure that he could deny culpability or malicious intent.

Finis origine pendet (the end is dependent on the beginning). Voyaging in the age of sail has been described as unbounded days of boredom punctuated by brief intervals of frenzied activity. In the case of the five naval officers whose brief biographical sketches are outlined here, a variation on this theme might be "long periods of contempt interrupted by short bursts of vindication."[16] As we have seen, naval leadership on each side of the Revolutionary War expressed authoritative personalities within the context of a microsociety. The noted contemporary British maritime historian Nichols A. M. Rodger considered the sailing navy "as a society in miniature, . . . very much a microcosm of . . . society in general. . . . In the last analysis, the wooden world [of ships] was built of the same material of the wider world."[17]

During the time of the Revolutionary War, the social order and its challenges were very different from those that the average American citizen faces today. The issues of an evolving society, changing mores of the late eighteenth century, and the unprecedented experience of an armed revolt against their king were exceptionally complex. The leadership traits of the Continental Navy's five officers presented here, four of whom were considered heroes, support the argument that some and probably many of the American naval officers were unusually irascible. The behavioral traits of these men appear to have had both emotional and social origins brought about by one or more particularly bothersome rivals and in some cases tormentors: Manley and McNeill, Talbot and Truxtun, Saltonstall and his two generals (Wadsworth and Lovell), Barney and Nicholson, Jones and Landais. The underlying psychological causes of their conduct cannot be definitively known but can be construed from historical evidence. The behavioral consequences of these dysfunctional "sons of the brine" that led to their individual victories and defeats are a provocative, understudied aspect of the maritime history of the American Revolution.[18]

Notes

Introduction

1. Putting this in perspective, the life expectancy for colonial men was around the early fifties.

2. Morison, *Maritime History of Massachusetts*, 160.

3. Crawford, *Autobiography of a Yankee Mariner*, 23.

4. Dickerson, *Navigation Acts*, 5–6.

5. Albion, Baker, and Labaree, *New England*, 21–44.

6. Nicholas Biddle served as a midshipman along with Horatio Nelson in the Royal Navy. Thomas Truxtun was impressed at the age of sixteen on board the 64-gun Royal naval ship *Prudent*.

7. Hearn, *George Washington's Schooners*, 1–4.

8. See Dudley Saltonstall Papers. On 13 July 1779 Saltonstall was ordered by the state of Massachusetts Council Chambers to "turn over such of the impressed men on board the *Warren* . . . to the Ship *General Putnam* & . . . deliver them to Capt. Waters accordingly. Attested by Sam Adams Secr[etary]."

9. France's interests were only marginally in support of the ideal of American independence. The French relished the opportunity of siding in a struggle against the British and to gain economic advantages in continental North America and the West Indies as well as to develop trade alliances with the united colonies.

10. Keegan, *Price of Admiralty*, 47.

11. These commodores include William Bainbridge, James Barron, Isaac Chauncey, Stephen Decatur, Jesse Duncan Elliott, Thomas MacDonough, Oliver Hazard Perry, David Porter, Edward Preble, John Rodgers, and Thomas Truxtun.

Chapter 1: Maritime Naval Service during the Revolutionary War

1. Lavery, *Nelson's Navy*, 41.

2. Some historians note that election to the Society of the Cincinnati, for some, evolved into a post–Revolutionary War military officer aristocracy.

3. Cordingly, *Billy Ruffian*, 164.

4. In addition many communities formed groups then commonly called "seafensibles," local militias composed mainly of fishermen and watermen who were charged to defend harbors and strategic coastal landmarks.

5. Lincoln, ed., *Naval Records,* 217–495.

6. Stark, *Abolition of Privateering,* 121.

7. Volo and Volo, *Daily Life,* 311. It should be noted that some of these vessels were recaptured by the British, so the data are better used as order of magnitude comparisons.

8. Lincoln, ed., *Naval Records,* 217–495.

9. Ibid.; Volo and Volo, *Daily Life,* 311.

10. Labaree et al., *America and the Sea,* 140.

11. The fleet's number is impossible to estimate because of the range of vessels that qualify as merchantmen.

12. Lovette, *Naval Customs,* 18.

13. Beck, *Correspondence of Esek Hopkins,* 22.

14. Ketchum, *Victory at Yorktown,* 285.

15. Pengelly, *First Bellerophon,* 209. This statement appears to refer to the fact that Captain James Cook, one of England's greatest seaman, learned the mariner's trade as the captain of a collier sailing out of Newcastle.

16. Clowes et al., *Royal Navy,* 3:83.

17. Berckman, *Nelson's Dear Lord,* 240.

18. Lewis, *Extracts,* 1:394.

19. Ketchum, *Victory at Yorktown,* 33–35.

20. Clinton to Germain, 30 April 1781, in Clinton, *The American Rebellion,* 516–17.

21. Hannay, *Viscount Hood Letters,* 15.

22. The most notorious exceptions to this were the misunderstood signals of Admiral Sir Thomas Graves off the Chesapeake during sea battle preceding the battle of Yorktown.

23. The origin of the phrase is William Shakespeare's *Henry IV,* 4.3.

24. Jennings, ed., *John Wilson Crocker Correspondence,* 1:287.

25. Rodger, *Command of the Ocean,* 386.

26. Ibid., 389.

27. Lewis, *Navy in Transition,* 37.

28. Lavery, *Nelson's Navy,* 90–99.

29. *Andrea Doria* journal, Public Record Office, Admiralty Documents 1/2678, Captain's Letters, John Borlase Warren, 1793.

30. Barnes and Owen, eds., *Private Papers of John Montagu, Earl of Sandwich,* 2:6.

31. Leech, *Thirty-five Years from Home,* 42.

32. Richardson, *Mariner of England,* 119.

33. Larrabee, *Decision at the Chesapeake,* 13.

34. Dudley Saltonstall Papers, 13 July 1779. A note from the state of Massachusetts Bay to Captain Saltonstall and signed by Sam Adams ordered Saltonstall to release impressed American sailors to another vessel.

35. Some data for approximations may be found in the "Muster Book and Pay Abstract of the Continental Frigate Deane S. Nicholson Esq Commr commencing

[May 1] 1781; ending May 31, 1782," in the *Revolutionary War Rolls,* 66:115–28, Massachusetts Archives, Massachusetts Historical Society. (Information courtesy of Michael J. Crawford, department head of the Early History Branch, Naval Historical Center, Washington, D.C. 20374–5060.)

Chapter 2: The Continental Army Commodore

1. Esek Hopkins was given the title of commodore in October 1775.

2. Butterfield, ed., *Diary and Autobiography of John Adams,* discourse of 7 October 1777, 2:198.

3. Journal of the Continental Congress, 18 July 1775.

4. McManemin, *Captains of the Continental Navy,* 281.

5. Hearn, *George Washington's Schooners,* 12.

6. Ibid., 83.

7. George Cockings, *The American War* (London, 1781), quoted in Greenwood, *Captain John Manley,* 25.

8. Peabody, *The Naval Career of Captain John Manley of Marblehead,* 5; Greenwood, *Captain John Manley,* 1–8.

9. John Paul Jones to Joseph Hewes, 12 January 1777, *Naval Documents of the American Revolution* (hereafter *NDAR*), 7:937.

10. Smith, *Fired by Manley Zeal,* 42.

11. Hearn, *George Washington's Schooners,* 100.

12. Ibid., 100.

13. Foster managed to throw a bundle weighted with small arms overboard; this bundle included the ship's signal book and other documents, but the signal book later washed ashore and proved to be valuable to the Continental Navy.

14. *NDAR,* 3:145.

15. Stephen Moylan to William Watson, 13 December 1775, ibid., 3:81.

16. Clark, *George Washington's Navy,* 3:228.

17. Ibid., 3:873.

18. On 22 December 1775 Esek Hopkins of Rhode Island was given the title of commander in chief of the Continental Navy, roughly equivalent to that of Washington's for the army. Commonly referring to himself as "commodore," Hopkins has been considered by many to be the first commodore of the Continental Navy.

19. Allen, ed., "Hector McNeill to the Marine Committee," 116.

20. John Paul Jones to Joseph Hewes, *NDAR,* 7:937–38.

21. Greenwood, *Captain John Manley,* 96.

22. McManemin, *Captains of the Continental Navy,* 284–85.

23. The original appointment was to Captain "William" Manley. The clerical error was corrected in three weeks. See *NDAR,* 6:1220. Manley was second in seniority behind James Nicholson and just ahead of Hector McNeill. John Paul Jones ranked eighteenth and was assigned to the 12-gun sloop *Providence.*

24. *NDAR,* 7:1303–4. The committee comprised Captains John Manley, Hector McNeill, Dudley Saltonstall, Elisha Hinman, Joseph Olney, John Roche, and John Paul Jones.

25. Samuel Cooper to Elbridge Gerry, 24 March 1777, John S. Barnes Collection, portfolio 316, New-York Historical Society.

26. McManemin, *Captains of the Continental Navy*, 288.

27. Ibid., 289.

28. Smith, *Fired by Manley Zeal*, 69.

29. The number of guns carried on the *Raleigh* is unknown.

30. Smith, *Fired by Manley Zeal*, 68.

31. McManemin, *Captains of the Continental Navy*, 291.

32. Smith, *Fired by Manley Zeal*, 70.

33. Laing, ed., *Life and Adventures of John Nichol*, 50.

34. "Papers of William Vernon and the Navy Board," 247. See also McManemin, *Captains of the Continental Navy*, 293.

35. Cohen, *Yankee Sailors in British Gaols*, 190.

36. Morgan, *Captains to the Northward*, 215.

37. James Warren to Samuel Adams, 25 August 1778, in Massachusetts Historical Society, *Warren-Adams Letters*, 2:43.

38. *Massachusetts* magazine, February 1793.

Chapter 3: The Army Privateer

1. Eastman, *Some Famous Privateers*, 48; Fowler, *Silas Talbot*, 1–6.

2. Dunworth's first name is unknown.

3. *NDAR*, 10:503–5.

4. Ibid., 10:112.

5. Ibid., 10:122–23.

6. Eastman, *Some Famous Privateers*, 49.

7. Norton, "The Second Captain," 37–38. This vessel was named for Sir Robert Pigot, the British commanding general of Newport.

8. Tuckerman, *Life of Silas Talbot*, 221; Eastman, *Some Famous Privateers*, 50.

9. Tuckerman, *Life of Silas Talbot*, 226.

10. Eastman, *Some Famous Privateers*, 50.

11. Ibid.

12. Talbot was heartbroken but after a year rejoined the social scene. In 1783 he took a new bride, Rebecca "Becky" Morris, the daughter of the prominent Philadelphia merchant Morris Morris.

13. Norton, "The Second Captain," 38.

14. Guttridge and Smith, *Commodores*, 43.

15. Fowler, *Silas Talbot*, 144.

16. Morgan, *Captains to the Northward*, 180.

17. Tuckerman, *Life of Silas Talbot*, 240.

18. *London Courant and Westminster Chronicle*, 29 December 1780; Footner, *Sailor of Fortune*, 76.

19. Norton, "The Second Captain," 38.

20. Secretary Stoddert to Silas Talbot, 29 May 1799, in *Naval Documents Related to the Quasi-War*, 3:203.

21. Harris, *"Old Ironsides,"* 16.

22. Guttridge and Smith, *Commodores*, 44.

23. Ibid.

24. The firing of a salute on the 4th of July is still a custom on the *Constitution* during its annual summer turnaround. The salvos are now twenty-one in groups of seven, but the gun deck of the ship still echoes Captain Talbot's orders.

25. Tuckerman, *Life of Silas Talbot*, 254.

26. Ibid., 255.

27. Norton, "The Second Captain," 128.

28. *Putnam's* 1 (May 1853): 476.

29. Porto Plata is about 130 miles northwest of Santo Domingo in the Dominican Republic.

30. Document of tribute from the merchants of Santo Domingo, 22 July 1800, *Naval Documents Related to the Quasi-War*, 6:166.

31. Secretary Stoddert to Silas Talbot, 3 September 1800, *Naval Documents Related to the Quasi-War*, 6:315.

32. Eastman, *Some Famous Privateers*, 48.

Chapter 4: The Naval Patrician

1. Field, *Esek Hopkins*, 82n–83n.

2. Middlebrook, *Maritime History of Connecticut*, 2:163–64.

3. Butterfield, ed., *Diary and Autobiography of John Adams*, 3:350.

4. In conjunction with the nepotism of the time, Hopkins was a cousin of Saltonstall.

5. *NDAR*, 5:18.

6. Bryant, *Sea and the States*, 78–79.

7. Variolation was a subcutaneous inoculation with fluid from a smallpox-infected blister and was a preventive measure against the disease used from the first quarter to the end of the eighteenth century. In 1796 Dr. Edward Jenner discovered the more effective smallpox vaccination process extracted from bovine virus.

8. The *Andrew Doria* technically was the first hospital ship of the American navy.

9. Miller, *Sea of Glory*, 111–15.

10. While they were there, Major Silas Talbot was in New London arranging to transport a large contingent of army troops across Long Island Sound for what would later be known as the Battle for Long Island.

11. *NDAR*, 5:1029.

12. There are many spelling variations in the historical record of this peninsula, such as Pentagöet, Magabagaduce, Majabigwaduce, Majorbagwayduce, Majibagquiaduce, Maja Biguyduce, Maj Bigueduce, Machebiggaduce, Bagadoose, and more.

13. *Journals of the House of Representatives of Massachusetts*, vol. 54.

14. James Sullivan to John Sullivan, 30 August1779, in Coffin, *Life of James Sullivan*, 2:376–78. James Sullivan stated that the British occupation of Bagaduce greatly alarmed Boston and neighboring seaports because of the prospect of a scarcity of timber.

15. Kevitt, *General Solomon Lovell*, 1.

16. Taylor, ed., *Papers of John Adams*, 8:269.

17. On 12 April 1777 Saltonstall temporarily commanded another vessel, also called the *Trumbull*. He captured two unidentified British transports, of 8 and 10 guns respectively, off the Virginia capes. This has been the source of minor historical confusion, but apparently Saltonstall briefly took command of the 10-gun Connecticut privateer *Trumbull* to keep his men sharp and provide some much-needed prize revenue.

18. Taylor, ed., *Papers of John Adams*, 8:30.

19. Kevitt, *General Solomon Lovell*, 174–75. In July 1780 Dr. John Calef went to England as agent for the Loyalists in Penobscot with a memorial to the king requesting that this district be severed from the province of Massachusetts Bay. Calef actively supported the formation of New Ireland, extolling the virtues of a tract of land much like a modern developer selling a project. The petition plan was drawn up and approved by the cabinet in August 1780 and signed by the king. In spite of cabinet approval, the king's signature, and Calef's efforts, the project failed because of the economic pressures brought about by the Revolution.

20. The Massachusetts State Navy vessels were the 16-gun *Active*, the 16-gun *Tyrannicide*, and the 10-gun *Hazard*.

21. Kevitt, *General Solomon Lovell*, 65, 69–70.

22. Ibid., 72–73.

23. De Koven, *Life and Letters of John Paul Jones*, 1:100; Kevitt, *General Solomon Lovell*, 170–72; Wheeler, *History of Castine, Penobscot, and Brooksville*, 38.

24. Morison, *John Paul Jones*, 42–43.

25. Bradford, ed., *Papers of John Paul Jones*, reel 1, doc. 23; *NDAR*, 5:151–52.

26. Bradford, ed., *Papers of John Paul Jones*, reel 1, doc. 17.

27. Morison, *John Paul Jones*, 56.

28. Lorenz, *John Paul Jones*, 61.

29. Ibid., 72.

30. *NDAR*, 5:294–95.

31. Ibid., 5:64–65.

32. Dudley Saltonstall Papers; Cayford, *Penobscot Expedition;* Kevitt, *General Solomon Lovell*.

33. *Proceedings of the General Assembly . . . of the State of Massachusetts-Bay*, 30 December 1779, 1st series, no. 16847, 29–40.

34. Bailyn et al., eds., *Journals of the House of Representatives of Massachusetts*, 55:70.

35. Revere's unit had four 18-pounders with six hundred rounds, one 12-pounder fieldpiece with eighty-four rounds, two 9-pounders with six hundred rounds, two 5 1/2-inch howitzers with two hundred rounds, and four 4-pounder fieldpieces with an unknown number of rounds. The unit contained approximately eighty men.

36. Smith, *Marines of the Revolution*, 207; deposition of Jeremiah Hill, 29 September 1779, Massachusetts Archives Collection, Boston, 145:284–300.

37. Colonel Paul Revere to General William Heath, 24 October 1779, Massachusetts Historical Society, Boston, microfiche box 19, vol. 14, September–December 1779, 374.

38. The following is an excerpt about the concern for secrecy (from the diary of John Trevett, a captain of marines, in Smith, *Marines of the Revolution*, 335): "Now is an Expedition out att Boston for PerNobscut and our sloop [*Providence*] Praparing to Join the Fleet now I have some buzness to Settel and have no Enclenaton to go [to] Pernbscut as I think the British well Get information Either att New York or Newport before tha Can Gett Redy to sail and if tha Due I now thre or fore Large British ships can Block them in and that will be the Lors of All our shiping."

39. Letter from David Perham giving Colonel John Brewer's reminiscences of the Penobscot Expedition, *Whig and Courier* (Bangor, Maine), 13 August 1846.

40. The appeal is as follows (from Cayford, *Penobscot Expedition*, 19):

"Hummbly sheweth. That we your petitioners, strongly impressed with the importance of the Expedition, and earnestly desiring to render to our country all the service in our power, would represent to Your Honor that the most speedy exertions should be used to accomplish the design we came upon. We think delays, in the present case, are extremely dangerous—as our enemies are duly fortifying and strengthening themselves, and are stimulated so to do, being in daily expectation of a reinforcement. We do not mean to advise, or censure your past conduct, but intend only to express our desire of improving the present opportunity to go immediately into the harbor, and attack the enemy's ships. However, we humbly submit our sentiments to the better judgment of those in superior command. We, therefore, wait your orders, whether in answer to our petition, or otherwise." [signed by David Porter, first lieutenant of the ship *Putnam*, and thirty others]

41. Deposition of Lieutenant George Little, 25 September 1779, in Papers Relating to the Penobscot Expedition, 1779, Transcripts from the Massachusetts Archives, New-York Historical Society.

42. Colonel Paul Revere to General William Heath, 24 October 1779.

43. Ibid.

44. Hoysted Hacker had an uncertain reputation as a captain. John Paul Jones noted on 27 October 1776 that Hacker hit a submerged rock and damaged his

ship the *Hampden* so that it could not be used in a naval mission. On 12 January 1777 Jones said that Hacker should have been court-martialed for deserting the *Hampden* during a snowstorm on 16 November 1776 off Nova Scotia.

45. Letter headed "Headquarters, Majabagaduce Heights, 11 August 1779," Dudley Saltonstall Papers:

> Sir,
>
> In this alarming posture of affairs, I am once more obliged to request the most speedy service from your department; and that a moment be no longer delayed to put into execution, what I have been given to understand, was the determination of your last council. The destruction of the enemy's ships must be effected at any rate, although it might cost us half our own. I cannot possibly conceive of that danger or that the attempt will miscarry. I mean not to determine upon your mode of attack; but it appears to me that any further delays must be infamous. I have it this moment, by a deserter from one of their ships, that the moment you enter the harbor, they will destroy themselves—which will effectually answer our purpose.
>
> The idea of more batteries against them was sufficiently reprobated. If the situation of ground would admit to such proceedings, it would not take up dangerous time, and we have already experienced their obstinacy in that respect. . . . My situation is confined, and while the enemy's ships are safe, the operations of the army cannot possibly be extended an inch beyond the present limits. The alternative now remains, to destroy the ships, or raise the siege.
>
> The information of the British ships at the Hook [probably those that sailed past Sandy Hook many days earlier] is not to be dispised [ignored], not a moment is to be lost. We must determine instantly, or it may be productive of disgrace, loss of ships and men. As for the troops, their retreat is secure, though I would die to save the necessity of it.
>
> I feel the honor of America is at stake, especially in an expedition which a nobler exertion had long before this crowned with success. I have now only to repeat the [a]bsolute necessity of undertaking the destruction of the ships, or quitting this place. I impatiently await your answer. I am, Sir, Your, etc.
>
> S. Lovell, Brig. Gen.

46. Kevitt, *General Solomon Lovell*, 101.

47. Miller, *Sea of Glory*, 415.

48. Colonel Paul Revere to General William Heath, 24 October 1779.

49. Measured today at two to three knots and occasionally up to five knots during flood tides.

50. Dudley Saltonstall Papers.

51. Revolution: Penobscot Expedition, Massachusetts Archives Collection, microfilm, box 19, 14:337. These actions led to Revere's court-martial for misconduct. Ultimately the well-known patriot was acquitted.

52. General S. Lovell, journal entry, 14 August 1779; in Kevitt, *General Solomon Lovell,* 50.

53. Papers of Nathan Dane, Esq, Massachusetts attorney, 14 July 1780.

54. Bailyn et al., eds., *Journals of the House of Representatives of Massachusetts,* 55:78.

55. In 1793 Massachusetts authorities succeeded in persuading Congress to partially reimburse the state for the cost of the expedition.

56. Kevitt, *General Solomon Lovell,* 133.

57. Ibid.

58. Ibid.

59. Cooper, *The History of the Navy,* 107.

60. Saltonstall, *Ancestry and Descendents,* 230.

61. Ibid., 231.

62. Captain Hoysted Hacker of the *Providence* faced a court of naval inquiry for his conduct during the expedition. The evidence showed that he consistently voted for offensive actions at the various Councils of War, clearing him of the charges against him.

63. Gurley, *Collection of Naval Manuscripts, 1734–1784,* 7a,b,c.

64. Admiralty to Navy Board, 25 January 1780, National Archives, Microfilm Publication Record Group 360, M 332, roll 6:249.

65. Buker, *Penobscot Expedition,* 163.

66. Forbes, *Paul Revere,* 306.

67. Dudley Saltonstall Papers, 1782–83.

Chapter 5: The Lieutenant Commodore

1. Although Barney evidently appealed to the patriotism of the Baltimore seamen, the Americans, like the British, frequently impressed seamen to naval duty. Since the colonists were in rebellion, acts of naval warfare against a Crown ship were considered piracy and punishable as such in court. Rebel soldiers fared much better in British captivity.

2. The ship's name also appears as *Andrew Doria* in some American naval historical records. The vessel was named after the renowned Genoese patriot and admiral Andrea Doria (1466–1560), but *Andrew* is the English equivalent of *Andrea.* Joshua Barney knew her by the Italian name. *NDAR,* 2:647, identifies the *Andrea Doria* as a 14-gun brigantine. Chapelle, in *History of the American Sailing Navy,* describes her as a brig. She is called a brig-of-war on other official documents. The vessel was most probably what might be called a hermaphrodite brig today. Robinson and Dow, in *Sailing Ships of New England* (28, 29), define the brig as a generic vessel with three spars on two masts

(fore and main) that were square-rigged. The brigantine also had two masts; the foremast carried two spars for square sails, and the main had a fore-and-aft sail. The hermaphrodite version had two square foresails, a square top mainsail, and a fore-and-aft gaft mainsail.

3. The Grand Union flag had thirteen stripes but displayed the British Union Jack as its canon.

4. Over the years this incident has grown in historical importance. In 1939 a plaque was presented to St. Eustatius bearing the signature of President Franklin D. Roosevelt, a Dutch descendant. It reads, "In commemoration of the salute of the flag of the United States fired at this fort November 16, 1776, by the order of Johannes de Graaff [Graef], Governor of St. Eustatius, in reply to the national gun salute fired by the Brig-of-War *Andrea Doria*. Here the sovereignty of the United States of America was first formally acknowledged to a national vessel by a foreign official." However, the historian J. F. Jameson has presented evidence that the Grand Union flag was first saluted in St. Croix by the Danes three weeks earlier, a view that has gained wide acceptance.

Most histories state that the first naval salute to the American flag was by the French fleet at Brest in Quiberon Bay on 14 February 1778. The recipient was the ship *Ranger,* under the command of Captain John Paul Jones. This was the first governmentally sanctioned salute to an American flag, but the flag was not the earlier Grand Union flag that was flown by the *Andrea Doria.* A motion by the Continental Congress on 14 June 1777 adopted a "flag of thirteen United states be thirteen stripes, alternate red and white; that the union be thirteen stars, white in a blue field representing a new constellation." In a curious historical coincidence, during that same hour Congress also ordered John Paul Jones to command the ship *Ranger.* He later sentimentally wrote, "that flag and I were twins; born in the same hour from the same womb of destiny. We cannot be parted in life or death. So long as we can float, we shall float together. If I must sink, we shall so drown as one." On 14 June, America still celebrates Flag Day in remembrance of the approval by Congress of the new official nation emblem, a variation of which Jones flew from the *Ranger.*

5. The conquest of a hostile capital usually caused surrender in a European military campaign. American society was so independent and diffusely organized that the capture of New York, Philadelphia, and later Trenton brought no such results as would have happened with the fall of Paris, Berlin, or Amsterdam.

6. Xebecs are lateen-rigged ships of Mediterranean or North African design.

7. The vessel was named for a Moslem ruler, Hyder-Ally (also spelled Haidar Ali), who led a courageous but unsuccessful 1781 revolt against the British in India.

8. The Pennsylvania legislature did not officially pass the resolution authorizing the purchase of the *Hyder-Ally* for the defense of Delaware until 9 April 1782. Thus it was not the property of the commonwealth when it won its most famous battle.

9. A poignant and ironic series of meetings of three ships, formerly commanded by three of the men whose biographies appear in this book, took place during the war. On 8 August 1781 the frigate *Trumbull*, Dudley Saltonstall's former ship, sailed as escort for a merchant convoy out of Philadelphia. On the night of 28 August the *Trumbull* was badly damaged in a storm. Now vulnerable, she was attacked the next morning by the British men-of-war *Iris* and *General Monk*. The *Iris* was the former *Hancock* that had been commanded by John Manley. Silas Talbot formerly commanded the *General Monk* under the name of the *General Washington*. Shortly thereafter Joshua Barney recaptured the *Monk*, and it was renamed *General Washington* for American naval service. The *Trumbull* was ravaged from her encounter and subsequently towed to New York to be broken up. The *General Washington* was sold in the summer of 1784. The French captured the *Iris* from the British on 11 September 1781 at the Battle of the Virginia Capes. The *Iris* was used as a hulk at Toulon and subsequently blown up at anchor by the British on 18 December 1793.

10. Unfortunately, this sword was later stolen in Paris. Barney prized it so much that he had a duplicate made.

11. Although Barney was addressed as captain, his Continental Navy promotion from lieutenant to captain did not come until 6 March 1784, about one and one-half years later.

12. Norton, *Joshua Barney*, 96.

13. Burnett, ed., *Letters of Members of the Continental Congress*, 6:70–75.

14. Barney, *Biographical Memoir of the Late Joshua Barney*, 150–51.

15. Norton, *Joshua Barney*, 112–23.

16. Barney and Talbot, whose lives crisscrossed in many coincidental ways, were strikingly alike in character and accomplishment. Barney's place in American naval history might have become even greater had he not gotten into this quarrel about seniority.

17. Footner, *Sailor of Fortune*, 93.

18. Benjamin Stoddert to Thomas Truxtun, *NDAR*, 1:427.

19. Footner, *Sailor of Fortune*, 226.

20. Ibid., 263.

Chapter 6: Captain Paul

1. Many of the captains who served in the Continental Navy did a stint in the slave trade, a common way to gain maritime experience, if only for a short time.

2. Parkinson, *Trade in the Eastern Seas*, 194.

3. The addition of the surname Jones, a variant of his father's Christian name John, to his name was a patronymic custom common in Wales and not unusual in the section of Scotland from which John Paul emigrated.

4. *NDAR*, 5:1029.

5. John Paul Jones to Joseph Hewes, 19 May 1776, John Paul Jones Papers.

6. Thomas, *John Paul Jones*, 80.

7. John Paul Jones to Joseph Hewes, 19 May 1776, John Paul Jones Papers.

8. Thomas, *John Paul Jones,* 54.

9. Ibid., 55.

10. John Paul Jones to Joseph Hewes, 17 August 1777, John Paul Jones Papers.

11. A snow is a variation of a brig. It has square sails on both masts but has a small trysail mast and boom stepped just abaft of the mainmast. A trysail is hooped to this auxiliary mast.

12. Jones, *Memoirs,* ed. Levy, 45–49.

13. The first recognized naval salute to an American vessel was given to the *Andrea Doria* when she sailed into the harbor of the Dutch island of St. Eustatius.

14. Barnes and Owen, eds., *Private Papers of John Montagu, Earl of Sandwich,* 1:236.

15. Other American captains had captured British ships off their coast, but this was the first loss of a man-of-war.

16. Butterfield, ed., *Diary and Autobiography of John Adams,* 16 July 1778, 2:166.

17. Thomas, *John Paul Jones,* 152.

18. Morison, *John Paul Jones,* 170.

19. *NDAR,* 10:961–62. The name Landais is spelled variously as Lundy, Landai, and Landi in documents of this period.

20. Landais's French 20-gun ship was the *Heureux,* whose name was later changed to the *Flamand.*

21. John Paul Jones to Benjamin Franklin, 14 May 1779, John Paul Jones Papers.

22. Butterfield, ed., *Diary and Autobiography of John Adams,* 12 May 1779, 2:368.

23. Abigail Adams to James Lovell, 13 December 1779, in Butterfield, ed., *Adams Family Correspondence,* 3:248.

24. Thomas, *John Paul Jones,* 170.

25. According to the formal dueling code, the challenged person, if he accepted, had the choice of weapons. Since Jones essentially refused the challenge by putting it off, the sword issue may have been Landais's way of continuing his threat to Jones.

26. Jones, *Memoirs,* 1:163.

27. Gawalt, ed., *John Paul Jones' Memoir of the American Revolution,* 29.

28. Cooper, *The History of the Navy,* 97.

29. Morison, *John Paul Jones,* 235.

30. Seitz, *Paul Jones,* 88; quoted from the *London Evening Post,* 12 October 1779.

31. When everyone had returned home, the British Admiralty honored the defeated Captain Pearson for his gallantry.

32. Jones, *Memoirs,* 1:194–95.

33. John Paul Jones to John Brown, 13 March 1781, John Paul Jones Papers.

34. Franklin to the Officers of the *Alliance,* 12 June 1780, *Papers of Benjamin Franklin,* 32:508.

35. Jones, *Memoirs,* 1:192.

36. Landais had one more encounter with Jones in New York City during the autumn of 1787. They met on the street, and Landais challenged Jones to the previously promised duel by spitting on the ground near Jones and uttering, "I spit in your face," as a sign of contempt. A verbal duel about exactly what took place in this altercation in the street appeared in the *New York Journal and Weekly.* Jones avoided Landais's sword for the last time by sailing to Paris a few days after the encounter.

37. *Papers of Benjamin Franklin,* 33:28.

38. Morison, *John Paul Jones,* 92.

39. Frost, *Pictorial Book of the Commodores,* 31.

40. Nicholson was not court-martialed for the loss of the *Virginia,* but Congress instituted an inquiry and acquitted him of blame. He would later lose the frigate *Trumbull,* on 9 August 1781.

41. Morison, *John Paul Jones,* 315; Thomas, *John Paul Jones,* 249.

42. Morison, *John Paul Jones,* 334.

43. Journal of the Campaign of the Liman, 10, John Paul Jones Papers.

Chapter 7: Issues of Leadership, Personality, and Psychology

1. Sun Tzu, *Art of War.*

2. In six years this document proved unsatisfactory and necessitated the Constitutional Convention of 1787.

3. Article 42 of the *Argus* orders of 1811, rules and regulations of the sloop *Argus,* William M. Crane, Commander, Naval Records Collection.

4. MacLiesh and Krieger, *Privateers,* 46.

5. Boswell, *Life of Johnson,* quotation from March 1759, 1:403.

6. Carr, *Coming of War,* 354.

7. "Narcissism" seems a particularly appropriate term because of its maritime connection. In Greek mythology Narcissus was the son of the river god Cephissus and the water nymph Liriope.

8. Taylor, ed., *Papers of John Adams,* 7:244.

9. John Paul Jones served as a member of this committee.

10. The *Code Duello* provided specific rules for engaging and conducting duels for the preservation of honor. The earliest known *version* was the Renaissance-era *Flos Duellatorum in Armis,* written down in Italy (circa 1410). The Italian dueling codes and manuals became the basis of the complex French eighty-four-rule code. The twenty-six-commandment Irish *Code Duello* of that was adopted at the Clonmel summer assizes in 1777. Gentlemen delegates of five Irish counties codified the settling of affairs of honor to be conducted outside of the law.

11. By the end of November 1781 the Britons whose property he had confiscated on the island were suing Rodney. News of the admiral's act of singling out

the Dutch Jews for the harshest punishment reached the British Parliament. Edmund Burke, a member of Commons and an eloquent sympathizer of the American cause, was known for uncharitable statements toward Jews, and yet he reproved Rodney for his mistreatment of the Jews of St. Eustatius. Burke was likely more concerned with Britain's image of ethical lapse as seen by Rodney's actions than with the plight of the Jews. Still, in recognizing Jewish vulnerability, Burke implied that the plight of the Jews might be solved if they had a state of their own.

Jews ultimately returned to St. Eustatius. The Honen Dalim synagogue still stands in ruins there, a forlorn and solemn monument to both a significant and an unfortunate moment in history. Ten months later the French, allies of the Dutch in this war, conquered the island. The Dutch regained command over the island in 1784.

12. Ironically much of the spoils never reached there. A convoy laden with his treasures was intercepted in the English Channel by a French squadron, and the valuables fell into French hands. The estimated value of the cargo and maritime prizes in the harbor amounted to more than three million pounds sterling. See Clowes et al., *Royal Navy*, 3:480.

13. Millon and Radovanov. "Passive-Aggressive (Negativistic) Personality Disorder," 321; Millon, *Personality and Psychopathology*, 198.

14. Millon and Davis, "Evolutionary Theory of Personality Disorders," 309.

15. Beck and Freeman, *Cognitive Therapy*, 46.

16. Brooks, "Our Way: Root and Hoot," A25.

17. Rodger, *Wooden World*, 346.

18. "Sons of the Brine" is a phrase from Gilbert and Sullivan's *H.M.S. Pinafore*.

Bibliography

Primary Sources

Archival Materials

Andrea Doria Journal, Public Record Office, Admiralty, London.

John S. Barnes Collection, New-York Historical Society.

Joshua Barney. Defense of the *Chesapeake.* Manuscript Division, Library of Congress.

Joshua Barney Papers, Dreer Collection, Pennsylvania Historical Society.

Nathan Dane Papers, Massachusetts Historical Society.

John Paul Jones Papers, Library of Congress.

Journal of the Continental Congress, Library of Congress.

Naval Records Collection of the Office of Naval Records and Library, U.S. National Archives.

Papers Relating to the Penobscot Expedition, 1779, Transcripts from the Massachusetts Archives, New-York Historical Society.

Revolution: Penobscot Expedition, 1779. Massachusetts Archives Collection (microfilm).

Dudley Saltonstall Court-Martial, Collection of Naval Manuscripts, 1734–1784, edited by Jacob B. Gurley, Connecticut State Library.

Dudley Saltonstall Papers, private collection, Bloomfield, Conn.

Published Sources

Allen, Gardiner W., ed. "Hector McNeill to the Marine Committee, 25 August 1777." *Massachusetts Historical Society Proceedings* 3rd series, 55 (1923):116.

Bailyn, Bernard, et al., eds. *Journals of the House of Representatives of Massachusetts.* Vol. 55. Boston: Massachusetts Historical Society, 1990.

Barnes, George Reginald, and John H. Owen, eds. *The Private Papers of John Montagu, Earl of Sandwich, First Lord of the Admiralty, 1771–1782.* 4 vols. London: Navy Records Society, 1932–38.

Beck, Alverda S., ed. *The Correspondence of Esek Hopkins Commander in Chief of the United States Navy.* Providence: Rhode Island Historical Society, 1933.

Bradford, James C., ed. *The Papers of John Paul Jones*. 10 reels. Alexandria, Va.: Chadwych-Healy, Microform, 1986.

Burnett, Edmund Cody, ed. *Letters of Members of the Continental Congress*. 8 vols. Baltimore: Lord Baltimore Press, 1934.

Butterfield, Lyman Henry, ed. *Diary and Autobiography of John Adams*. 4 vols. Cambridge, Mass.: Belknap Press of Harvard University Press, 1961.

Butterfield, Lyman Henry, et al., eds. *Adams Family Correspondence*. 8 vols. Cambridge, Mass.: Belknap Press of Harvard University Press, 1963–2007.

Clinton, Sir Henry. *The American Rebellion: Sir Henry Clinton's Narrative of His Campaign, 1775–1782*. Ed. William B. Wilcox. New Haven, Conn.: Yale University Press, 1954.

De Koven, (Mrs.) Reginald. *The Life and Letters of John Paul Jones*. 2 vols. New York: Scribners, 1913.

Dudley, William S. *The Naval War of 1812*. Washington, D.C.: Naval Historical Center, Department of the Navy, 1985.

Ferguson, E. James, and John Catanzariti, eds. *The Papers of Robert Morris*. 1781–84. Pittsburgh: University of Pittsburgh Press, 1980.

Fitzpatrick, John C., ed. *The Diaries of George Washington*. 39 vols. Boston: Houghton Mifflin, 1925.

Franklin, Benjamin. *Papers of Benjamin Franklin*. Edited by Leonard W. Labaree et al. 38 vols. New Haven, Conn.: Yale University Press, 1959–2006.

Gawalt, Gerald, ed. *John Paul Jones' Memoir of the American Revolution Presented to King Louis XVI of France*. Washington, D.C.: Library of Congress, 1979.

Hannay, David R., ed. *Letters Written by Sir Samuel Hood (Viscount Hood) in 1781–1783*. London: Navy Records Society, 1895.

Jennings, Louis J., ed. *The Correspondence and Diaries of the Late Right Honorable John Wilson Crocker*. 3 vols. London, 1884.

Jones, John Paul. *Memoirs of Rear Admiral Paul Jones*. 2 vols. Edinburgh: Oliver & Boyd, 1830. Repr., 1 vol. Edited by Leonard W. Levy. New York: Da Capo Press, 1972.

Lewis, Theresa. *Extracts of the Journals and Correspondence of Miss Berry*. London: Longmans, Green, 1865.

Lincoln, Charles Henry, ed. *Naval Records of the American Revolution 1775–1788*. Washington, D.C.: U.S. Government Printing Office, 1906.

Massachusetts Historical Society. *Warren-Adams Letters, Being Chiefly a Correspondence among John Adams, Samuel Adams, and James Warren*. 2 vols. Boston: Massachusetts Historical Society Collections, 1917, 1925.

Naval Documents of the American Revolution. Vols. 1–4, *December 1, 1774–September 2, 1775*, edited by William Bell Clark; vols. 5–9, *May 9, 1776–September 30, 1777*, edited by William James Morgan; Vols. 9–11, October 1, 1777–December 31, 1777, edited by Michael J. Crawford. Washington, D.C.: Naval Historical Center, Department of the Navy, 1964–2005.

Naval Documents Related to the Quasi-War between the United States and France, Naval Operations from February 1797 to December 1801. 7 vols. Edited by Dudley W. Knox. Washington, D.C.: U.S. Government Printing Office, 1935–38.

"Papers of William Vernon and the Navy Board." *Publications of the Rhode Island Historical Society* 7 (January 1901):1–282.

Proceedings of the General Assembly and of the Council of the State of Massachusetts Bay Relating to the Penobscot Expedition and the Orders of the Continental Navy Board to the Commander of the Naval Forces. Boston: Printed by J. Gill, 1780. Worcester, Mass.: Early American Imprints, 1970.

Taylor, Robert J., ed. *The Papers of John Adams.* 8 vols. Cambridge, Mass.: Belknap Press of Harvard University Press, 1977.

Secondary Sources

Adams, William Frederick. *Commodore Joshua Barney.* Springfield, Mass.: Privately printed, 1912.

Albion, Robert G., William A. Baker, and Benjamin W. Labaree, *New England and the Sea.* Middletown, Conn.: Wesleyan University Press, 1972.

Ansted, A. *A Dictionary of Sea Terms.* Glasgow, U.K.: James Brown & Son, 1919.

Axelrad, Jacob. *Philip Freneau: Champion of Democracy.* Austin: University of Texas Press, 1967.

Barney, Mary. *Biographical Memoir of the Late Joshua Barney: From Autobiographical Notes and Journals in Possession of His Family, and Other Authentic Sources.* Boston: Gray & Bowen, 1832.

Beck, Aaron T., and Arthur Freeman. *Cognitive Therapy of Personality Disorders.* New York: Guilford Press, 1990.

Benjamin, Lorna Smith. *Interpersonal Diagnosis and Treatment of Personality Disorders.* New York: Guilford Press, 1993.

Berckman, Evelyn. *Nelson's Dear Lord.* London: Macmillan, 1962.

Bienkowski, Lee. *Admirals in the Age of Nelson.* Annapolis, Md.: Naval Institute Press, 2003.

Bixby, W. K., ed. *Letters and Recollections of George Washington.* New York: Page, 1906.

Boswell, James. *Life of Johnson.* 6 vols., edited by George Birkbeck Hill. New York: Bigelow, Brown, 1925.

Bourne, Russell. *Cradle of Violence: How Boston's Waterfront Mobs Ignited the American Revolution.* Hoboken, N.J.: Wiley, 2006.

Bradford, James C. *Command Under Sail: Makers of the American Naval Tradition 1775–1785.* Annapolis, Md.: Naval Institute Press, 1985.

Brooks, David. "Our Way: Root and Hoot," *New York Times,* 14 October 2003, A25.

Bryant, Samuel W. *Sea and the States.* New York: Crowell, 1967.

Buell, Richard Jr. *In Irons*. New Haven, Conn.: Yale University Press, 1998.

Buker, George E. *The Penobscot Expedition: Commodore Saltonstall and the Massachusetts Conspiracy*. Annapolis, Md.: Naval Institute Press, 2002.

Carr, Albert Z. *The Coming of War: An Account of the Remarkable Events Leading to the War of 1812*. Garden City, N.Y.: Doubleday, 1960.

Carroll, John Alexander, and Mary Wells Ashworth. *George Washington*. Vol. 7. New York: Scribners, 1957.

Cayford, John E. *The Penobscot Expedition*. Orrington, Maine: C&H Publishing, 1976.

Chapelle, Howard I. *The History of the American Sailing Navy: The Ships and Their Development*. New York: Bonanza Books, 1949.

Clark, William B. *George Washington's Navy: Being an Account of His Excellency's Fleet in New England Waters*. Baton Rouge: Louisiana State University Press, 1960.

Clowes, William Laird. *The Royal Navy: A History from the Earliest Times to the Present*. 7 vols. London: Chatham, 1901.

Coffin, Thomas. *Life of James Sullivan: With Selections from His Writings*. Boston: Phillips, Sampson, 1859.

Coggins, Jack. *Ships and Seamen of the American Revolution*. Harrisburg, Pa.: Stackpole, 1969.

Cohen, Sheldon S. *Yankee Sailors in British Gaols: Prisoners of War at Forton and Mill, 1777–1783*. Newark: University of Delaware Press / London & Cranbury, N.J.: Associated University Presses, 1995.

Commager, Henry Steele, and Richard B. Morris. *The Spirit of 'Seventy-six: The Story of the American Revolution as Told by Participants*. New York: Bobbs-Merrill, 1958.

Cooper, James Fenimore. *The History of the Navy of the United States of America*. Philadelphia: Thomas, Cowperthwait, 1845.

Cordingly, David. *The Billy Ruffian: The Bellerophon and the Downfall of Napoleon*. London: Bloomsbury, 2003.

———. *Under the Black Flag*. New York: Random House, 1995.

Crawford, Michael J. *The Autobiography of a Yankee Mariner: Christopher Prince and the American Revolution*. Washington, D.C.: Brassey's, 2002.

DeConde, Alexander. *The Quasi-War: The Politics and Diplomacy of the Undeclared War with France 1798–1801*. New York: Scribners, 1966.

De Selincourt, Aubrey. *The Book of the Sea*. New York: Norton, 1961.

Dickerson, Oliver M. *The Navigation Acts and the American Revolution*. Philadelphia: University of Pennsylvania Press, 1951.

Durant, Will, and Ariel Durant. *The Age of Napoleon: A History of European Civilization from 1789 to 1815*. New York: Simon & Schuster, 1975.

Eastman, Ralph Mason. *Some Famous Privateers of New England*. Boston: Privately printed for the State Street Trust, 1928.

Eller, Ernest McNeill, ed. *Chesapeake Bay in the American Revolution*. Centreville, Md.: Tidewater Publications, 1981.

Ferreiro, Larrie D. *Ships and Science: The Birth of Naval Architecture in the Scientific Revolution, 1600–1800.* Cambridge, Mass.: MIT Press, 2007.

Field, Edward. *Esek Hopkins: Commodore in Chief of the Continental Navy during the American Revolution, 1775–1778.* Providence, R.I.: Preston & Rounds, 1898.

Footner, Hulbert. *Sailor of Fortune: The Life and Adventures of Commodore Joshua Barney.* New York: Harper, 1940.

Forbes, Esther. *Paul Revere and the World He Lived In.* Boston: Houghton Mifflin, 1942.

Fowler, William M., Jr. *Jack Tars and Commodores: The American Navy 1783–1815.* Boston: Houghton Mifflin, 1984.

———. *Rebels under Sail: The American Navy during the Revolution.* New York: Scribners, 1976.

———. *Silas Talbot, Captain of Old Ironsides.* Mystic, Conn.: Mystic Seaport Press, 1995.

French, Allen. *The First Year of the American Revolution.* Boston: Houghton Mifflin, 1935.

Freneau, Philip. *Poems of the American Revolution.* New York: W. J. Widdleton, 1865.

Frost, John. *The Book of the Navy.* New York: Nafts & Cornish, 1845.

Garitee, Jerome R. *The Republic's Private Navy.* Mystic, Conn.: Mystic Seaport Press, 1977.

Garland, Joseph E. *The Fish and the Falcon: Gloucester's Resolute Role in America's Fight for Freedom.* Charleston, S.C.: History Press, 2006.

Gilbert, William S., and Arthur Sullivan. *H.M.S. Pinafore.* London: Metzler, 1887.

Greene, George Washington. *Historical View of the American Revolution.* Boston: Ticknor & Fields, 1865.

Greenwood, Isaac J. *Captain John Manley Second in Rank in the United States Navy 1776–1783.* Boston: C. E. Goodspeed, 1915.

Guttridge, Leonard F., and Jay D. Smith. *The Commodores: The U.S. Navy in the Age of Sail.* New York: Harper & Row, 1969.

Harris, John. "Old Ironsides," *Boston Globe,* special supplement, 16 October 1977.

Harrison, Peleg D. *The Stars and Stripes and Other American Flags.* Boston: Little, Brown, 1906.

Hearn, Chester G. *George Washington's Schooners: The First American Navy.* Annapolis, Md.: Naval Institute Press, 1995.

Herold, J. Christopher. *The Age of Napoleon.* New York: American Heritage, 1963.

Hickey, Donald. *The War of 1812: A Forgotten Conflict.* Urbana: University of Illinois Press, 1989.

Jameson, J. Franklin. "St. Eustasius in the American Revolution." *American Historical Review* 8 (1903): 691.

John Paul Jones: Commemoration at Annapolis 24 April 1906. Washington, D.C.: U.S. Government Printing Office, 1907.

Journals of the House of Representatives of Massachusetts. Vol. 54, *1778–1779.* Boston: Massachusetts Historical Society, 1989.

Kantor, Martin. *Diagnosis and Treatment of the Personality Disorders.* St. Louis: Ishiyaku EuroAmerica, 1992.

Keegan, John, *The Price of Admiralty: The Evolution of Naval Warfare.* New York: Viking, 1988.

Kennedy, Paul. *The Rise and Fall of British Naval Mastery.* New York: Scribners, 1976.

Ketchum, Richard M. *Victory at Yorktown: The Campaign That Won the Revolution.* New York: Henry Holt / John Macrae Books, 2004.

Kevitt, Chester B. *General Solomon Lovell and the Penobscot Expedition, 1779.* Weymouth, Mass.: Weymouth Historical Commission / C. B. Kevitt, 1976.

King, Dean. *A Sea of Words.* New York: Holt, 1995.

King, Irving. *Washington's Coast Guard.* Annapolis, Md.: Naval Institute Press, 1978.

Kurlansky, Mark. *Cod.* New York: Penguin, 1997.

Labaree, Benjamin, William Fowler Jr., John Hattendorf, Jeffrey Safford, Edward Sloan, and Andrew German. *America and the Sea: A Maritime History.* Mystic, Conn.: Mystic Seaport Press, 1998.

Laing, Alexander, ed. *The Life and Adventures of John Nichol, Mariner.* New York: Atlantic Monthly Press, 1999.

Langguth, A. J. *Patriots: The Men Who Started the American Revolution.* New York: Simon & Schuster, 1988.

Langley, Henry David. *Social Reform in the United States Navy, 1798–1862.* Urbana: University of Illinois Press, 1967.

Larrabee, Harold A. *Decision at the Chesapeake.* New York: Bramhall House, 1964.

Lavery, Brian. *Nelson's Navy: The Ships, Men and Organization 1793–1815.* Annapolis, Md.: Naval Institute Press, 1989.

Leech, Samuel. *Thirty-five Years from Home, or a Voice from the Main Deck.* Boston: C. Tappan, 1843.

Lewis, Michael. *England's Sea Officers.* London: Allen & Unwin, 1939.

——. *The Navy in Transition, 1814–1864: A Social History.* London: Hodder & Stoughton, 1965.

Lord, Walter. *The Dawn's Early Light.* New York: Norton, 1972.

Lorenz, Lincoln. *John Paul Jones, Fighter for Freedom and Glory.* Annapolis, Md.: United States Naval Institute, 1943.

Lovette, Leland P. *Naval Customs, Traditions, and Usage.* Annapolis, Md.: United States Naval Institute, 1939.

Maclay, Edgar Stanton. *A History of American Privateers.* New York: D. Appleton, 1899.

——. *A History of the United States Navy from 1775 to 1898.* 2 vols. New York: D. Appleton, 1898.

MacLiesh, Fleming, and Martin L. Krieger. *The Privateers: A Raiding Voyage to the Great South Sea.* New York: Random House, 1962.

McManemin, John A. *Captains of State Navies during the Revolutionary War.* Ho-Ho-Kus, N.J.: Ho-Ho-Kus Publishing, 1984.

——. *Captains of the Continental Navy.* Ho-Ho-Kus, N.J.: Ho-Ho-Kus Publishing, 1982.

——. *Captains of the Privateers of the War of 1812.* Springdale, N.J.: Ho-Ho-Kus Publishing, 1994.

Middlebrook, Louis A. *Maritime History of Connecticut during the American Revolution 1775–1783.* 2 vols. Salem, Mass.: Essex Institute, 1925.

Miller, John F. *American Ships of the Colonial and Revolutionary Periods.* New York: Norton, 1978.

Miller, Nathan. *Broadsides: The Age of Fighting Sail, 1775–1815.* New York: Wiley, 2000.

——. *Sea of Glory.* New York: David McKay, 1974.

Millon, Theodore. *Personality and Psychopathology: An Evolutionary Model.* New York: Wiley, 1996.

Millon, Theodore, and Roger Davis. "An Evolutionary Theory of Personality Disorders." In *Major Theories in Personality Disorders,* ed. John F. Clarkin and Mark F. Lenzenweger. New York: Guilford Press, 1996.

Millon, Theodore, and Jelena Radovanov. "Passive-Aggressive (Negativistic) Personality Disorder." In *Personality Disorders,* ed. John W. Livesley. New York: Guilford Press, 1995.

Morgan, William James. *Captains to the Northward: The New England Captains in the Continental Navy.* Barre, Mass.: Barre Gazette, 1959.

Morison, Samuel Eliot. *Dudley Saltonstall and the Penobscot Expedition.* Trumbill, Conn.: Connecticut History, 2003.

——. *Henry Mowat—Miscreant of the Coast of Maine.* Portland, Me.: Maine History Quarterly, 2007.

——. *John Paul Jones: A Sailor's Biography.* Boston: Little, Brown, 1959.

——. *Joshua Barney: Hero of the Revolution and 1812.* Annapolis, Md.: Naval Institute Press, 2000.

——. *The Maritime History of Massachusetts.* Boston: Houghton Mifflin, 1921.

Norton, Louis Arthur. *The Continental Navy Brig Andrew (Andrea) Doria.* Salem, Mass.: American Neptune, 2001.

——. *The Penobscot Expedition: A Tale of Two Indicted Patriots.* Boston: Revere House Gazette, 2000.

——. *The Penobscot Expedition: A Tale of Two Indicted Patriots.* Ottawa: Northern Mariner / Le Marin du nord, 2006.

——. "The Second Captain: Silas Talbot of the USS Constitution." *Sea History* no. 81 (Spring 1997): 37–39.

Ott, Thomas O. *The Haitian Revolution, 1789–1804.* Knoxville: University of Tennessee Press, 1973.

Paine, Ralph D. *The Fight for a Free Sea: A Chronicle of the War of 1812.* New Haven, Conn.: Yale University Press, 1921.

——. *Joshua Barney, Forgotten Hero of the Blue Water.* New York: Century, 1924.

Palmer, Michael A. *Stoddert's War: Naval Operations during the Quasi-War with France, 1798–1801.* Columbia: University of South Carolina Press, 1987.

Parkinson, C. Northcote. *Trade in the Eastern Seas, 1793–1813.* Cambridge: Cambridge University Press, 1937.

Pattee, Fred Lewis, ed. *The Poems of Philip Freneau, Poet of the American Revolution.* 3 vols. Princeton, N.J.: Princeton Historical Association, University Library, 1902–7.

Peabody, Robert Ephraim. *The Naval Career of Captain John Manley of Marblehead.* Salem, Mass.: Essex Institute Historical Collection, 1909.

Pengelly, Collin. *The First Bellerophon.* London: Baker, 1966.

Peterson, Charles J. *The American Navy: Being an Authentic History of the United States Navy and Biographical Sketches of American Naval Heroes, from the Formation of the Navy to the Close of the Mexican War.* Philadelphia: James B. Smith, 1858.

Pitch, Anthony S. *The Burning of Washington: The British Invasion of 1814.* Annapolis, Md.: Naval Institute Press, 1998.

Pool, J. Laurence. *Fighting Ships of the Revolution on Long Island Sound 1775–1783.* Torrington, Conn.: Rainbow Press, 1990.

Potter, E. B. *Sea Power: A Naval History.* Annapolis, Md.: Naval Institute Press, 1981.

Preston, Anthony, David Lyons, and John H. Batchelor. *Navies of the American Revolution.* Englewood Cliffs, N.J.: Prentice-Hall, 1975.

Richards, Henry Jay. *Therapy of the Substance Abuse Asyndromes.* Northvale, N.J.: Jason Aronson, 1993.

Richardson, William. *A Mariner of England: An Account of the Career of William Richardson from Cabin Boy in the Merchant Service to Warrant Officer in the Royal Navy as Told by Himself.* London: John Murray, 1908.

Robinson, John, and George Francis Dow, *The Sailing Ships of New England, 1607–1807.* Salem, Mass.: Marine Research Society, 1922.

Rodger, Nichols A. M. *The Command of the Ocean. A Naval History of Britain, 1649–1815.* New York: Norton, 2004.

——. *The Wooden World: An Anatomy of the Georgian Navy.* Annapolis, Md.: Naval Institute Press, 1986.

Royster, Charles. *A Revolutionary People at War: The Continental Army and the American Character, 1775–1783.* Chapel Hill: University of North Carolina Press, 1979.

Saltonstall, Richard. *The Ancestry and Descendants of Sir Richard Saltonstall.* Boston: Printed at the Riverside Press, 1897.

Scharf, J. Thomas. *Chronicles of Baltimore.* Baltimore, Md.: Turnbull Brothers, 1874.

Scott, Sybil, ed. *A Book of the Sea.* Oxford: Oxford University Press, 1918.

Seitz, Don C. *Paul Jones: His Exploits in English Seas during 1778–1780.* New York: Dutton, 1917.

Shay, Frank. *An American Sailor's Treasury.* New York: Norton, 1948.

Shomette, Donald G. *Flotilla Battle for the Patuxent.* Solomons, Md.: Calvert Marine Museum Press, 1981.

Sioussat, Annie Leakin. *Old Baltimore.* New York: Macmillan, 1931.

Smelser, Marshal. *Congress Founds the Navy, 1787–1789.* South Bend, Ind.: University of Notre Dame Press, 1959.

Smith, Charles R. *Marines of the Revolution.* Washington, D.C.: History and Museum Division, U.S. Marine Corps, U.S. Government Printing Office, 1975.

Smith, Page. *A New Age Now Begins.* New York: McGraw-Hill, 1976.

Smith, Philip Chadwick Foster. *Fired by Manley Zeal: A Naval Fiasco of the American Revolution.* Salem, Mass.: Peabody Museum of Salem, 1977.

Sobel, Dava. *Longitude.* New York: Walker, 1995.

Sprout, Harold, and Margaret Sprout. *The Rise of American Naval Power.* London: Oxford University Press, 1939.

Stacton, David. *The Bonapartes.* New York: Simon & Schuster, 1966.

Stark, Francis R. *The Abolition of Privateering and the Declaration of Paris.* New York: Columbia University Press, 1897.

Statham, E. P. *Privateers and Privateering.* New York: James Pott, 1910.

Stone, Michael H. *Abnormalities and Personality, within and beyond the Realm of Treatment.* New York: Norton, 1993.

Sun-Tzu. *The Art of War.* Trans. Yuan Shing and J. J. L. Duyvendak. Ware, Hertfordshire, U.K.: Wordsworth-Editions, 1998.

Syrett, David, and R. L. DiNiro. *The Commissioned Sea Officers of the Royal Navy: 1660–1815.* Aldershot, U.K.: Scolar Press for the Navy Records Society / Brookfield, Vt.: Ashgate, 1994.

Thomas, Evan. *John Paul Jones: Sailor, Hero, Father of the American Navy.* New York: Simon & Schuster, 2003.

Toll, Ian W. *Six Frigates: The Epic History of the Founding of the U.S. Navy.* New York: Norton, 2006.

Trumbull, John. *Reminiscences of His Own Times from 1756 to 1841.* New York & London: Wiley & Putnam, 1841.

Tuchman, Barbara W. *The First Salute.* New York: Knopf, 1988.

Tuckerman, Henry Theodore. *The Life of Silas Talbot, a Commodore in the Navy of the United States.* New York: J. C. Riker, 1850.

Vassa, Gustavus. *The Interesting Narrative of the Life of Olaudah Equianon or Gustavus Vassa.* London: Cradock and Joy, 1814. Repr. in Henry Louis Gates, ed., *The Classic Slave Narratives.* New York: Penguin Books, 1987.

Volo, Dorothy D., and James M. Volo. *Daily Life during the American Revolution*. Westport, Conn.: Greenwood Press, 2003.

Ward, Christopher. *The War of the Revolution*. New York: Macmillan, 1952.

Wells, Gerard. *Naval Customs and Traditions*. London: Philip Allan, Camelot Press, 1930.

Wheeler, George W. *History of Castine, Penobscot, and Brooksville, Maine*. Bangor, Maine: Burr & Robinson, 1875.

Newspaper and Journal Sources

Boston Globe

London Courant and Westminster Chronicle

London Evening Post

Massachusetts magazine

New York Journal and Weekly

New York Times

Putnam's

Index

Page numbers in italics refer to illustrations.

Active (Massachusetts State Navy brigantine), 152n20
Active (Royal Navy warship), 116
Acts of Trade and Navigation. *See* Navigation Acts
Adams, John, 69; adversaries, 134; and Barney, 98; and British Admiralty Code, 17; and Hopkins, 69; and Jones-Landais dispute, 120, 121; as narcissist, 138; on naval officer disputes, 120; on Saltonstall's appointment as captain, 65; and Talbot, 58; and Talbot-Truxtun dispute, 59, 60
Adams, Samuel, 44, 147n8, 148n34
Adams, Winborn, 33
Admirals in the Age of Nelson (Bienkowski), 4
Adventurer (Royal Navy warship), 44 aggression, 137, 144–45
Albany (Royal Navy warship), 70
Alexander, Charles, 92–93
Alfred (Continental Navy warship): court-martial of crewman, 41; and *Glasgow* incident, 67, 68; Hinman as captain, 116–17, 142; Jones as captain, 116; Jones as first lieutenant, 65, 73, 91, 112; Jones's leaving, 73, 114; in Nassau Expedition, 65–66, 91, 112, 113; Saltonstall as captain, 65, 68, 73, 91, 113

Algiers, dey of, 90, 131
Algiers, Treaty of (1795), 58
Alicante, Spain, 89, 90
Alliance (Continental Navy warship), 7–8, 98, 121, 123, 124–27
Amelia (ship), 62
America (Continental Navy warship), 128
American Revolution: American privateers treated as pirates during, 15; beginning, 48, 90; British desertions during, 26; British officer quarrels during, 19; economic causes, 2–3, 29–31; end, 44, 143; as first American naval war, 22; first significant vessel confiscation during, 34–35, 44; first successful American naval raid during, 48, 66; founding fathers' animosity, 134; France as ally, 147n9; last significant vessel confiscation during, 44; maritime warfare options, 13–14; Philadelphia campaign (1777–78), 94–95; prejudicial atmosphere at outset, 18; social order during, 145–46; tactical problems, 46; warfare theory, 4. *See also specific battles and people*
Amphitheatre (schooner-rigged tender), 62

Andrea Doria (Continental Navy warship): Barney as first lieutenant, 50, 93–95; Biddle as captain, 67; burning, 95; in Continental Navy fleet, 112; as first American hospital ship, 151n8; first formal gun salute as U.S. vessel, 93, 156n4, 158n13; *Glasgow* incident and, 67; as hermaphrodite brig, 155–56n2; name, 155n2; in Nassau Expedition, 65–66, 67, 91; in Philadelphia campaign (1777–78), 50, 93–95
anti-Semitism, 142–43, 159–60n11
Arbuthnot (merchant ship), 85
Arbuthnot, Marriot, 19, 55
Argo (sloop), 54
Ariel (French frigate), 128
aristocracy, 10, 11, 140, 147n2 (ch. 1)
arms smuggling, 121
Art of War, The (Sun Tzu), 133
Articles of Confederation, 126, 134, 159n2
Asia (Royal Navy warship), 48–49, 63, 140
Augusta (Royal Navy warship), 50

Babcock, Adam, 85
Babcock, Frances, 64, 85
Babcock, Joshua, 64
Bagaduce (Castine) peninsula of Maine, 70, 75–76, *76*, 152n14. *See also* Penobscot Expedition (1779)
Baille (Royal Navy warship), 29, 44
Baltimore, Md., 90, 102–3, 106–7
Baltimore Committee of Safety and Defense, 107
Barbados, 43
Barbary corsairs, 90, 132
Barbary States, 104
Barbary War (1801), 60–61
Barney, Frances, 87

Barney, Joshua, 27, 28, *88;* aggressiveness, 144; as *Andrea Doria* first lieutenant, 93–95; appearance, 97; appointed captain in French navy, 105, 143; appointed captain in U.S. Navy, 104–5; awards, 101, 107; background, 28, 87; birth, 87; business pursuits, 103, 106; capture and imprisonment, 87, 95–96, 97, 103, 104; capture and parole, 94; as commodore of Chesapeake flotilla (War of 1812), 106–7; congressional campaigns, 106; death, 107; defense mechanisms, 145; duels, 106, 141; early seamanship experience, 87–90; as *General Mercer* first lieutenant, 96–97; 101–2; *General Washington* recaptured by, 55, 100, 104, 139, 157n9; as *Hornet* mate, 65, 91–92; hot temper, 87, 92, 107; and Jones, 102, 128, 129; marriages, 97, 106; as narcissist, 139, 140, 141, 142, 143; and Nassau Expedition, 48, 91; and Nicholson, 28, 95–96; prison escapes, 97–98; privateering career, 96–97, 106; promotion to lieutenant in Continental Navy, 93; ruses, 100; and Talbot, 58, 59, 60, 95, 104–5, 157n16; tried for piracy, 103; as *Wasp* mate, 92–93; word of honor, 94; wounds suffered, 106, 107, 140
—commands: *General Washington,* 101–2; *Hyder-Ally,* 98–101; *L'Insurgente,* 105; *Sachem,* 93; *Sampson,* 103; *Sidney,* 88–90;
Barney, William, 87
Barry, John, 93, 104, 127
Bay of Biscay, 123
Beaumarchais, Pierre Augustin Caron de, 121
Bedford, Anne, 97, 106

Benbow, John, 25
Benson, Robert, 109
Betsey (sloop), 37
Betsy (merchant ship), 54, 111
Beverly, Mass., 33, 37
Biddle, Nicholas, 67, 73, 147n6
Bienkowski, Lee, 4
Black Prince (privateer), 72
Bladensburg, Battle of (1814), 106–7
Blonde (Royal Navy warship), 80
Bolton (Royal Navy warship), 67
Bonhomme Richard (Continental
    Navy warship), 7–8, 120–25, *125*,
    126, 128
Boston (Continental Navy warship),
    41–43, 62
Boston, Mass., 31–32, 33, 37
Bradley, Omar N., 133
Brewer, John, 77
Brisbane, John, 42
Britain. *See* Great Britain
Britannia (brigantine whaler), 116
Britannia (collier sloop), 42
Britannia (Royal Navy warship), 65
British Admiralty: Barney tried for
    piracy by, 103; and Continental
    Navy, 18; convoy duty assignment,
    117; goal, 25; and Jones, 119;
    naval officer procurement system,
    20; and seamen, 24–25; and Tal-
    bot, 53
British Admiralty Code, 17
British Parliament, 30
Brooklyn Heights, N.Y., 48
Broughton, Nicholas, 27, 32–33, 39
Brown, Daniel, 44
Browne, Montfort, 66
Bunker Hill, Battle of (1775), 90
Burke, Edmund, 159–60n11
Burr, Aaron, 134
Byron, John "Foul Weather Jack," 96

Cabot (Continental Navy warship),
    65–66, 67, 91, 112

Calef, John, 152n19
camels, 69
Camilla (Royal Navy warship), 80
cannon bounty, 54
Cape Henlopen, 98
Cape May, 92, 98
Captains to the Northward (Mor-
    gan), 6
Castine peninsula. *See* Bagaduce
    (Castine) peninsula of Maine
Catherine the Great of Russia, 129–31
Cerberus (Royal Navy warship), 33,
    34–35, 116
Cerf (Continental Navy warship), 121
Champlain, Samuel de, 70
Charles II of Spain, 121
Charleston, S.C., 94
Charming Molly (merchant ship), 97
Charming Polly (privateer), 82
Charming Sally (merchant ship), 99
Chase, Samuel, 31
Chesapeake (U.S. Navy warship),
    60–61
Chesapeake Bay, 87, 90, 94, 143
Chesapeake flotilla, 106–7
chevaux-de-frise, 49, 50
Clinton, Henry, 19
Coale, Harriet, 106
Code Duello, 140, 141, 159n10
Coit, William, 27
Collier, George, 42, 80, 81
Collingwood, Cuthbert, 18–19
Columbus (Continental Navy war-
    ship), 65–66, 67, 68, 91, 112
Command of the Ocean, The
    (Rodgers), 4
Commodores, The (Guttridge and
    Smith), 5, 6
Concord (British ship), 36
Concord, Battle of (1775), 48, 90
Confederacy (Continental Navy war-
    ship), 98
Connecticut River, 68–69
Conrad, Joseph, 17

Constellation (U.S. Navy warship), 58, 59, 105

Constitution (U.S. Navy warship), 46, 59–60, 61–62, 151n24

Constitutional Convention (1787), 159n2

Continental Army, 3–4; in Battle of Rhode Island (1778), 51–52; competition with Continental Navy, 12; establishment, 31; recruitment, 32; slave battalion, 52; strategies, 85

Continental Congress: Continental Army established by, 31; Continental Navy authorized by, 90; fiscal restraints imposed by, 69; flag adopted by, 156n4; and Jones, 120, 128; and Manley, 39; naval officer connections to, 11, 17–18, 86, 112; naval officers paid by, 13; and need for navy, 3–4, 112; officer impatience with, 45; privateer fleet authorized by, 9, 13–14, 16, 32; recompenses paid by, 49, 57, 83, 84; state navies authorized by, 13, 31; and Talbot, 52, 54–55

Continental Navy: administration, 64; and British Admiralty Code as standard of conduct, 17; British condescension toward, 18; and British Philadelphia campaign (1777–78), 49–51, 94–95; competition with Continental Army, 12; desertions from, 26–27; discipline, 13; European operations, 117; first officer list, 112; first successful raid, 48, 66; fleet decimations, 51, 82, 95, 98; formation, 29, 39, 90, 112, 138; and impressment, 3, 26, 72, 147n6, 148n34, 155n1; leadership style, 12; mission, 13; motivations for joining, 10–11; need for, 3–4, 112; official vessel-capture policy, 36; privateers commissioned for, 15–16; procurement system lacking in, 20; and Royal Navy, 9, 18; rules and regulations, 96; sailors' trade backgrounds, 1–2; salaries, 13; scholarship on, 5–6; sea victories, 120; seamen, 26–27, 136, 137; ship shortages, 22; tactics, 23; wardroom culture, 20

Continental Navy Board, 68–69, 71

Continental Navy officers, 4, 5; animosity among, 7–8, 16–17, 27–28, 133–35; aristocratic hierarchy among, 147n2 (ch. 1); battle experience, 23; education, 23, 134–35; intrepidity, 46; leadership skills, 28, 135–37; logs, 26–27; motivations, 10–11, 16; payment of, 57; Royal Navy officers compared to, 22–23; selection, 9, 10, 11–12, 17–18, 65, 69, 86; slave trade experience, 157n1; standardized uniforms, 40; treatment of subordinates, 12; turnover among, 22; wardroom culture, 20

convoy system, 69, 117, 123–24

Conyngham, Gustavus, 117

Cook, James, 25, 148n15

Cooper, James Fenimore, 61, 83–84, 124

Cooper, Samuel, 40

Copenhagen, Denmark, 129

Cornwallis, Charles, 143

Countess of Scarborough (Royal Navy warship), 123–24

courts-martial, 27, 41, 43, 68, 74, 96, 126

Craik, William, 108, 110

crimps, 24

Culloden (Royal Navy warship), 55

Culloden, Battle of (1746), 108

Cumberland (privateer), 43

Dale, Richard, 104, 126

Davidson, Julian O., *125*

Deane (Continental Navy warship), 44, 85, 98

Deane, Barnabas, 40
Deane, Silas, 64, 65, 68
Decatur, Stephen, 140
Decision at the Chesapeake
    (Larrabee), 5–6
Declaration of Independence, 12, 113
Degge, J. A., 127
Delaware, 13, 156n8
Delaware (Continental Navy war-
    ship), 94
Delaware Bay, 91, 92
Delaware River, 49–51, 94–95,
    113
desertions, 26–27, 29, 79, 106
Diligent (brig), 71
discipline, 135–36, 144
Dominican Republic, 62
"Don't Tread on Me" flag, 91
Doria, Andrea, 155n2
Dragon (Royal Navy warship), 54
Drake (Royal Navy warship), 118,
    119–20
Drysdale, Thomas, 88, 90
Dublin (Royal Navy warship), 35, 54
Duc de Duras (French navy ship),
    120. See also *Bonhomme Richard*
dueling: as aristocratic concept,
    140–41; of Barney, 106, 141; of
    Jones, 122, 141, 158n25, 159n36;
    of Manley, 44, 141; role in Ameri-
    can history, 140–41; rules, 140–41,
    158n25, 159n10; of Talbot, 48
Dunsmore, Lord, 113
Dutch Jews, 142–43, 159–60n11
Dutch West Indies, 93

Eisenhower, Dwight D., 133
Eliz (schooner). See *Franklin*
    (schooner)
Ellsworth, Oliver, 57
Elphinstone, George Keith, 94
Emerald (Royal Navy warship), 96
esprit de corps, 135
Estaing, Charles Hector, comte d', 51,
    101

Esther (schooner), 62
Eustis, William, 49

Fair American (British privateer),
    98–99
Favourite (Royal Navy warship), 116
Fisheries Bill (1775), 30
fishermen, 32, 147n4 (ch. 1)
fishing, British regulation of, 30
fishing boats: captains, 1; crews, 2;
    naval officers from, 10; quasi-
    democratic leadership on, 12
Flamand (French navy ship), 158n20
flogging, 110, 135
Flora (Royal Navy warship), 24, 42,
    52
Flos Duellatorum in Armis (dueling
    code), 159n10
Fly (Continental Navy warship),
    65–66, 91, 94, 112, 113
Fort George (Bagaduce peninsula),
    70, 75, 78, 79, 86
Fort Mercer, 49, 50, 51, 95
Fort Mifflin, 49, 50, 95
Fort Montagu, 66
Fort Nassau, 66
Foster, Robert, 36
Fotheringham, Patrick, 42
founding fathers, animosity among,
    134
Fowler, William, 6
Fox (Royal Navy warship), 42
France: as American ally, 3, 51,
    147n9; Barney's return of French
    officers to, 101–2; ports as bases
    for raids, 117; and Quasi-War
    (1798–1800), 58, 59, 61–62,
    105–6; St. Eustatius conquered
    by, 160n11; wars with Britain,
    103–4, 117
Franklin (Continental Navy
    schooner), 32–33
Franklin, Benjamin, 56, 120–21,
    126–28, 134, 138
French Admiralty, 105

French and Indian War (1756–63),
17, 32, 65, 113
French navy, 104, 143
French Revolution, 103, 105
Friendship (merchant ship), 108–9

Galatea (Royal Navy warship), 116
Gates, Horatio, 84, 134
General Greene (Pennsylvania State
Navy), 99
General Mercer (privateer), 96–97
General Monk (Royal Navy warship),
98–100, *100*, 139, 157n9. See
also *General Washington*
General Putnam (privateer), 72,
153n40
General Washington (Rhode Island
privateer, Pennsylvania State Navy
warship, and Continental Navy
warship): Barney as captain,
101–2; Barney's recapture, 55,
100, 100, 101, 104, 139, 157n9;
captured by British, 55, 98; con-
verted to packet ship, 101–2, 129;
renaming, 98; sale, 102, 157n9;
Talbot as captain, 55, 98, 104,
157n9. See also *General Monk*
(Royal Navy warship)
George III of England, 9, 23, 33–34,
47–48
Germain, George, 19
Ghazi Hassan, 131
Gibraltar, 89
Gilbert, W. S., 132
Glasgow (Royal Navy warship), 67,
68, 113–14
Glover, John, 32
Graaf, Johannes de, 93, 156n4
Grand Union flag, 156nn3–4
Grasse, François-Joseph-Paul, Compte
de, 143
Graves, Thomas, 32, 148n22
Great Britain: and colonial natural
resources, 1; France as American
ally against, 147n9; maritime policy,
58; trade taxation, 2–3, 29–30;
and War of 1812, 106–7; wars
with France, 103–4, 117; wars
with Holland, 142. *See also* Royal
Navy
Greene, Nathanael, 48
Greyhound (Royal Navy warship), 80
Gulf of St. Lawrence, 14
Guttridge, Leonard, 5, 6

Hacker, Hoysted, 79, 116,
153–54n44, 155n62
Hague (Continental Navy warship),
44
Hamilton, Alexander, 134, 140
Hampden (privateer), 72, 82,
153–54n44
Hancock (Continental Navy
schooner), 32–33, 39
Hancock (Continental Navy warship),
40, 41–43, 68, 98, 115, 157n9.
See also *Iris* (Royal Navy warship)
Hancock, John, 40, 112
Hannah (Continental Navy
schooner), 32
Hannah (merchant vessel), 85
Hannah (Royal Navy warship), 54
Hawk (Royal Navy warship), 67
Hawke (sloop), 52–53, 54
Hazard (brig), 83, 152n20
Hazard (British privateer), 44
Hazard, John, 67, 68, 74
Hazard, Stanton, 54
Hector (privateer), 72
Hesburgh, Theodore, 133
Heureux (French navy ship), 158n20
Hewes, Joseph, 73
Hickman, Martha, 35
Hinman, Elisha, 41, 69, 116–17, 142
Holland, 142
Hood, Samuel, 19, 25
Hope (Royal Navy warship), 39
Hopkins, Esek (Ezek): appointed
commander-in-chief of Continental
Navy, 17, 18, 149n18; appointed

commodore of Continental
Navy, 149n1, 149n18; background,
17–18; and Jones,112–13, 116–17;
as Nassau Expedition commodore,
48, 66–68, 91, 112–13; repri-
mand, 27, 113–14; as *Warren*
captain, 69. *See also* Nassau
Expedition (1776)
Hopkins, Stephen, 18, 113
Hopper, Grace, 133
Hornet (Continental Navy warship),
65–66, 91–92, 94, 112, 113
Hortalez et Cie, 121
Houdon, Jean-Antoine, *109*
Howe, Richard, 19, 49
Howe, Tyringham, 67, 113
Howe, William, 37, 48, 94
Hull, Isaac, 61, 62
Hunter (privateer), 72, 82
Hunter, Robert, 34
Hyder-Ally (Pennsylvania State
Navy warship), 98–101, *100*,
156nn7–8
Hydman, Michael, 42

impressment, 3, 24, 25–26, 30, 58,
72, 104, 147n6, 148n34
Indien (Continental Navy warship),
117
insubordination, 81–82, 110
Intolerable Acts (1774), 30
Intrepid (Royal Navy warship), 97
Iris (Royal Navy warship), 98, 157n9.
See also *Hancock* (Continental
Navy warship)
irritability, 144–45
Isis (Royal Navy warship), 50

Jameson, J. F., 156n4
Jason (privateer), 43–44
Jay, John, 56
Jefferson, Thomas, 132
Jenner, Edward, 151n7
Jenny (British ship), 36, 37
Jersey (British prison hulk), 55

Jervis, John, 19, 144
John (brig), 109–11
Johnson, Samuel, 136
Jones, John Paul, 40, 74, *109, 130;*
aggressiveness, 144; as *Alfred*
first lieutenant, 65, 73, 91, 112;
appointed admiral in Russian navy,
129–31; appointed American consul to Algeria, 131–32; appointed
captain in Continental Navy, 112;
audacity, 123; awards and honors,
126, 128, 129, 131; background,
12, 28, 108; and Barney, 102,
128, 129; birth, 108; combat
style, 116; death, 132; defense
mechanisms, 145; denigrated by
Hacker, 153–54n44; denigrated
by Hopkins, 112–13; disputes
with crewmen, 110, 111, 120,
121, 122–23, 130; duels, 44, 122,
141, 158n25, 159n36; early seamanship experience, 108–10;
Franklin's reprimand, 127–28;
as *Friendship* apprentice, 108–9;
humor, 123; and Landais, 7–8,
28, 122, 123, 124–27, 158n25,
159n36; leadership flaws, 128;
and Manley, 35, 36, 38, 41, 115;
name change, 112, 157n3; as narcissist, 139, 140, 141, 142, 143; in
Nassau Expedition, 48; and James
Nicholson, 128–29; promotion to
admiral denied, 128–29; psychological warfare, 117–19, 140, 143;
and Saltonstall, 65, 73, 113, 114,
115, 121–22; seniority rank,
149n23; snobbery, 115, 129–30;
snobbery as viewed by, 65, 115;
tried for assault and cruelty, 110;
tried for piracy, 103; viewed by
British as pirate, 119, 123, 129;
Virginia home, 109, 111–12; as
war hero, 27, 132; wartime recompense sought, 101–2, 129; wounds
suffered, 140

Jones, John Paul (*continued*)
—commands: *Alliance,* 126–27;
   Betsy, 111; *Bonhomme Richard,*
   7–8, 120–25, *125; John,* 109–10;
   Providence, 114, 115–16, 149n23;
   Ranger, 117–20, 156n4
Jones, William, 94, 106
Jordan, Nathaniel, 74
Jupiter (British privateer), 56–57

Kentucky, 57
King George (Royal Navy warship),
   54, 109
Kingfisher (Royal Navy warship), 90
Kingston, Jamaica, 109
Kirkland, Moses, 37
Knox, Henry, 49, 69, 104–5

Landais, Pierre: background, 121;
   court-martial, 27;and Jones, 8, 28,
   121, 122, 123, 126–27, 141,
   158n25, 159n36
—commands: *Alliance,* 7–8, 121,
   122, 123, 124–27; *Heureux,*
   158n20
Larrabee, Harold, 5–6
Laurens, Henry, 54–55, 102
Lavery, Brian, 4
leadership, 1; and aggression, 137,
   144–45; applications of, 135–37;
   in Continental Navy versus Royal
   Navy, 12; deference as principle,
   135; definitions, 86, 133; and discipline, 135–36; education in,
   134–35; and mutual respect, 27;
   and narcissism, 137–43, 159n7;
   and officer quarrels, 28, 133–35;
   and perfectionism, 137, 143–44
Lee (Continental Navy schooner),
   33–35
Lestock, Richard, 19
letters of marque, 14, 32, 62, 103
Lexington (Continental Navy warship), 92

Lexington, Battle of (1775), 48, 90
L'Insurgente (French frigate), 59, 105
Linzee, Robert, 44
Little Hannah (brig), 36–37
Lively (Royal Navy warship), 54
Liverpool (Royal Navy warship), 92
Lloyd's of London, 16
Long Island, Battle of (1776), 151n10
Long Island Sound, 47, 54, 68,
   151n10
Lord Harlow (Royal Navy warship),
   24
L'Orient (France), 126, 127
Louis XVI of France, 126, 127, 129
Lovell, Solomon: background, 84; on
   Penobscot Expedition failure, 82;
   and Penobscot Expedition investi-
   gation, 84–85; as Penobscot Expe-
   dition land forces commander,
   74–76, 78–82; and Saltonstall,
   19, 28, 78, 79, 154n45
Lowrie, James, 36
Loyalists, 152n19. *See also* Tories
Lynch, William, 89

Maine militia, 74–75
Manley, John, *30;* admiration for,
   44–45; aggressiveness, 144;
   appointed captain in Continental
   Navy, 39–40; appointed commodore of schooner fleet, 29, 38;
   background, 27–28, 35; bravery,
   140; British denigration of, 38–39;
   capture and imprisonment, 42–43,
   44, 52, 56, 97; as Continental
   Army captain, 29, 38; correspondence, 35–36; court-martial, 43;
   death, 44, 45; defense mechanisms, 145; duels, 44, 141; and
   Jones, 35, 36, 38, 115; leadership
   skills, 37–38, 139; marriage, 35;
   and McNeill, 28, 35, 38, 41–43,
   115; name changes, 35; as narcissist, 139–40, 142; number of

vessels captured, 37; postwar civilian activities, 44; as Royal Navy deserter, 29, 35, 115; ruses, 34, 36, 37; and Saltonstall, 40; seniority rank, 149n23; standardized officer uniforms designed by, 40; and Talbot, 52; and Washington, 29, 33–34, 38, 39, 139–40
—commands: *Hancock* (Continental navy warship), 40, 41–43, 68, 98, 115, 157n9; *Hancock* (schooner), 39; *Jason,* 43–44; *Lee,* 33–35, 36–37
Manley, John (Royal Navy officer), 35
Marblehead, Mass., 34
Marchand, Henry, 54
Marine Committee: animosity within, 27; administration of Continental Navy, 64; and Barney, 95; and captains' personnel logs, 27; and *Hancock* (Continental Navy warship) arming, 40; investigation of *Glasgow* incident, 68, 113–14; and Jones, 115, 116–17, 142; naval officer connections, 11, 18, 64; orders for British transport interceptions, 68; revision of seniority list, 115; and Saltonstall, 68–69; and Talbot, 52–53, 54, 57
marine committees, state, 13, 98
Maryland militia, 106–7
Massachusetts, coastal defense of, 70
Massachusetts Bay Colony, 64, 152n19
Massachusetts Board of War, 70
Massachusetts Continental Army, 32
Massachusetts Council Chambers, 147n6
Massachusetts General Court, 70, 71, 82, 84
Massachusetts House of Representatives, 82–83, 84
Massachusetts Navy Board, 72

Massachusetts State Navy, 71, 72, 84, 152n20
Masters, Robert, 36
Maxwell, Mungo, 110
Maxwell, Robert, 110
McAdam, Samuel, 109–10
McCloud, Kenneth, 73–74
McGlathry, William, 33
McLean, Francis, 70, 75
McNeill, Hector, 27, 35, 38, 41–43, 115, 149n23
Mellish (British armed transport), 116
merchant ships: manning of, 2; naval officer pool from, 10; quasi-democratic leadership style on, 12
merchant trade, 2
Metcalf, George, 57–58
midshipmen, 20, 21–22, 141
military ceremonies, 143–44
Minerva (Connecticut privateer brigantine), 85
Mississippi Packet (merchant sloop), 66
Montagu, John, 31, 118
Montgomery (Pennsylvania State Navy), 94
Morgan, William James, 6
Morison, Samuel E., 73, 128
Morris, Rebecca "Becky," 150n12
Morris, Robert, 44, 128, 129
Mowat, Henry, 70, 75, 76–77, 78–79, 80, 83
Moylan, Stephen, 37
Murray, John, 70
mutinies, 43, 87, 96, 121, 122–23, 127
Mystic Seaport Museum, 139

Nancy (brig), 34–35, 44
Napoleonic Wars, 4
narcissism, 137–43, 159n7
Narragansett Bay, 47, 51–52, 53, 54, 68

Nassau Expedition (1776), 28, 48, 65–68, 112–15
Nassau-Siegan, Charles, 131
Nautilus (Royal Navy warship), 70
Nautilus Island, 76–77, 78
Naval Committee, 18, 39, 65, 112
Navigation Acts, 2, 30
Navy Act (1794), 104
Nelson, Horatio, 4, 18–19, 67, 138, 140, 147n6
Nelson's Navy (Lavery), 4
nepotism, 11, 17–18, 59, 65, 72, 84, 134
New England Restraining Act (1775), 30
New Hampshire State Navy, 72
New Ireland, 69, 152n19
New Jersey, 13
New London, Conn., 48, 54, 64, 67–68
New Providence, Bahamas, 66, 91, 113
New York, Battle of (1776), 48
New York, N.Y., 39
New York Assembly, 57
Newburyport, Mass., 40
Newport, R.I., 51, 52
Nice, France, 89
Nicholson, James, 27, 28, 95–96, 128–29, 149n23
Nicholson, Samuel, 59, 104
Nithsdale clan, 110
North (Royal Navy warship), 70
North, Frederick, 118
North Sea, 123
Nymph (brig), 62

Old Mill Prison, Plymouth, England, 44, 56, 58, 97, 104
Olney (*Queen of France* captain), 69
Otter (Royal Navy warship), 80

Pallas (privateer brig), 82, 121, 124, 125

Paris, Treaty of (1783), 101
Patton (film), 138
Patton, George, 138
Paul, John. *See* Jones, John Paul
Paul, William, 109
Paulus Hook, N.Y., 48
Peace Establishment Act, 63
Pearson, Richard, 124, 125, 158n31
Penelope (Royal Navy warship), 103
Pennsylvania Commission, 101
Pennsylvania State Navy, 94, 98, 101
Penobscot Bay, 75, 80
Penobscot Expedition (1779), 14, 114; American losses, 82–83, 86, 121; American retreat, 80–82; amphibious assaults, 75–77; British reinforcements, 80; commanding officers, 74; councils of war, 75, 79, 155n62; courts-martial for, 155n62; fleet assembled for, 71, 72–73, 74, 153n38; formation, 71, 74; historical debate over, 83–85; insufficient land force for, 74–75; and Jones, 121–22; leadership deficiencies, 77–80, 144, 153n40, 154n45; mission, 73; privateer participation, 77–78, 79; reimbursement for, 155n55; Saltonstall as commodore of, 71–72, 73, 74, 153n40; secrecy surrounding, 153n38
Penobscot River, 69–70, 81
perfectionism, 137, 143–44
Perseus (Royal Navy warship), 94
personnel logs, 2, 26–27
Philadelphia, Pa., 90, 93, 101
Philadelphia campaign (1777–78), 49–51, 94–95
Pigot (Royal Navy warship), 52–53, 54, 140
Pintard, Eliza, 63
piracy, 15, 103, 155n1
Polly (merchant sloop), 34
Pomona (Royal Navy warship), 43

Poor Richard's Almanack (Franklin), 120–21

Porter, David, 153n40

Potemkin, Grigory Alexandrovich, 131

President (U.S. Navy warship), 58

press gangs, 24

prison hulks, 55–56, 96

privateering, 13–14, 32

privateers, American: arming of, 15, 16, 34, 40, 72; as coastal defense, 70; commissions, 14–15; first, 32; fishing and trade backgrounds, 3; government authorization, 9, 13–14, 32; impressment, 72; investment in, 15; Manley as role model for, 37–38; military significance, 13–14, 15–16, 69; as naval officer pool, 10; need for, 3; noncommissioned, 15; as pirates, 15, 32; recruitment, 14, 37–38; role in Penobscot Expedition, 77–78, 79; strategies, 14, 15, 34, 53–54

privateers, British, 16

prize money, 27, 39, 129

"Proclamation for Suppressing the Rebellion and Sedition," 33–34

promotions, 35

Providence (Continental Navy warship): and *Glasgow* incident, 67, 68; Hacker as captain of, 79, 116, 155n62; Hazard as captain of, 67, 68; Jones as captain of, 114, 115–16, 149n23; in Nassau Expedition, 65–66, 91, 112; in Penobscot Expedition, 71, 79, 153n38

Providence, R.I., 47–48, 51, 68

Province Island, 49–50

Prudent (Royal Navy warship), 147n6

punishment, 110, 135

quarrelsomeness, 144–45

Quasi-War (1798–1800), 58, 59, 61–62, 105–6

Quebec (Royal Navy warship), 98–99, 100

Queen of France (Continental Navy warship), 69

Racehorse (Royal Navy warship), 94

Rainbow (Royal Navy warship), 42

Raisonable (Royal Navy warship), 80

Raleigh (Continental Navy warship), 41

Raleigh (Royal Navy warship), 97

Randolph, Edmund, 134

Ranger (Continental Navy warship), 117–20, 156n4

Ranger (lumber sloop), 33

rations, 25–26

Ravené, Abraham, 93

Read, Thomas, 128–29

Rebels under Sail (Fowler), 6

Red Bank, N.J., 49, 95

Renown (privateer), 82

Renown (Royal Navy warship), 53–54

Revere, Paul: insubordination, 81–82; as Penobscot Expedition artillery commander, 74, 76, 78, 153n35; on Penobscot Expedition councils of war, 75; on Penobscot Expedition failure, 79, 80; as Saltonstall privateering investor, 85

Revolutionary People at War, A (Royster), 6

Revolutionary War. *See* American Revolution

Rhode Island (island), 51

Rhode Island, Battle of (1778), 51–52

Rhode Island Colonial Assembly, 17

Rhode Island Continental Army, 48

Rhode Island General Assembly, 64

Rhode Island Militia, 17–18, 48, 64

Rhode Island State Navy, 55. See also *Providence* (sloop)

Rhode Island Supreme Court, 64

Richardson, William, 26

Richmond, Anna, 47, 48, 57

Robbins, Robert, 33

Robinson, Isaiah, 93, 94, 96

Robinson, Robert, 123

Rodger, Nichols A. M., 4, 145

Rodney, George Brydges, 19, 142–43, 159–60n11

Roebuck (Royal Navy warship), 50, 91–92

Romney (Royal Navy warship), 123

Roosevelt, Franklin D., 156n4

Rotheram, Edward, 18–19

Royal Navy: control of Boston harbor, 32; control of Narragansett Bay, 51–52, 53, 68; compared to Continental Navy, 9, 18; desertions, 26, 29; impressment practices, 3, 24, 25–26, 30, 58, 104; leadership style, 12; limitations, 31; motivations for joining, 25; officer selection, 9–10; in Philadelphia campaign (1777–78), 49–51, 94–95; power, 9, 29, 31, 69–70; procurement system, 20; promotion within, 19, 21–22, 25, 35; scholarship on, 4; seamen, 24–26, 136; shipboard life, 24, 25–26, 136; tactics, 23; traditional culture, 18; wardroom culture, 19–20

Royal Navy Academy, Portsmouth, England, 21

Royal Navy officers, 4; animosity among, 18–19, 134; battle experience, 23; camaraderie among, 19–21; compared to Continental Navy officers, 22–23; education, 21; promotion, 19, 21–22; selection, 9–10, 20, 22, 31; social standing, 11, 21–22

Royal Sovereign (Royal Navy warship), 19

Royster, Charles, 6

Rule of 1756, 103

Rules and Regulations of the Navy of the United Colonies, 96

Russian navy, 129–31

Sachem (Continental Navy warship), 93

Sackville, Lord, 19

St. Croix, West Indies, 156n4

St. Eustatius, West Indies, 93, 142–43, 156n4, 158n13, 159–60n11

St. John (Royal Navy warship), 66

Sakonnet River, 52

Sally (brigantine slave ship), 17

Sally (British sloop), 62

Saltonstall, Dudley, 19, 27; adversaries, 28; aggressiveness, 144; appearance, 64; appointed captain in Continental Navy, 65; aristocratic lineage, 64, 71–72, 83, 141; arrogant demeanor, 65, 73–74, 86, 114; background, 28, 64–65; congressional investigation of, 68, 113; court-martial, 85; courts-martial conducted, 74; death, 86; defense mechanisms, 145; dismissed from Continental Navy, 85; historical debate over, 83–85; impressed sailors under his command, 147n6, 148n34; ineptitude, 68–69, 77, 83–85, 86, 115, 122; and Jones, 114, 115, 121–22; and Lovell, 19, 28, 78, 79, 154n45; and Manley, 40, 43; marriage, 64; as narcissist, 139, 142; in Nassau Expedition, 48, 65–68; privateering career, 85; as slave trader, 85–86. *See also* Penobscot Expedition (1779)

—commands: *Alfred,* 65–66, 67, 68, 91, 113; *Minerva,* 85; *Trum-bull* (Continental Navy warship), 68–69; *Trumbull* (privateer), 152n17; *Warren* (Continental Navy warship), 69, 71–72, 85

Saltonstall, Gurdon, 64

Saltonstall, Gurdon, Jr., 64

Saltonstall, Richard (ancestor of Dudley), 64

Saltonstall, Richard (descendant of Dudley), 84
Sampson (merchant ship), 103
Sandwich (sloop), 62
Sandwich, Lord, 31, 118
Santa Margaretta (Royal Navy warship), 61
Saratoga (Continental Navy warship), 97, 98
Schuykill River, 49, 95
Scott, George C., 138
Sea Nymph (merchant ship), 116
seamen, 23–27, 136, *137*
sedition, 96
Selkirk, Earl of, 119, 129
Selman, John, 32–33
seniority lists, 27, 58, 59–60, 98, 104–5, 115
Serapis (Royal Navy warship), 7–8, 123–25, *125*
Seven Years' War (1756–63), 9. *See also* French and Indian War
Shakespeare, William, 9
shipwrecks, 87
Sidney (merchant brig), 88
Simpson, Thomas, 120
Six Frigates (Toll), 5
slave trade, 2, 17, 18, 85–86, 109, 157n1
smallpox, 66–67, 151n7
Smith, Daniel, 98
Smith, Jay, 5, 6
Smith, John, 90
Smith, Robert, 60–61
Smith, Samuel, 34, 107
smuggling, 121
Society of the Cincinnati, 47, 147n2 (ch. 1)
Solebay (Royal Navy warship), 116
Somerset (Royal Navy warship), 50
Speedwell (fishing schooner). See *Hancock* (schooner)
Stamp Act (1765), 30
state navies: congressional authorization, 13, 31; Massachusetts, 71,

72, 84, 152n20; military significance, 13; and multiple enlistments, 26; New Hampshire, 72; Pennsylvania, 94, 98, 101; Rhode Island, 55
Stevens, Thomas, 33
Stewart, Potter, 133
Stoddert, Benjamin, 59–60, 61, 62, 105
Stone, William, 91–92
Sullivan, James, 152n14
Sullivan, John, 51
Sun Tzu, 133, 135
Surprise (Continental Navy warship), 92, 94
Surprise (Royal Navy warship), 44
Swift (schooner), 62

Talbot, Silas, 27, *47;* aggressiveness, 144; appointed captain in Continental Army, 48; appointed captain in Continental Navy, 54–55, 104; background, 28, 46–48; and Barney, 58, 59, 60, 95, 104–5, 157n16; in Battle of Long Island (1776), 151n10; in Battle of Rhode Island (1778), 51–52; birth, 46; and British Philadelphia campaign (1777–78), 49–51, 95; capture and imprisonment, 55–57, 58, 97, 104; congressional commendations, 49, 52; defense mechanisms, 145; duel, 48, 141; illegitimate daughter, 57; leadership skills, 53–54; and Manley, 52; marriages, 47, 48, 57, 63, 150n12; as narcissist, 139, 142; pension, 54; postwar political career, 57–58; privateering career, 54, 57, 61–62; promotion to lieutenant colonel in Continental Army, 52; promotion to major in Continental Army, 49; resignation from U.S. Navy, 62–63; and Truxtun, 28, 58–61; as U.S. Navy

Talbot, Silas (*continued*)
  founder, 63; and Washington, 50;
  wounds, 49, 50, 54, 63, 104, 140
—commands: *Argo,* 54; *Constitution,*
  59–60, 61–62, 151n24; *General
  Washington,* 55, 157n9; *Hawke,*
  52–53, 54
taxation, 2–3, 10, 29–30
Taylor, Lemuel, 106
Thomas (merchant ship), 94
Thompson, Thomas, 41, 115
timber, 1, 66, 152n14
tobacco, 1
Tobago, 110–11
Toll, Ian, 5
Tories, 10, 37, 54, 69
trade, transatlantic: British and
  French privateer attacks on,
  103–4; Royal Navy control of, 9,
  29, 69, 70; sailors' backgrounds,
  1–2; taxation, 2–3, 29–30
Trafalgar, Battle of (1805), 4,
  18–19
Treaty of Algiers (1795), 58
Treaty of Paris (1783), 101
Trevett, John, 153n38
tributes, 104
Trisden, John, 33
Trumbull (Connecticut privateer),
  152n17
Trumbull (Continental Navy war-
  ship), 68–69, 98, 157n9
Trumbull, John, 64
Truxtun, Thomas, 28, 58–61, 104,
  105, 147n6
Tuckerman, Henry, 55
Turkish navy, 131
Two Angels (ship), 62
Two Friends (merchant brig), 93,
  109
Two Sisters (fishing schooner),
  33–34
Tyrannicide (Massachusetts priva-
  teer), 152n20

United Colonies of America: and
  Articles of Confederation, 134;
  economic recession, 2; natural
  resources, 1; shipbuilding restric-
  tion, 31; social order, 11; taxation,
  2–3, 10
United States (U.S. Navy warship),
  58
United States, formal recognition of
  independence, 93
United States Congress, 104, 107,
  129, 141, 155n55
United States House of Representatives, 57–58
United States Naval Academy, 139
United States Navy, 59, 60, 63, 104,
  141
United States War Department,
  104–5

Vengeance (Continental Navy war-
  ship), 121, 125
Vermont, 13
Vernon, Edward, 25
Victor (Royal Navy warship), 42
Victory (Royal Navy warship), 138
Vigilant (Royal Navy warship), 50
Virginia, 109, 111–12
Virginia (Continental Navy warship),
  95–96, 128
Virginia (Royal Navy warship), 50
Virginia Capes, Battle of the (1781),
  157n9

Wadsworth, Peleg, 28, 74, 81, 83,
  84–85
Wallabout Bay, 55
War of 1812, 106
Ward, Artemas, 83
wardroom culture, 19–20, 141
Warren (Continental Navy warship),
  71; Hopkins as captain, 114;
  impressed sailors aboard, 147n6,
  148n34; in Penobscot Expedition,

72, 75, 85; Saltonstall as captain, 69, 71–72, 75, 85, 147n6, 148n34

Warren (schooner), 33

Warren, James, 44–45, 69, 138

Washington, D.C., burning of, 106

Washington, George, 9, 23; adversaries, 134; appointed Continental Army commander, 31; appointment of Jones as Algerian ambassador, 131–32; appointments of commodores, 29, 38; and formation of Continental Navy, 29; headquarters moved to New York, 39; and Manley, 29, 33–34, 38, 39, 139–40; Massachusetts garrison commanded by, 31–32; paranaval fleet envisioned by, 34; schooner fleet, 29, 33, 37, 38, 39; supply lines to, 68, 114–15; Talbot commanded by, 50; vessel-capture policy, 36

Wasp (Continental Navy warship), 65–66, 91, 94, 112

Waterloo, Battle of (1815), 4

Weare, Mesech, 72

West Indies, 14, 36–37, 61, 86, 93

Whipple, Abraham, 27, 68

Wickes, Lambert, 92, 117

Williams, John, 83

Winthrop, John, 64

Winthrop, Mary, 64

Wooden World, The (Rodgers), 4

Yarmouth (British prison hulk), 55–56

yellow fever, 67

Yorktown, Battle of (1781), 6, 101, 143

Young, James, 97

Younger, James, 108–9

About the Author

A native of the old seaport of Gloucester, Massachusetts, LOUIS ARTHUR NORTON is a professor emeritus at the University of Connecticut. Norton writes frequently on maritime history topics, and he was awarded the 2002 and 2006 Gerald E. Morris Prizes for maritime historiography for articles published in the *Log of Mystic Seaport*. His previous books are *Joshua Barney: Hero of the Revolution and 1812, Sailors' Folk Art under Glass: A Story of Ships-in-Bottles*, and the children's book *New England's Stormalong*.